Am I
My Brother's
Keeper?

Am I My Brother's Keeper?

EDUCATIONAL OPPORTUNITIES AND OUTCOMES FOR BLACK AND BROWN BOYS

Adriana Villavicencio

HARVARD EDUCATION PRESS

Cambridge, Massachusetts

Paperback ISBN 978-1-68253-621-6
Library Edition ISBN 978-1-68253-622-3

Library of Congress Cataloging-in-Publication Data is on file.

Published by Harvard Education Press,
an imprint of the Harvard Education Publishing Group

Harvard Education Press
8 Story Street
Cambridge, MA 02138

Cover Design: Wilcox Designo
Cover Image: Hill Street Studios/DigitalVision via Getty Images

The typefaces in this book are Minion Pro, Legacy Sans, and Milo.

CONTENTS

FOREWORD

WHEN I WAS CONDUCTING my own research on Black men and boys more than a decade ago, this was the book that I was searching for but could not find. Books that love us are rare, perhaps because it's easier, or more acceptable, to write about what afflicts us young Black and Brown men and boys than about what heals us. Nevertheless, writing this book could not have been easy, because doing so must have meant contending with this tragic mix of deeply engrained biases—that is, confronting the scars. Researching and writing about Black and Brown men and boys is about balance. One must hold onto the pain while uplifting the heavy wounds, stare at the naked corpse of our bodies thoroughly bruised while listening to the shrill but silent cries of agonies rehearsed over and again while no one ever hears.

Black and Brown men and boys have grown accustomed to not being heard. But with *Am I My Brother's Keeper?* Adriana Villavicencio listens. She cares. In a world too often bent on devaluing Black and Brown life, this book declares that we matter.

Yet, declaring our worth is not the book's most significant contribution. In this moment in which murdered Black bodies pepper our news screens and innocent Brown children cry out in cages, during this time when our collective consciousness can no longer refuse the empirical realities of anti-Blackness and white supremacy, perhaps more valuable is this book's insistence on helping us atone for our irrational sins—this consented-to belief that something about Black and Brown people is broken.

This book is audacious and hopeful, and it is strategic in moving us past our biases and deficit logics, past our fetish for Black and Brown suffering and our strange fixation on filtering the world through the white gaze. This radical book is about humans. Perhaps the most significant contribution of this book, then, is its alchemy, its ability to turn lead to gold, to see as human people we too frequently strip of humanity. In doing so, each chapter of this delicately woven narrative elevates human sciences above human biases, raising the stakes of research closer to the possibilities of BIPOC bodies released from the narratives of contempt and disdain. It is with care and elegance that Villavicencio writes a study that feels like a song, a book that is fresh and penetrating, research that peers into the educational lives of young Black and Latinx men and boys in ways that allow us to see them not for their problems but for their possibilities.

With thoughtful and heartfelt honesty, the book raises a set of serious questions about threads of racial bias woven deeply into the fabric of social research, where Black and Latinx men and boys have usually been seen as problems to be solved or as broken objects that need to be fixed. This dehumanization fastened to the flesh of children leaves us with a moral problem—empirical objectification, which, left unchecked, has given us traditions of educational research insufficient for understanding Black and Latinx men and boys. By contrast, Villavicencio weaves a new narrative that painstakingly details the story of the Expanded Success Initiative (ESI), leading readers to a set of powerful ideas about how Black and Brown men and boys learn and how schools can be shaped around them. Indeed, these ideas start with a recalibration of our gaze to focus on the cast of players who love and refuse to give up on these students.

Villavicencio's findings do not come out of a randomized trial or some other statistical analysis but, rather, from hours spent sitting with people and listening to them. She aimed to converse with people who felt ignored but who knew more about the educational experiences of young Black and Brown men and boys than our sciences or schools do. These people knew young Black and Brown men and boys personally; they worked with them and dared to bend straighter a crooked system that was in opposition to their needs and dismissive of their cultural backgrounds.

I am glad that the book privileges thick description over randomization. When used to understand racial inequity—something that is neither random nor incidental—I maintain that randomization can only reinforce racist ideas because a random sample of a social distortion can only yield a distorted result. To locate promise and possibility—to understand how Black and Brown men and boys might succeed in US schools, for example—the science seeking to find them cannot be random, because, in a racist world, Black and Brown success does not happen randomly. Thus, the project of the researcher who dares to understand the question of how to transform education, to fix a broken system, to sustain Black and Brown men and boys is a deep dive into uncertainty that requires vulnerability, self-examination, and reflection. Villavicencio offered the young men and boys she writes about the space to enter into a deep but humanizing introspection. Some of the most moving passages of the book were those in which I could feel her feminine presence engage the age-old dyad of I/us, with *I* at its eternal core, elongate—as Audre Lorde puts it—and flatten out into the elegantly strong braiding of sisters reflecting their brothers' pains.

This story becomes the elegant heuristic for a new type of methodology that moves from within narratives of joy to locate the external realities of lives younger, perhaps tinier, yet more innocent than we have cared to acknowledge. One idea from the book lingers: the many similarities shared by young Black and Brown men and boys—in spite of potential differences in social class, family background, and age, to name but a few—and how they relate to interactions are central to understanding Black and Latinx men and boys, particularly those deemed "at risk" or difficult to educate.

Of course, as Villavicencio notes, the questions raised in this book "are by no means comprehensive, but they are inspired by listening to hundreds of policy folks, researchers, parents, educators, and students talk about how we should be thinking about change and what it will take to make differences that are meaningful and enduring." This is because human science is complex, produced interactively, dependent on not only the questions of the researcher but the experiences we share with those we research. Thus, any practice of inquiry is likely to be influenced by who we are in relationship to who we study. Despite the dismal statistics and the growing reality that Black and Latinx men and boys are vanishing or missing from our universities and schools, from labor markets, and from the communities where we were raised, it would be a mistake to treat us merely as victims.

This is not a book about victims but about victories. It is about locating the triumphs of the human spirit, the possibilities that sit between voice and silence where a voice-centered methodology of inquiry makes it possible for us to build theory from listening. This is what Villavicencio has done: she listened. And in so doing, she created a space where Black and Brown men and boys could express what's too often taken off the table for us: success and second chances, desires and fears, pains and hopes and eventual prosperity. She created an opening for Black and Brown men and boys to escape the stereotypical images and all of the layers of baggage that lay atop us.

This is why this book is so important. It is a provocative and inspiring account of humans and human victories that provides us with the opportunity to listen to and learn from the voices of young Black men and boys—the victors—who are finally heard speaking not of eternal struggle but of expanded success.

David E. Kirkland
New York University

CHAPTER 1

Not a Moment but a Movement

The Story of ESI

> It is the hope of the ESI team that lessons learned through its implementation can influence the work of schools in New York City and beyond as we improve the educational opportunities for Black and Latino young men nationwide. As was its hope, ESI has supported the movement, not just this moment.
>
> —Lillian Dunn, Elise Corwin, and John Duval, "Creating a Movement, Not a Moment: New York City's Efforts to Implement an Initiative Focused on Young Men of Color"

I WANT TO TELL you a story that does not often get told in education. In the relatively small number of cases when an education policy meets its intended goals, it is widely shared with the scholarly community in peer-reviewed journals and at academic conferences. It is celebrated in the media with inspired headlines and quotes from those deemed responsible for the success. When policies and programs fail, however, they go out with a whisper, dismissed as having been misguided from the start or otherwise quietly disregarded as yesterday's news. We rarely take the time to examine what occurred or attempt to learn what might be useful to our communities of education scholars, policy makers, and practitioners. We quickly move on to the next policy, the future study, the new administration, the current crisis.

While looking ahead is important and—from the position of those on the ground—attending to the here and now is critical, allow me to turn our attention to another time, another moment, as an opportunity to learn from what can only be observed in retrospect. This is the story of an education initiative that was hard won and hard fought, which shot high and fell short, even while managing to effect meaningful change. The Expanded Success Initiative (ESI), a predecessor to My Brother's Keeper and one of many racial equity policies in districts around the country, was a signature policy of the New York Department of Education (NYC DOE). It was one part of a four-strand effort to close gaps for young men of color in the areas of education, health, employment, and criminal justice. Under the umbrella of the Young Men's Initiative (YMI), ESI set out to not only improve graduation rates (which had already been increasing in NYC for all groups) but to improve postsecondary outcomes, setting the bar higher than previous mayoral administrations had. It was also part of a broader plan to change the narrative about young men of color—from a deficit lens to an asset-based one, from "preventing dropout" to "expanding opportunities for college." It sought to shift the question from "Why are boys of color lagging behind?" to "Why are schools failing to raise them up?"

Despite an investment of $24 million, the backing of the mayor and other leaders, and a robust infrastructure of school support, ESI did not achieve its ultimate goal of increasing college enrollment. It did, however, improve teachers' ability to connect with their students as well as students' sense of belonging, noteworthy in itself considering how schools can often be spaces of alienation for Black and Brown boys. Yet, these changes alone did not improve some key outcomes that the funders, program leaders, and schools expected after four years of tremendous dedication and effort. This book helps explain why the initiative did not achieve all of its goals while providing insight into the important ways ESI changed school culture and touched the lives of many students across multiple schools. This study makes clear how ESI did indeed change the conversation. ESI informed the work of the district's Office of Equity and Access and inspired countless educators through its Critical and Courageous Conversation series. It made space for district leaders to speak candidly about the city's racial segregation and provide antiracism and equity training for all its teachers. So while this book focuses on what may have limited the impact of ESI, it nonetheless highlights the initiative's promise and aims to inform the work of other scholars, policy makers, and practitioners dedicated to improving opportunities and outcomes for boys of color.

HISTORICAL AND ENDURING OPPORTUNITY GAPS

For decades, documenting education "achievement gaps" between Black and Latinx students and their White and Asian counterparts has been commonplace in education research. Some argue that it only serves to reaffirm entrenched biases against students of color while ignoring the social contexts in which these gaps are formed over time. Black scholars have challenged this discourse by recasting disparate outcomes in the context of the historical, persistent (and intentional) educational inequity in the United States. In her 2006 Presidential Address to the American Education Research Association, Gloria Ladson-Billings declared, "We do not have an achievement gap; we have an education debt," calling attention to the ways Black, Latinx, and Native American communities have been systematically denied the educational opportunities that White students have been granted.[1] Jacqueline J. Irvine pushes back on the achievement gap frame by calling attention to other gaps that are sometimes ignored in our conversations about student performance, including the teacher quality gap, school funding gap, and the digital divide gap, to name a few.[2] Richard Milner provides scholars with an opportunity gap explanatory framework to name and explain education practice beyond the achievement gap, calling explicit attention to "(a) color blindness, (b) cultural conflicts, (c) myth of meritocracy, (d) low expectations and deficit mindsets, and (e) context-neutral mindsets and practices."[3] This lens allow scholars to shift the focus from documenting when students are not meeting expectations to exploring how schools are failing to serve them effectively. The entrenched system of exclusion in the American education system and the ways these traditions still play out in schools today lead some to argue that the system isn't broken; rather, it is working as intended.

Even within these systems, many Black and Latinx males succeed in ways that present a counternarrative to how they are typically described in the public or in education research.[4] Without diminishing these success stories, however, scholars have long chronicled the ways boys of color, in particular, have been marginalized in schools.[5] In this book I touch on only a few dimensions of schooling that intersect with the initiative and its underlying theory of action. One prominent locus of inequitable treatment in schools centers on issues of discipline, behavior, and biased perceptions of boys of color. (These perceptions apply to Black girls as well.[6]) Education researchers have long documented an overrepresentation of Black and Latinx males who are referred to for disciplinary actions, suspended, or expelled.[7] For Black boys, in particular, the intense scrutiny can begin as early as preschool. Data from the US Department of Education Office for Civil Rights reports that while Black children account for roughly 19 percent of all preschoolers, they make up nearly half of preschoolers who get suspended. A recent study showed that when expecting challenging behavior, teachers stared longer at Black children, especially Black boys.[8] School suspensions or removal from classrooms may have a profound impact on a child's educational experience. When students are removed from their regular classrooms, they miss instruction, opportunities to learn, and support from their teachers. Repeated removals from school can set a student further and further behind, making it more likely that a student will disengage from school entirely. It is no wonder why boys of color are less satisfied with school, even as early as during the transition into kindergarten.[9]

In addition to these potentially harmful perceptions of Black and Latinx boys, there is a corresponding deficit view of their academic abilities, work ethic, and overall capacity to do well in school.[10] Black boys are underrepresented in gifted and talented courses and are more likely to be overrepresented in special education.[11] Race and gender may play a role in how students are perceived and treated by teachers and administrators who have considerable discretion over which students are classified as requiring special education. The fact that a disproportionate number of male students of color receive special education services may suggest that these students are being misdiagnosed and designated to special education classrooms for reasons other than special needs. In related research on suspensions, studies suggest that boys are sometimes labeled as special education students because of perceptions of their behavior.[12]

The mislabeling of boys of color based on assumptions of their misbehavior and the cumulative effect of lower expectations by teachers and other adults helps establish schools as places of alienation. Compounding this experience is the fact that boys of color are not likely to see teachers who look like them. The idea of "windows and mirrors" began as a metaphor to understand curricula that could both reflect students' experiences and provide them insight into the world of others, but it has also become a lens through which to understand whom students are exposed to in their classrooms and schools.[13] The cultural mismatch between the teaching profession and the country's student population has been well documented. While students of color make up slightly more than 50 percent of the total student population in the US, the teacher workforce is 82 percent White.[14] In more than thirty states, there is a demographic divide between teachers and students of twenty percentage points or greater.[15] The dearth of teachers of color is important considering the mounting evidence showing the positive effects of same-race teachers. Studies have found that teachers of color not only improve nonacademic outcomes, such as improved attendance and reduced suspensions, but they can also boost the academic performance of students of color.[16] In fact, Seth Gershenson and colleagues found that having just one Black teacher in elementary school reduced Black boys' probability of dropping out of high school by 39 percent.[17] In New York City, where 85 percent of students are Black or Latinx and 42 percent of teachers are White, students are more likely than in other districts to have teachers of color.[18] But the dearth of *male* teachers of color makes it unlikely that boys of color will encounter windows and mirrors in their classrooms. Only 3.7 percent and 3 percent of the teacher workforce are Black and Latinx males, respectively.[19]

Intersecting with these in-school factors are a host of other challenges that boys of color face outside of school, including a level of surveillance and police violence against Black and Brown bodies. Policies like stop-and-frisk and the arming of regular citizens have made it dangerous to engage in everyday activities while being Black—playing (Tamir Rice), jogging (Ahmaud Arbery), standing (Eric Garner), wearing a hoodie (Trayvon Martin), playing loud music (Jordan Davis), being in your own apartment (Botham Jean). A recent study found that "about 1 in 1,000 Black men and boys can expect to die as a result of police violence over the course of their lives—a risk that's about 2.5 times higher than their white peers."[20] Domestic and international protests over the murder of George Floyd captured the public's growing rage at these injustices, though it is unclear whether efforts to meaningfully reform the police will be enacted. As a result of the threats to one's life and the chronic stress it causes, Black males suffer greatly in quality-of-life indicators, including physical and mental illness.[21] Long-time educator and school leader Sharif El-Mekki labels the experience of living as a Black male in the United States as PTSD—*persistent*-traumatic stress disorder.[22] For many Black and Brown boys, school does not necessarily provide an escape from the world that perceives them as a threat but, rather, as yet another place where they might be unfairly targeted and penalized. Indeed, the school-to-prison pipeline may be tolerated because of who it affects the most.[23]

It is important in this context to consider two things: discussions of "achievement gaps" are limited in what they can tell us about the intersecting ways that historical, current, and persistent inequities are shaping those gaps, and efforts designed to close achievement gaps will be limited to the extent that they do not consider the gaps in opportunity and the forces (color blindness, cultural mismatch, deficit mind-sets, xenophobia, structural racism, anti-Blackness) that make them so. The severity of these inequities should also raise questions about the potential of any one initiative or set of policies to unweave the web of institutional inequities across multiple generations. To some, these efforts may seem like "band-aids on bullet holes." But for others, the hard truths of the country's education debt only magnify our collective responsibility to acknowledge its impact, undo its harm, and ultimately seek justice.

THE EDUCATION LANDSCAPE FOR YOUNG MEN OF COLOR IN NEW YORK CITY

New York City's educational landscape prior to the launch of ESI served as the impetus for the initiative. A large body of research has documented the relationships between socioeconomic status and educational performance.[24] Nationally, children of color are disproportionately represented among those living in poverty. More than one in three Black and Latinx children are living in poverty (defined as a $23,000 annual income for a family of four), compared to one in ten White children.[25] Though NYC is one school district, there is incredible disparity among the boroughs and the neighborhoods within the boroughs. According to the 2010 US Census, the percentage of individuals living in poverty is 30.2 in the Bronx, 23 in Brooklyn, 16.4 in Manhattan, 15 in Queens, and 11.8 in Staten Island.[26] While, overall, 14.5 percent of individuals across all boroughs live in poverty, there are higher percentages of poverty in the Bronx and in Brooklyn, where the majority of the population is Black or Latinx. At the time of the study, about 80 percent of Black and Latinx students qualified to receive free or reduced-priced lunch.

Examining the performance trends of Black and Latinx male students in New York City masks differences among subgroups of students, particularly students who are immigrants and newcomers. The academic experiences of immigrant students are inherently different than those of their native peers. For example, in one national cohort of graduates who identified as Latinx male aged 16–25, only 12 percent of native-born students had dropped out of high school, as compared to 37 percent of foreign-born students.[27] Immigrant students are also more likely to experience interruptions in their formal education, higher rates of depression, and other psychosocial issues.[28] Moreover, immigrant students who are also English learners or emergent bilinguals must acquire a new language while learning the social cues, norms, and culture of American schools.[29] At the same time, many are forced to abandon their own languages, cultures, and customs to become assimilated into their new environments (especially in increasingly immigrant-hostile political environments).[30] Thus, there are distinct challenges for the many Black and Latinx male students who are also immigrants and/or emergent bilinguals. In 2011, roughly 11 percent of Black and 15 percent of Latinx students were born abroad, and over 60 percent of Latinx students (and about 7 percent of Black students) in NYC schools were from homes with a dominant language other than English.

Acknowledging that factors such as poverty and immigration status affect student outcomes should not blind us to the ways their experiences *in* schools help limit or expand their potential to succeed there. In *Moving the Needle: Exploring Key Levers to Boost College Readiness Among Black and Latino Males in NYC*, our research team provided evidence of the overrepresentation of boys of color in special education and their underrepresentation in gifted and talented programs—assignments that depend heavily on the decisions of individual teachers.[31] Black and Latinx male students made up the largest portion of special education students in NYC schools, representing 51 percent of all of students receiving these services and yet only 34 percent of the student population. And while Black and Latinx students represented 24 percent and 41 percent of all kindergarteners, respectively, only 8 percent and 10 percent were placed in gifted and talented programs. Suspensions rates were also telling. After an analysis of ten years of discipline data for NYC schools, the New York Civil Liberties Union found that Black students accounted for 53 percent of all suspensions.[32] (In contrast, Latinx students were suspended at a rate roughly proportional to their share of the overall population.) These rates were comparable to national figures.

In *Moving the Needle*, we also analyzed schools' access to higher-level curricula prior to ESI because of its relationship to college-readiness and enrollment. In particular, Algebra II continues to be a strong predictor of college enrollment and success and is a basic requirement for admittance to all state flagship schools.[33] But among NYC public schools serving the largest populations of Black and Latinx students, only 22 percent offered Algebra II at the time.[34] By omitting Algebra II from high school degree requirements, these schools automatically disqualified a large pool of Black and Latinx male students from applying for admission to many four-year institutions (postsecondary institutions in New York State require at least three years of mathematics). Moreover, even in schools that did offer Algebra II, Black and Latinx male students did not enroll in these courses in the same numbers as their White and Asian counterparts. And even among those males of color who did complete Algebra II, many did not take the Algebra II Regents exam. Of the 55 percent of Black and 57 percent of Latinx males eligible to take the exam, only about 20 percent did so.[35]

In addition to these demographic factors and school-based practices, the establishment of ESI was motivated by some key outcomes. In NYC in 2010, the high school graduation rates for Black and Latinx males were below 60 percent, though they had been steadily increasing over the prior decade.[36] This was comparable to national rates. According to the Schott Foundation's *50 State Report*, 52 percent of Black males and 58 percent of Latinx males who started high school in 2009 graduated.[37] At the same time, however, college-readiness rates for Black and Latinx graduates were only at 7 percent and 9 percent, respectively. Thus, while more Black and Latinx males were graduating from high school, many fewer were prepared to enter and persist in college. There is an important distinction between college-readiness and college enrollment. In NYC, college-readiness is defined as earning a New York State Regents Diploma and receiving a score of 80 or higher on a

Mathematics Regents exam and a score of 75 or higher on an English Language Arts (ELA) exam. The rationale behind this definition is that without these scores, students admitted to the City University of New York (CUNY) system would be required to enroll in remedial courses, which has shown to be negatively associated with college completion.[38]

By this definition, college-readiness hovered below 10 percent for this population. However, the percentage of students who enrolled in college was higher than the fraction of students who were deemed college-ready. In other words, many young people who did not meet the college-readiness benchmark enrolled in college. In the years prior to ESI, almost 30 percent of Black and Latinx young males were enrolled in a postsecondary institution five years after entering high school, mirroring the national college enrollment rate of 33 percent for Black and Latinx males.[39] At the same time, their female counterparts enrolled at significantly higher rates. For young Black women, college enrollment rates were eleven percentage points higher, at 39 percent; for Latina students, college enrollment rates were nine percentage points higher, at 37 percent. Another dimension of the college enrollment picture was the type of college selected by Black and Latinx males. Of the Black and Latinx men who enrolled in college, a sizable fraction of them attended less-competitive institutions. For example, Latinx students showed a particularly strong preference for enrolling in two-year institutions. The choice between two- and four-year institutions has implications for college completion, since evidence suggests that students are less likely to earn a bachelor's degree if they start at a two-year college.[40] Thus, it was important not only to ensure that Black and Latinx males had the opportunity to enroll in college but to also support their decision-making about the type of institution they would attend.

The patterns in NYC did not differ substantially from the national averages. Black and Latinx males were more likely to be economically disadvantaged, to be from immigrant households, to be overrepresented in special education classrooms and among students suspended, and yet to be underexposed to high-level coursework in math and science. Their rates of high school graduation (while on an upward trajectory) and college enrollment were also similar to national figures. However, one statistic proved particularly alarming (while also highlighting an opportunity to intervene): disaggregated college-readiness levels by prior performance. Figure 1.1 shows that a substantial racial gap persisted even among students scoring at higher levels of proficiency. In particular, even among the students with the highest level of proficiency (level 4) in the eighth-grade ELA exam, there was a twenty percentage point gap in college-readiness rates by the time they reached twelfth grade. To some extent, eighth-grade ELA test scores can help predict the likelihood that students will graduate college-ready. But if those test scores explained the entire college-readiness gap, there would be a much smaller disparity between different groups by race. The fact that even those eighth-grade boys who scored a 3 or 4 were not graduating college-ready suggested that the disparities existed in high school even for students who came in relatively well prepared.

At the time these numbers were released, district leaders saw that even high-performing boys of color were falling behind upon entering

FIGURE 1.1   NYC's college-readiness gap

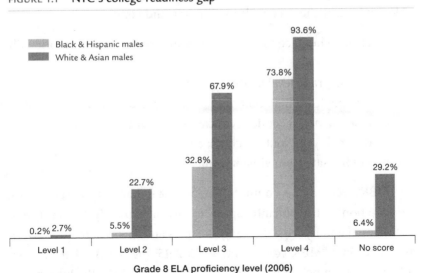

Grade 8 ELA proficiency level (2006)

Source: NYC DOE

high school. Some, however, saw it as an opportunity, believing that those numbers suggested that some traction could actually be made during the high school years. While sobering, these patterns indicated to the NYC DOE that some investment at the high school level could help close the gap between Black and Latinx young men's high school graduation and college-readiness rates. This figure was thus used to motivate and contextualize ESI as a college-readiness effort focused on the four years of the high school experience.

THE YOUNG MEN'S INITIATIVE AND MY BROTHER'S KEEPER

To understand ESI, it is important to contextualize it within broader efforts to improve opportunities and outcomes for young men of color. In 2014, President Obama launched My Brother's Keeper (MBK) to improve the opportunities and outcomes of Black and Latinx young men. Based on data from the Departments of Justice, Education, and Health and Human Services, as well as new databases created under the auspices of MBK, the initiative identified the widest gaps facing men of color and established six goals for children and youth:

- entering school cognitively, physically, socially, and emotionally ready;
- reading at grade level by third grade;
- graduating from high school;
- completing postsecondary education or training;
- being employed if out of school; and
- remaining safe from violent crime.

MBK secured the commitment of more than fifty corporations, organizations, and philanthropists to invest explicitly in Black and Latinx men and issued a challenge to cities and towns across the country to become "MBK communities." In 2015, the My Brother's Keeper Alliance was launched to sustain the mission of MBK. By 2016, nearly 250 communities in all fifty states, nineteen Tribal Nations, the District of Columbia, and Puerto Rico had taken on this designation and in so doing committed to addressing one or more of the six milestones through a detailed action plan agreed on by a group of diverse stakeholders.[41] With the change in presidential administrations, this effort now falls under the purview of the Obama Foundation, but it continues to focus largely on the same goals through community-based mechanisms. In particular, its goals center on closing gaps in education and the labor force through locally developed initiatives and programs as well as partnerships between nonprofit organizations, philanthropies, and municipal leaders.

Though MBK is widely known, New York City's Young Men's Initiative preceded MBK by two years. In 2012, the city launched YMI under Mayor Michael Bloomberg. As the largest investment ever focused on young men of color at the time, YMI served as a banner program for My Brother's Keeper and also inspired some of the building blocks of the national effort, including focusing on a range of life outcomes and engaging community partnerships across different sectors. YMI was unprecedented not only in the amount of money it invested in males of color ($127 million) but in how it brought more than twenty city agencies together to create a broad-based approach to improving outcomes for Black and Latinx males in education, health, employment, and criminal justice.

It is important to consider YMI in light of the political context and unrest in NYC at the time. In particular, Mayor Bloomberg's stop-and-frisk, one of his signature policies (and a source of contention in his 2020 presidential bid), complicated the public reaction to YMI, especially when Black and Brown male students were often victims of stop-and-frisk. Joscha Legewie and Jeffrey Fagan, for example, found stark disparities in police exposure among young people in the city: fifteen-year-old Black males are stopped 2.7 times more than their Latinx counterparts and 5.9 times more than their White counterparts.[42] Data suggest that "students heavily exposed to stop-and-frisk are more likely to struggle in school and more likely to experience symptoms of anxiety and depression."[43]

Neither YMI nor MBK have been without controversy. Both efforts have received criticism for not addressing the struggles of Black and Latina women.[44] While many of the disparities in outcomes are more severe for males, much remains to be done to understand and better address the unique challenges confronting women of color. (NYC launched the Young Women's Initiative in 2015, though it was not nearly as well funded or resourced.) Others have pointed out that neither MBK nor YMI goes far enough to address the systems that deepen inequality or to promote local and state policies that undo them (including stop-and-frisk). Michael Dumas, for example, faults efforts like MBK for highlighting deficit-based representations of young men of color and for "locating the problem within (the bodies of) Black boys and young men rather than in the social and economic order."[45] Yet, the ways stakeholder groups in communities like New York City, Oakland, Milwaukee, Chicago, and Austin framed and implemented these efforts appear to be more complex than does some of the rhetoric employed by initiatives for young men of color. Many of these local implementers—including those in NYC—explicitly rejected deficit perspectives in favor of calling out the structural racism embedded in schooling.

THE EXPANDED SUCCESS INITIATIVE: IMPORTANT GAINS AND LESSONS LEARNED

While the primary outcome of the Expanded Success Initiative, YMI's educational component, was college- and career-readiness, early documentation describes multiple intermediary and long-term goals, including providing students with socioemotional supports, improving access to high-level coursework, increasing teacher capacity to make curriculum and pedagogy relevant to boys and young men of color, and broadly changing the narrative from one that focused on students' low college-readiness rates to understanding how schools were failing to support them toward college. To that end, ESI provided a combination of funding ($250,000, or about 3–10 percent of a school's annual budget), professional development, and ongoing support to forty public high schools with relatively high graduation rates for Black and Latinx males but college enrollment rates that were on par with the rest of the city. The four-year initiative was designed to begin with a ninth-grade cohort and end when that cohort was ready to enroll in college. ESI schools were charged with creating and expanding services and supports for male students of color in three broad domains that the NYC DOE saw as important for increasing college-readiness: academics, youth development, and school culture (see figure 1.2). In addition, ESI placed a heavy emphasis on the principles of culturally relevant education undergirding all three domains.

Unlike other similar efforts across the country, ESI was subject to rigorous research from the outset. A multiyear study documented the design, launch, and implementation, of the initiative, examining ESI practices in all forty participating schools (serving roughly fifteen thousand students) to capture how it was being enacted on the ground and to assess the quality of implementation across schools.[46] Using a set of comparison schools, the study also measured ESI's impact on graduation rates, college enrollment, attendance, suspension rates, and a host of other related outcomes (e.g., self-efficacy, sense of fair treatment, postsecondary planning).

The story of ESI's "results" is a mixed one. Of the design and roll-out, the study found that ESI represented a significant investment of resources and buy-in; it was characterized by strong centralized support while encouraging school-level autonomy and experimentation. On the ground, implementation was strong in the second year but diminished somewhat in Years 3 and 4 as funding levels declined. Moreover, implementation varied across schools, as did levels of participation among Black and Latinx male students. For example, a group of nine schools exhibited relatively strong and consistent alignment with the ESI principles and average participation rates of 50 percent or higher across the four years of the initiative, while seven schools had consistently low alignment and average participation rates below 30 percent; the remaining twenty-one schools had alignment and participation rates that fell somewhere in the middle. Still, educators and students across

FIGURE 1.2   Evaluating NYC's Expanded Success Initiative: Findings from Year 1

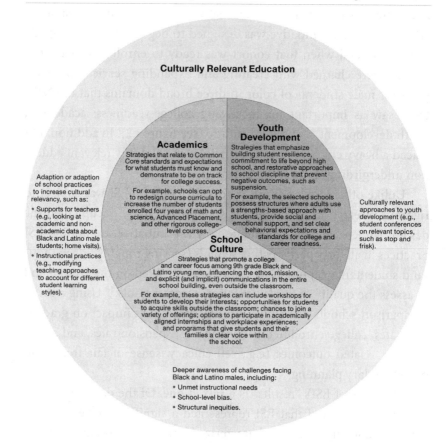

Source: Reproduced from "Definitions of Academics, Youth Development, and School Culture from NYC DOE" (report, Research Alliance for NYC Schools, New York, 2013).

schools consistently reported meaningful changes to school culture and relationships as a result of ESI. Three areas of school change stood out across schools and years of the initiative: the development of a culturally relevant orientation to teaching and learning, improved school relationships, and a stronger schoolwide commitment to supporting students' postsecondary goals. Notably, these reported changes reflect fundamental shifts in educators' mind-sets and beliefs about their students, as opposed to just the addition of new programming. Taken together, these findings suggest that ESI changed the culture of schools in ways that particularly benefited Black and Latinx young men.[47]

ESI also increased student participation in a range of activities. An annual student survey revealed that Black and Latinx young men in ESI schools were more likely than their counterparts in non-ESI comparison schools to participate in activities associated with the three domains and culturally relevant education. The largest and most consistent differences occurred in students' participation in college and career preparation activities (e.g., college trips, college advising, work-based learning) and in youth development activities (e.g., mentoring programs, youth groups, student advisory programs). Black and Latinx young men in ESI schools were more likely to participate in academic support activities (e.g., tutoring programs, Regents prep services, Advanced Placement or International Baccalaureate classes) than in college preparation or youth development activities, but the differences between ESI and non-ESI schools were generally smaller, since academic activities were common for both groups. Finally, in keeping with the study's findings from interviews and focus groups, Black and Latinx young men in ESI schools were more likely than their counterparts in non-ESI schools to report being exposed to culturally relevant materials in their classes. Beyond exposure and participation, Black and Latinx young men in ESI schools were more likely than similar students in non-ESI comparison schools to respond positively on measures of fair treatment and belonging in their schools, especially in grades 11 and 12. This finding is particularly important given past research showing that high schools are often alienating spaces for young men of color.[48]

More directly related to ESI's focus on college-readiness and enrollment, ESI increased students' interaction with adults around discussing plans for their future. Black and Latinx young men in ESI schools were consistently more likely than their counterparts in non-ESI comparison schools to engage in conversations with adults in their lives about college and careers. ESI students were also more likely to take the SAT. Yet, ESI had little or no systematic impact on high school graduation, college-readiness, or college enrollment rates. Just over two-thirds of the Black and Latinx young men in *both* ESI and non-ESI schools graduated with a Regents diploma within four years of entering high school. In addition, ESI and comparison students applied for college, pursued financial aid options, or were accepted into college at similar rates. Students in both sets of schools applied to an average of about five colleges, and more than three-quarters of both groups reported being accepted to at least one. However, less than 20 percent of these students met the New York State college-readiness standard, suggesting that most of these high school graduates likely required remediation if they enrolled in college. About a quarter of Black and Latinx male students in both sets of schools enrolled in a four-year college immediately following high school graduation. While graduation and college enrollment rates for Black and Latinx young men in both ESI and non-ESI schools were higher than citywide averages for this demographic, they were still substantially lower than rates for Black and Latinx females and White and Asian males.[49]

The fact that ESI accomplished what it did in the face of historical patterns of disenfranchisement among young males of color is noteworthy and suggests that certain elements of the initiative should be emulated elsewhere. But making sense of why and how ESI missed the mark is also a learning opportunity. Where did the breakdowns in the theory or the implementation occur? Which decision points could have made a difference for the potential success of the initiative?

In this book I argue that ESI's ambitious goals, its success in providing protective environments for marginalized students, and its limited success in meeting other outcomes provide a set of concrete lessons for other districts about how to maximize the impact of similar initiatives. I reflect on some of the larger lessons learned from the NYC model about how districts and schools can create and implement systemic initiatives focused on better serving Black and Latinx male students, including attending to issues such as system-level buy-in, school-level support, and a focus on school culture to address the multiple barriers facing young men of color in schools. These components, among others, serve as important dimensions of a model that school districts should consider in their own efforts to improve outcomes for historically underserved students.

ABOUT THE STUDY

This work is based on a four-year study of ESI conducted by the Research Alliance for New York City Schools. The study was designed to answer two broad sets of research questions:

- What services and programs did ESI schools provide to their staff and students as a result of this initiative? What challenges did schools face in implementing these programs, and how did they attempt to address those challenges?
- Did ESI impact students' academic outcomes (e.g., credit accumulation, graduation rates, and college-going rates) and socioemotional outcomes (e.g., sense of belonging, sense of fair treatment)?[50]

As such, the study consisted of two core components: an implementation study and a study of impacts on students. Both components drew on a sample of 80 regular public high schools across the 5 boroughs (with the exception of Staten Island)—40 ESI schools and a set of 40 comparison schools serving nearly 15,000 students. Black and Latinx males represented at least 30 percent of the population in every school in the study (nearly all qualified for free and reduced-priced lunch), though important differences existed among this group in terms of cultural backgrounds, immigrant status, and special education status.

The implementation study examined the services and supports that schools planned and implemented under the auspices of ESI, the challenges schools confronted along the way, and the strategies they used to address those challenges. As part of this study component, the research team also explored the supports and training offered by the district to understand its role in implementation. The data draw on more than five hundred interviews with key school actors (e.g., principals, teachers, guidance counselors, deans, students) and extensive document review (e.g., school-based action plans, program questionnaires, curricula) used to develop an understanding of the types of programming and supports for Black and Latinx males in their schools. In Years 3 and 4 of the study, we conducted additional interviews, observations, and document reviews in a set of eight case study schools. In each year of the evaluation we used a multistep process to analyze interview and focus group data through transcript coding and a combination of reflection and analytic memo writing.

The impact study was designed to determine whether students who were exposed to ESI-related interventions and supports achieved better outcomes than they would have if their school had not been involved in ESI. The research team drew data for the impact study from administrative data, including attendance, credit accumulation, graduation rates, and college enrollment, and from student surveys to measure nonacademic outcomes, such as sense of belonging, racial and gender climate, and postsecondary aspirations. We conducted analysis of the academic outcomes using a comparative interrupted time series design, which allowed for the best comparison of ESI schools to non-ESI schools in the absence of random assignment. For the survey analysis, we assessed the impact of ESI on students' responses using regression analyses, comparing the differences of students in participating ESI schools with students in comparison schools.

In both its breadth and depth, the study offered a unique opportunity to examine a set of underlying principles and everyday strategies aimed at improving schooling and outcomes for Black and Latinx young males. In addition, the heterogeneity of the school sample—in size, years of existence, population, etc.—speaks to the potential for generalizing the findings to other contexts. (See the appendix for more details about the study's design, data collection, and analysis.)

MY POSITIONALITY

As the principal investigator on this study, and given its focus on race and gender, it is important to describe my own motivation and approach in leading this work and how they were informed by my identities and experiences.

First and foremost, I identify as a Latina and a daughter of immigrants. In their early twenties, my parents emigrated from Ecuador to Toronto, Canada, before moving on to Buffalo, then traversing the United States, and finally landing in Southern California, where I was born. Though not my own journey, the immigrant experience is so strongly etched into my psyche (en mi sangre) that I constantly carry the feeling of being an outsider, of being exposed for not knowing the right words or for failing to carry myself in ways that are expected in predominantly White spaces. It took me two years before I uttered a word in my college classes, and I remained similarly hesitant to speak in my first year as a research associate at the Research Alliance at New York University. At the same time, I am aware that my fear of being seen as an imposter is tempered by the fact that I may or may not be perceived as different by the outside world. Since my ethnicity is invisible or ambiguous to many, I am granted privilege to move freely in most spaces, to be in the university without standing out too much, to not worry about my own safety with police or other authority figures—which I can't say is the case for my partner, who had a gun pulled on him by an officer in the subway. In fact, the juxtaposition of how the world may perceive us—including in circles where he is met with much more trust—makes me aware on a daily basis of the limitations of fully knowing another community or their lived experiences. And so it is with humility that I write about experiences I may not have had myself and also with much gratitude for the hundreds of young people who have shared their voices and first-hand accounts with me.

I also approach my work as a scholar with the heart of a teacher. I was a middle and high school teacher for five years in Brooklyn, New York, and Oakland, California, before deciding to pursue an advanced degree. Research suggests it takes at least five years to become an effective teacher, so I do not pretend to have been a great success in the classroom. But my students taught me a great deal. They taught me to appreciate young people—to sit back and listen, to let my students take the lead, to share my own passions as a way of creating space for theirs.

We had lively conversations about *Hamlet* and *Things Fall Apart*. We read *Their Eyes Were Watching God* and reenacted scenes from *Death of a Salesman*. Despite what I had heard from my peers in their student teaching programs (I started teaching without the benefit of one), my students weren't unmotivated. (And they didn't lack any "grit," despite the scholarship that suggests they do.) Moreover, their backgrounds and experiences were too varied to say anything universal about "these kids." If I think back on the boys in my classroom, I remember Christian, who the dean told me was an "asshole," who was hand-picked by other staff to be in the new teacher's classroom.[51] I remember how much he made me laugh and how good he was at impressions. I remember Daniel, a Latinx who grew up in a Black neighborhood. He liked to fix bikes, paint his nails, and listen to alternative rock. I remember Anthony, who did SAT tutoring with me after school. Years later he became an educator himself and remained devoted to his mom and little sister. James, who was only in my class for a few months, was far more mature than the other eighth graders in his class. I learned after he left the school that his mother had died of HIV when he was a young boy. Andre wasn't at school very often because he was taking care of his younger siblings, but he wrote tender poetry and ended up marrying his high school sweetheart. Tony was always in school and completed every assignment with meticulous handwriting. He went on to Stanford and now owns his own business.

When I became a researcher and saw NYC DOE's call to study this initiative for Black and Latinx males, I thought back to the experiences of these boys. I wondered what this type of initiative might have meant for them. I was heartened by ESI's foregrounding of race and the fact that it was led by Black and Latinx males. I approached my work as a researcher with the tools and training I received from my mentors and with the expectations and support of an organization that prides itself on the rigor of its research. But this work was also personal, grounded in my own drive to understand, name, and address education inequity and to uncover the many ways schools can simultaneously serve as sites that reproduce or interrupt injustice.

A NOTE ON TERMS AND STUDENT IDENTITIES

I use the terms *Black* and *Latinx* to describe the student population that is the focus of the book, which is consistent with those used by the initiative. I use the gender-neutral label *Latinx* as a term of inclusion, while acknowledging that the individuals I write about here may self-identify with other terms (e.g., *Latino, Hispanic, Chicano*) and that new language and labels (e.g., *Latine*) may continue to evolve over time.[52] I use *Brown* to signify Latinidad while recognizing that Latinx students are not monolithically Brown, particularly when a quarter of Latinos in the US identify as Afro-Latinos.[53] I also use *boys* in an attempt to reclaim some of the childhood and adolescence that is robbed from Black and Brown boys who are often perceived as being older than they are and as less innocent than their White peers.[54]

Based on the target population of the initiative, I use *boys* or *young men of color* synonymously with *Black and Latinx young men*, even though *students of color* might typically be used to refer to Indigenous students and students of Asian descent as well. I acknowledge these terms are unsatisfying, inadvertently hold up model minority myths, and mask both the heterogeneity within these labels and the intersectionality of students' identities.[55] On student surveys, for example, many students checked off multiple racial and ethnic categories, and on modified student surveys in later years, students often opted to write in their country of origin versus checking off a categorical label. In New York City in particular, where 40 percent of the population is foreign born, it is important to not universalize the Black or Latinx experience as monolithic. The experience of a Black student whose family has lived in Harlem for generations may differ greatly from that of a student who is newly arrived from Haiti, even though a school survey may label them similarly. In the same vein, a Puerto Rican student from the Bronx may not be able to identify with an Ecuadorian peer living in Queens, even if both their families speak Spanish at home. The diversity of Black and Latinx boyhood should be an important dimension of efforts designed to speak to students' racial and ethnic identities and is one that did emerge in the case of ESI.

ORGANIZATION OF THE BOOK

Am I My Brother's Keeper? Educational Opportunities and Outcomes for Black and Brown Boys leads readers through a journey—not a moment but a movement.[56] It begins with a look at the design of the initiative and examines the layers of support undergirding its implementation. It also examines closely the internal workings of schools, the work of educators, and the experiences of students. Just as these components are all essential to the success of the initiative, so are they necessary dimensions of developing and implementing any policy initiative aimed at transforming districts and schools for traditionally underserved students.

I have organized the book into two parts. Part I focuses on the actions of district and program leaders by highlighting important strategic decisions made around the rollout, launch, and implementation of ESI. Chapter 2 examines the strengths and limitations of the initiative's initial design and argues that initiatives such as these be grounded in theory, led by love, and sustained by commitment. It describes the ways the initiative, while informed by prior evidence, lacked a concrete enough theory of action to drive implementation across forty schools. It did, however, benefit from a strong network of partnerships and resources and from a dynamic leadership that resisted deficit-laden narratives about boys of color and imbued the initiative with passion and purpose. Chapter 3 describes the support provided to schools that served as the foundation for the entire effort, including partnerships with external organizations, capacity building through targeted professional development, and experiential learning through professional community. This chapter also explores how the lack of more prescriptive standards or accountability measures limited ESI's ability to maximize the potential of its model and discusses specific ways to address these shortcomings.

Part II examines the ecological approaches enacted within schools addressing systemic inequalities experienced by Black and Latinx boys. Chapters 4–6 explore how schools can address multiple dimensions of the student experience by attending to students' academic needs and postsecondary goals, shifting teachers' mind-sets and beliefs about their students, and creating protective environments for boys of color. The chapters in Part II draw careful portraits of effective practices related to each of these and utilize case studies of particular schools to illustrate how to implement these approaches and strategies across different school settings.

Finally, in considering the last years of the initiative and its legacy, chapter 7 highlights strategies for sustaining change and describes how the lessons learned from this work may inform broader equity-based policy and practice in NYC DOE and other districts. Indeed, ESI has morphed from an initiative located in forty schools to a movement whose principles have spread to schools across the district and permeated multiple offices of the Department of Education and the city. This final chapter also raises critical questions about how to recast or reimagine education and efforts to restore racial justice for students and communities.

When presenting findings from this study at local, regional, national, and international conferences, I observed that policy makers, educators, and researchers engaged in these efforts share a desire to learn from other districts that are facing the same challenges and are committed to the same outcomes. In this political context especially, when some educators and members of the broader public are increasingly recognizing the need for honest conversations about race and the biases facing Black and Brown boys in particular, this book can provide a framework for districts committed to addressing long-standing inequities as well as a set of evidence-based approaches for schools and educators. To that end, the book is written for a variety of audiences, including local and state policy makers working on issues of equity and access; superintendents and district leaders designing initiatives focused on improving outcomes for young men of color in their own districts; scholars studying high schools, college-readiness, and postsecondary opportunities for males of color; and school-level administrators and teachers interested in supporting their Black and Latinx male students in ways that are meaningful. In addition, *Am I My Brother's Keeper?* documents the design and realization of a research study on a districtwide effort to target Black and Latinx males. As such, it can also be a valuable contribution for education researchers who undertake other efforts to study similar endeavors and their impacts on students.

While the context for this work is New York City, a metropolis unique in its size and population, the very heterogeneity of its schools and the competing priorities of such a large district provide an opportunity to highlight how the successes and limitations of this model may be applicable in multiple contexts with different student populations. The lessons I describe here also highlight the ways districts and schools can embed educational equity into the principles and policies that guide their work with students, in contrast to implementing stand-alone "initiatives" that may come and go. In essence, this book takes the reader from research to practice and provides a level of depth and specificity necessary for other districts and schools to take up similar efforts in their own context with even more robust results. Ultimately, it aims to inform the implementation and impact of other large-scale district-community partnerships that are designed to improve opportunities and outcomes for young people who have systematically been denied both.

PART I

Designing and Implementing
a Racial Equity Initiative at
the District Level

CHAPTER 2

Grounded in Theory and Led by Love

As we look at ESI and look at what we're learning, it's not even just about a particular school; it's about a structure for a community and not just these 40 schools, but throughout New York City and as the nation looks at New York City, across the country.

—*Paul Forbes, ESI director*

THE MEDIA AND POPULAR CULTURE are filled with stories of miracle schools, pockets of educational success that capture the public's imagination around the exceptional versus systems that work. Yet, many of us in education know that these stories often hide the more complicated realities behind their claims of success (e.g., a 100 percent graduation rate of a class that is only a fraction of the number of students who started there) and that we must do more than focus on individual schools without investigating the larger contexts in which they operate. Focusing only on individual schools or the exceptional school leader diverts our attention from the policies, levers, and funding elements that create an ecosystem in which schools either fail or thrive. School districts and their superintendents, local school boards, city governments, and state policies all profoundly influence how schools operate, which goals they prioritize, and how they allocate resources. This chapter surfaces important insights from the NYC school district about the mission and mechanics of designing a district-level approach to address race and gender disparities, paying particular attention to the ways a large system can utilize a racial equity perspective in its work.

When the New York City Department of Education launched ESI in 2012, it was the largest private-public partnership aimed at addressing health, education, and employment gaps for Black and Latinx young men in the country. Though NYC is now only one district among many committed to closing opportunity gaps for males of color, its particular characteristics may help maximize our learning about how other districts can accomplish this work. First, NYC is not only the largest district in the country, but it also serves a population of students that is 70 percent Black and Latinx. Perhaps because of its size and population, other large urban school districts look to NYC to understand district efforts to improve a system of schools that serves a significant population of low-income students of color. Of course, its size makes it singular in ways that other districts might not relate to. At the same time, when an initiative is implemented across eighteen hundred schools, it provides some evidence or proof points that it can also be instituted (and perhaps more strongly implemented) in smaller districts. Second, NYC is a district where education is highly political, since the city's mayor is the formal head of the Department of Education. This context highlights the ways educators can work within or against the political realities as well as the constraints they face in their decision-making and daily work.

Over the course of the five-year study by the Research Alliance for New York City Schools, and through talking to district and program leaders as well as the school leaders, teachers, and students who participated in the program, those of us on the research team learned a great deal about the kind of leadership and strategy that can drive a large-scale initiative focused on Black and Latinx young men. It is critical to examine these efforts on the ground to understand how districts can create a vision for supporting young men of color that is rooted in understanding and attending to the structural barriers that students and their families navigate. In addition, we must also consider the strategic decisions of design and implementation to ensure that the vision can manifest in ways that improve opportunities and outcomes for students.[1]

DESIGNING A MODEL GROUNDED IN THEORY AND EVIDENCE

Identifying a Central Goal

The NYC school district saw a steady rise in graduation rates from 2003 to 2010 for *all* cohorts of students, including Black and Latinx young males.[2] The district credited a constellation of reforms for this improvement, including the closing of large comprehensive schools whose graduation rates hovered around 30 percent for decades; the opening of small schools in their place, bolstered by research on their effectiveness for low-income students of color; and two sets of reorganizations that provided schools and experienced school leaders with more autonomy.[3] While critics raise important questions about each of these policies, even the DOE acknowledged at the time that certain students had not benefited similarly from the reforms, in particular Black and Latinx males. Both high school graduation and college-readiness rates for these young people were substantially lower than those of their female counterparts. Moreover, even Black and Latinx males who entered the ninth grade at the highest level of proficiency were still much less likely to graduate college-ready. Transparency around this data—even if it shed unfavorable light on the district—helped establish and communicate a rationale for focusing on a particular set of outcomes for a specific population of students.

The focus on college-readiness received some pushback. One of the primary funders of this work, the Open Society Foundation, viewed the "problem" largely through the lens of the school-to-prison pipeline. Its concern for the health and well-being of students and their ability to attend school in the first place framed the problem differently and may have shifted the nature of the intervention considerably. Months of discussion yielded an initiative that still focused on college-readiness gaps but acknowledged the complex set of dynamics and antecedents that predict college-readiness. In addition, there was always steady pushback on the initiative's exclusion of young women. While the district's response could not satisfy all these critics, the focus on the data from the district and the city proved to be critical in messaging the rationale for the focus on boys. As the initiative evolved over time, there was a shift toward framing these choices as "targeted universalism," a system by which improving a district's most underserved groups will improve academic and socioemotional outcomes for all of its students.[4]

Despite the multiplicity of viewpoints, the district showed how disaggregating data by race and gender could help identify blind spots or gaps for specific populations that might be overlooked if more attention is being paid to the overall improvement of a system. (Schools used the same strategy later on to examine patterns of suspension and course enrollment.) This process also revealed how different stakeholders may define problems differently and how important it is for a community to wrestle with interpreting what the data actually mean. Noticing the college-readiness gaps, for example, does not address the root causes of the problem, only the symptoms. Educators looking at the same data may either assume the locus of the problem is in the students or situate it in schools. In the case of ESI, the search for the solution focused attention not only on the goals they wanted to achieve but also on some of the factors underlying the racial and gender disparities.

Creating an Evidence-Based Intervention

District leaders create or select existing interventions based on a number of different inputs—advice from a trusted source, reports, policy briefs, prior evidence, personal experiences, etc. In the case of ESI, the district's process of creating an intervention showed an interest in establishing a response informed by research rather than their own assumptions about what it takes to improve outcomes for Black and Latinx boys. The team began its search for an intervention by reviewing the literature to ensure that the program's design aligned with existing evidence, focusing on three areas of research: preparing students for college and careers, supporting young men of color, and identifying particular needs of first-generation college-goers and immigrant students.[5]

What emerged from this review was a focus not on a single intervention but on a combination of supports in academics, youth development, and school culture shown to contribute positively to college-readiness among young men of color. Underlying this selection was a recognition that no one intervention would be sufficient on its own to improve college-readiness outcomes and that improving academic outcomes necessitated attention to the whole child as well as the larger school environment. The district described the three domains:[6]

- *academics.* Strategies that relate to state standards and expectations for what students must know and demonstrate to be on track for college success. For example, schools can opt to redesign course curricula to increase the number of students enrolled in four years of math and science, Advanced Placement, and other rigorous college-level courses.[7]
- *youth development.* Strategies that emphasize building student resilience, commitment to life beyond high school, and restorative approaches to school discipline that offer alternatives to prevent negative outcomes, such as suspension. For example, the selected schools possess structures where adults use a strengths-based approach with students, provide social and emotional support, and set clear behavioral expectations and standards for college- and career-readiness.[8]
- *school culture.* Strategies that promote a college and career focus among ninth-grade Black and Latinx young men, influencing the ethos, mission, and explicit (and implicit) communications throughout the school building, even outside the classroom. For example, these strategies can include workshops for students to develop their interests and opportunities for students to acquire skills outside the classroom; chances to join a variety of extracurricular offerings;

options to participate in academically aligned internships and workplace experiences; and programs that give students and their families a clear voice within the school.[9]

In sum, the academic domain was a call to increase academic rigor and provide more opportunities for students to take advanced course-work. Youth development largely focused on attending to students' socioemotional well-being and creating alternatives to suspension. And the school culture domain was centered on an environment and a set of supports targeted at postsecondary-readiness, including student leadership. The district hypothesized that a combination of all three domains would increase both high school graduation rates and college-readiness rates among Black and Latinx males. Culturally relevant education (CRE) also emerged in Year 1, though not as a fourth domain as much as an overarching principle to inform the realization of the other three domains.

It is important to acknowledge that this framework, while grounded in evidence, was not articulated as a full-fledged theory of action or change. In part, this was because there was an interest on the part of some of ESI's architects to engage with the initiative as a research and development effort, one that encouraged schools to innovate, make mistakes, and learn from failure. Through the privilege of hindsight, however, the Research Alliance team and the ESI team co-created a more refined version of ESI's theory of action (see figure 2.1).[10] This more detailed version may be helpful for understanding the underlying assumptions about how the initiative intended to meet its goals.

ESI's intended outcome was college-readiness, but the initiative was also designed to address a range of opportunity gaps and other educational disparities. Other priorities included decreasing suspensions, confronting teacher biases, and creating professional communities for educators committed to better serving young men of color. To meet these primary and secondary goals, ESI provided participating schools with a set of "inputs" that included funding, professional development, and a learning community of leaders and educators across ESI schools.

FIGURE 2.1   The ESI theory of action

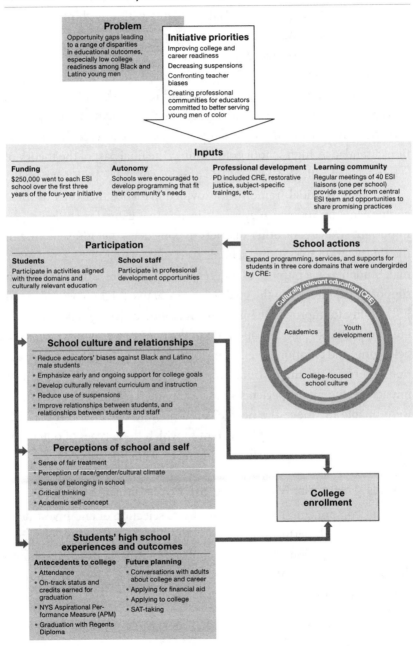

Schools were expected to draw on these resources to create and expand supports for Black and Latinx male students within each of ESI's core domains. Students and staff were to participate in the various programs, supports, and professional development offerings that schools and the ESI Central Team provided. This participation, in turn, would lead to improvements in overall school culture and relationships, better student perceptions of school and self, increased participation in future planning activities, and expanded "antecedents to college" (e.g., credit accumulation, attendance, high school graduation). The final part of the theory of action labeled college-readiness and enrollment as the long-term goal.

While this initial framework provided evidence that each of these components on its own may result in positive gains for students—an important strategy for other districts to consider—the diffuse nature of the intervention meant that schools were supporting Black and Latinx male students on a number of different fronts. A more targeted focus on supports tied directly to the goals of the initiative might have enhanced ESI's ability to improve the initiative's intended college-going outcomes but may have also paid less attention to the issues around safety, sense of belonging, and emotional well-being on which ESI was able to gain traction. Interestingly, and distinct from some prior research, ESI's positive impact on students' experiences in schools and relationships with adults were unable to "move the needle" on academic outcomes. These patterns raise questions about the extent to which these types of outcomes (on their own) are necessarily precursors to academic success.

Selecting Schools: Maximizing the Potential for Success

Another component of ESI's design was its selection of and investment in relatively high performing schools. The district established firm criteria for participation and used an application process to select schools that would be part of the initiative. In order to apply for ESI funding, schools had to meet the following criteria:

- student enrollment that included at least 35 percent Black and Latinx males;

- at least 60 percent of students qualifying for free and/or reduced-price lunch;
- a four-year graduation rate above 65 percent; and
- and an A or B rating on the district's most recent high school Progress Report.[11]

The rationale for targeting successful schools was twofold. First, while many other district-led reform efforts during and after this period targeted the lowest performing schools, the district believed that ESI would have more success in schools that displayed some level of stability and existing capacity to meet the initiative's goals. In other words, ESI's program team, known as the Central Team, viewed the application criteria as a readiness measure; schools that met the application criteria would have the necessary infrastructure in place to accomplish the central goals of ESI. By selecting schools with relatively high graduation rates, the initiative could focus on "reaching a new bar" (college- and career-readiness), which might have been too great a leap for struggling schools. Second, the district hoped to leverage the capacities and best practices developed in these relatively successful schools to effect change across the district. This selection model also represented a strategic use of resources for this set of goals. As one ESI leader described it, selecting struggling schools would have meant "spending all your money and resources trying to get a general level of stability."

The district also required interested schools to submit an application to participate in ESI. The application process, or Design Challenge, was another strategy by which the district could ensure commitment and readiness on the part of schools. It required schools to disaggregate their data by race and gender, submit detailed plans for how they would utilize their ESI funding, and articulate how those plans were grounded in the research embedded in the Design Challenge itself. Schools also had to submit a budget worksheet showing how they would use ESI funds to implement the proposed services and supports for Black and Latinx boys. These applications were subsequently scored by members of the DOE's Office of Postsecondary Readiness and representatives from several school networks and by faculty from CUNY, Harvard University, Howard University, New York University, and Columbia University's Teachers College. Scorers used a rubric that included nineteen items across four large "challenges": expanding success for Black and Latinx young men, aligning success with postsecondary-readiness indicators, building sustainable practices as part of the school organization, and capacity for implementation.

The fact that the forty ESI schools were not selected randomly from the eighty-one eligible schools raises a question around how representative those schools were of the broader population of NYC schools serving high school students. Our team, however, found that the ESI schools, with a few exceptions, were generally comparable to other NYC high schools in terms of student demographics (e.g., English language learner and special education statuses, overage for grade level, eligibility for free and/or reduced-price lunch) and school-level characteristics (e.g., size, configuration, location).[12] Given the selection criteria, ESI schools slightly outperformed non-ESI schools in the percentage of students on track for graduation and four-year graduation rates (68 percent versus 61 percent), but not in terms of the percentage of students meeting college-readiness measures.

A major takeaway from this aspect of the design is the importance of aligning the selection of sites for the intervention with the goals of the initiative. For example, when the district launched the Community Schools Model in 2014, it targeted schools serving the highest proportion of high-need students, because the initiative was focused on providing for the health and well-being of vulnerable students in underserved communities. ESI's Design Challenge may be useful for other districts aiming to assess schools' overall readiness and commitment to participate in a holistic model focused on racial equity. While it is prudent to select schools that appear to have the capacity to implement new programming, this aspect of ESI's design may have presented some trade-offs related to impact. By definition, schools that met ESI's eligibility criteria had less room to grow on outcomes related to the initiative. The school selection process also meant that Black and Latinx young men in the lowest-performing educational environments were not reached by the initiative, since ESI schools were required to show strong graduation rates.

LEADING WITH PURPOSE, LOVE, AND COURAGE

Shawn Dove, formerly of Open Society Foundation and the current CEO of the Campaign for Black Male Achievement, once said that the leadership we need resides in the "hands, heads, and hearts" of community leaders across the country.[13] While strategic planning is critical, the role of the heart cannot be overstated. Changing the trajectory of young people's lives is not merely a matter of education reform but a moral imperative. Moreover, centering love at the core of these efforts allows educators to see the young people they are serving, to understand the challenges they face while recognizing their unique promise. To quote Dove, "Kids don't need saviors; they need believers."

Na'ilah Nasire and Jarvis Givens assert that

> society and the schools embedded within it have made love a foreign thing for Black males," describing how "the American school, with few exceptions, is too often the place where Black students come to know that they are despised, feared, and deemed to be of little to no human value in the world. In this context, the gamble of love is high stakes. Yet those who care deeply for Black children, as extensions of ourselves, recognize that insisting on love anyhow is of the first order."[14]

Efforts designed to improve schools for young people who find them to be "sites of suffering" require individuals who can lead with love and a profound sense of purpose—to practice and preach what Chris Chatmon, the director of the African American Male Achievement in Oakland, calls a "conspiracy of care."[15]

Perhaps no one involved in ESI better embodied the mission of this work than its director, Paul Forbes, though his commitment was certainly reflected in the members of his team. When describing what drew him to ESI, Forbes said, "For me this is such a reality, it's my DNA, literally and figuratively. I am that young man. I take them all on as my own kids. In my mind, they are mine." Serving young people may be Forbes's profession, but the work is deeply personal. These qualities in a leader are not merely beneficial; they are essential for keeping the initiative and its implementers focused on the larger vision of racial equity, for pushing the conversation at multiple levels of leadership, and for challenging unspoken assumptions when they fall back on color blindness, stereotypes, and deficit thinking.

To be sure, I am not advocating for these responsibilities to fall on the shoulders of one person. Too often educational movements and transformational schools are centered on the power of a dynamic leader, a single individual who commands so much authority that they make change possible only to see improvements reverse when they leave. For system-level progress to be sustainable, movements need multiple champions—individuals who wake up thinking about the mission and who inspire others to do the same, teams of like-minded souls who push each other to think more deeply about the work and push the system to deliver on promises it would otherwise not keep.

Beyond College-Readiness: Reframing the Goals of ESI

The individuals leading ESI in the field consistently characterized the work in terms that extended beyond closing college-readiness gaps, and while the district leadership maintained a focus on college- and career-readiness for Black and Latinx males, ESI's mixed results should be understood in the context of the initiative's broader goals. Forbes admitted that while he considered the college-readiness goal "the mission on [his] shoulders," he always made clear that ESI was much more than that. In fact, the entire ESI team often described aspirations other than student outcomes when describing the initiative, including changing the mind-sets and behaviors of adults in the schools they were working with, in the central office, and in the larger school system. One team member said, "I think the goals of the initiative were to really push schools to raise school expectations to serve their young men of color better." Another admitted that while it was difficult to operationalize and harder to measure, the three domains (academics, youth development, and school culture) do not get at some of the underlying causes of the gaps in student outcomes—"It's about what people bring in every day and their implicit bias." As Forbes described:

> The mission of ESI is to raise awareness about how we bring the lived experiences of our young people into schools and classrooms and how we honor them and how we use that lens to inform our academics, youth development structures that you put in place, and school culture in general. If that's occurring, for me, we're achieving the goals of ESI . . . And yes, I'm focused on the young men because that's what we got funded for and we've been explicit about that, but for me this is about all of our young people and how we work with their families and community—how we honor their lived experiences where they don't have to check their authentic selves at the door but can bring that in and celebrate it in the school community. If that's happening, then its ESI for me.

His statement makes clear that the mission of ESI was not limited to addressing the symptom—the gaps in college-readiness rates—but was concerned with the root causes or the multiple ways boys of color experience alienation in schools. This stance also highlights the responsibility of the adults in those spaces to create a learning environment that works for students who typically do not feel seen, loved, or cared for in schools.

Because the ESI program team held these beliefs about the loftier purposes of ESI, they were instrumental in keeping district leaders, school leaders, and staff focused on issues like implicit bias, structural racism, and culturally relevant education. Interestingly, CRE was not a prominent component of the district's original Design Challenge, nor was it one of the three domains. It was through the insistence of ESI's director and the support of his team that it became a critical element around which professional development, partnerships with external organizations, and evaluation activities became centered. For these leaders, CRE was not merely a fourth domain but a foundational paradigm that helped define an effective school. Some of these shifts in focus and language surrounding the initiative required that its leaders confront pushback from inside the district about assumptions that had long been taken for granted. For example, what is a "highly qualified" teacher if the measures do not consider the extent to which their classrooms are responsive to the lives and identities of their boys of color? Forbes was always explicit about the initiative's role in shifting the mind-sets, beliefs, and practices of educators: "I keep saying, in my mind's eye, ESI won't end because, especially if I'm in this role, ESI can't end, because ESI is about a mind-set. It's the way in which we're thinking about the work that we do; it's the way that schools are positioning themselves to address the needs and concerns of their most vulnerable, historically underrepresented, and particularly their young men." This framing of ESI's goals does not mean the success of the initiative cannot be measured against its goal of closing the racial and gender college-readiness gaps, but it does help contextualize the design, implementation, and outcomes of the initiative. It also highlights the important ways to consider ESI's legacy beyond the four years of the initiative.

Courageous Conversations

These explicit and implicit goals emboldened ESI's leaders to keep issues of race, gender, and equity at the forefront in their work with schools and district leaders. In some contexts, pushing these conversations required courage to raise difficult questions and potentially yield dissent. But the ESI team viewed that at least part of their role was empowering others—especially school leaders and teachers in schools—to create opportunities to have "courageous conversations," and develop the skills to facilitate them with other educators in their buildings as well as with the students they served. District leaders reported that in places where people had avoided these difficult discussions in the past, "ESI allowed them to have conversations that they didn't know they'd have or didn't think they could have." The team recalled that when they were offered workshops and professional development on talking about race in schools, school leaders said things like, "We never knew that DOE offered this. We don't have workshops like this from the DOE," highlighting how this initiative was able to elevate the importance of talking about race and racism explicitly and openly with other colleagues.

Although it is difficult for some educators to engage in conversations about race, remaining silent fails to acknowledge that boys of color do not have the option of ignoring either the racism that is part of their lived experience or the acts of racism against Black and Brown bodies they witness on their phones and laptops. Two days before ESI's kickoff on February 26, 2012, Trayvon Martin was murdered by George Zimmerman. Forbes recalled individuals in several ESI schools asking if there would be a public response by the district or a gathering or demonstrations. The response he got when he asked the same questions of the central office was that they were not going to hold a public response or demonstration.[16] With some regret for having followed the recommendation, he "vowed" that he

> would never be in a place where a social action situation, something that affects our young people and our communities, that we wouldn't position ourselves as an ESI team, as a central team, in whatever role I'm in, that I'm not going to set up spaces for people to come together to have conversations . . . It could be four, it could be five, or four hundred—I don't care what it is. Have we created a space for conversation to occur?"

When Eric Garner died at the hands of police two years later, he recounted thinking that "I'm not waiting for other people. I'm not waiting, I'm not asking for permission.

Forbes's leadership extended to his role in working with ESI educators, as he and his team were committed to communicating the urgency of having these conversations in schools. He recalled that at one training he "let people know 'if you're not speaking about Michael Brown and Eric Garner in your classroom, you shouldn't be here.'" ESI training thus provided schools with resources to share with students, helped teachers develop skills to initiate these conversations, and invited schools to share their experiences in leading critical conversations with students. In December 2014, ESI hosted a Day of Action, bringing together five hundred young men to discuss current events related to police violence and how they might be change agents in their communities. The message was clear: "We don't know you, but we want you to know that we love you and we're here to support you. You're not alone." Though the gathering was not part of the initial budget, there was a core shared belief among team members that creating a safe space for students in that moment was essential. They walked over the Brooklyn Bridge in solidarity with students and their families, and they continued to gather as a community of young people, families, and schools to march in Black Lives Matter protests.

With the killing of George Floyd sparking protests of police violence against Black and Brown bodies in more than sixty countries and on every continent except for Antarctica, it becomes more evident why this type of leadership is always timely. Racial justice efforts require leaders who prioritize courage over comfort and their love for young people over making colleagues happy, leaders who see their roles as transformational in fulfilling goals that extend well beyond standard measures of achievement.

SUSTAINABILITY: CREATING CONDITIONS FOR SYSTEMWIDE CHANGE

Educators often lament the lack of sustainability or continuity of large-scale initiatives. For many, it seems like their schools and districts are always rolling out a "new" idea or set of solutions before they have had time to examine if the last one made a difference. Sustainability was intrinsic to ESI's design. Even though the initiative was implemented in forty schools, it was conceived as a strategy to improve outcomes and opportunities for NYC's Black and Latinx males by highlighting promising strategies that could be applied across schools and expanding communities of educators committed to better serving young men of color. This component of the initiative's design speaks to the potential for policy makers in other districts to address a broad challenge more systemically as opposed to improving individual schools, thereby sustaining change over time and across contexts.

Another design element targeted at increasing sustainability was its timeframe and funding structure. A four-year initiative that began with a cohort of ninth graders who would graduate at the end of the initiative, ESI gave each school $250,000 distributed over the first two and a half years. A member of the Central Team, Lillian Dunn, described how this decision was related to sustainability:

> ESI was always explicit. We are here for a certain number of years, that's it. There's a direct financial investment. That investment will go away, and so I think from the beginning, all the conversations with schools . . . were very explicit about that. Even when we started talking about things in Year 1, I remember Paul [Forbes] getting up front and saying, "And don't forget, this stuff will go away, so what are the structural changes you need to make at your school to make this intervention lasting?"

The district hoped that frontloading the funding would challenge schools to establish systems or programming in the first two years that would be sustainable beyond the funding period. However, this proved to be a big gamble. Though the ESI team developed ongoing communities and platforms for this work to continue past the funding period, data show that levels of implementation in ESI schools declined after Year 2, when the funding for ESI decreased. While sustainability was an explicit part of the initiative's design, there were some threats to the potential of this undertaking outlasting the life of the initiative.

Threats to Sustainability

District leaders and educators in the schools reported major challenges that threatened the potential for ESI to continue past the life of the initiative, namely turnover, finite resources, and new and competing priorities. Because these issues present themselves in any context, regardless of the nature of the district-led effort, they raise questions about how *any* systemwide change can be achieved and sustained.

Turnover. Over the course of the initiative, several schools experienced changes in their leadership, including the departure of two of the most committed and effective principals. (Both took on leadership roles at the district level.) The turnover of teachers across the forty schools varied widely, with some schools experiencing little change while others replaced two or three teachers a year. (The teacher turnover rate in NYC was close to 20 percent in the 2012–13 school year.[17]) In the central office, staffing was even more fluid. Many long-time district staff moved from one team to another, bringing their expertise to different areas of priority and expanding the purviews of their responsibility overall, while many less-experienced staff remained at the district for only a few years. These patterns may play out differently in other districts, but the impact of turnover on effecting and sustaining change in schools and across systems is considerable. At the school level, when principals, assistant principals, and key staff who lead their school's participation in racial equity work leave, their efforts are more likely to dissipate. At the district level, staffing changes may shift priorities completely or represent a loss in political will to engage in previous reform efforts. Even if the will does remain, the internal capacity, institutional knowledge, and shared memory of collective decision-making is lost, thereby limiting the extent to which teams can learn from and build on what has already been done.

Finite resources. Systemwide change requires financial investment to provide for the human capital to oversee this work, to create district-level positions for individuals who can champion these efforts, and to develop capacity across multiple roles and offices within the district. Resources also allow schools to prioritize these goals rather than having to opt out based on budget constraints. Healthy investments can act as incentives for schools and educators who may be reluctant to participate, and they can serve as important signals of what matters most to district leaders. The amount of money ESI schools received represented 3–10 percent of the schools' budgets, depending on their enrollment size—not a huge amount but enough for some schools to have the freedom to innovate and direct their time toward the initiative's goals. (One ESI leader believed that decreasing the number of schools and thus the resources for each would have increased this behavior substantially.) Since resources were not distributed equally across the three years, their participation was uneven; only a few schools were able to sustain a high level of programming alignment through the third and fourth years. The fact that many districts are always facing difficult budgetary decisions, especially those serving predominantly low-income students, highlights the need to maximize any infusion of resources by using them to establish policies and practices that will outlive the resources invested.

New and competing priorities. Even when district leaders can agree on a set of priorities, they may think differently about where to invest time and attention. In the case of ESI, for example, one of the funding institutions wanted to prioritize attendance supports and drop-out prevention, viewing the situation through a school-to-prison pipeline lens; the district, however, wanted to focus more on academic rigor and college-going. These priorities were somewhat reflected in the final design of the initiative, but they limited the potential for the initiative to outlast the people who were originally at the table making these compromises. Districts must also contend with other external shifts, policies, or mandates. At the time of the initiative, for example, the district was still ramping up teachers and standards to comply with the Common Core State Standards. They also adopted the application of the Danielson Framework in 2013 (subsequently revised) in their teacher evaluation system and in 2015 incorporated the Framework for Great Schools into their school evaluation process. New administrations can also threaten the sustainability of initiatives created under their predecessor. This is perhaps especially true in New York City, where politics play a prominent role in education policy due to mayoral control. Because a mayor's reelection can be hindered or helped by what they are able to accomplish in schools during their time in office, it becomes important to establish a set of goals (and a corresponding narrative) that is uniquely their own. One ESI leader said that "education is still politics, and politics is about breaking away from what your predecessor did." Given these shifting priorities, as well as a tendency to latch on to new ideas when previous policies grow stale, it is difficult to envision how initiatives can survive for very long. Thus, it becomes imperative to focus not only on the initiatives themselves but on the mind-sets, practices, and policies that stem from them.

Strategies to Sustain Change in Schools

Despite the decreasing levels of participation among many ESI schools in the last years of the initiative, our study also revealed a number of important strategies some schools used to sustain the intent and energy of the first two years. We also documented some important cultural shifts across schools that have the potential to outlive ESI.

Integrating ESI into the school's core mission and programming. A measure we called *programmatic cohesion* signified the extent to which schools had, after Year 1, integrated ESI into their everyday practice and overall culture. Cohesion required the involvement of multiple staff members in ESI meetings and professional development; ESI-related activities that were built into the school day or infused into classes; and widespread communication to teachers and staff about the rationale behind ESI and how its goals could be explicitly incorporated into the school mission and strategic vision. Explicit training around building programmatic cohesion (versus offering several stand-alone programs or services) also helped inform schools' decision-making around what *not* to do—an essential strategy when working within budget constraints. In schools demonstrating a high level of programmatic cohesion, the influence of ESI, especially on school culture, seemed to persist in the face of decreasing funding, staff turnover, and other districtwide changes.

Generating buy-in and designating leadership roles among staff. In Year 1, staff from twenty-four schools cited aspects of stakeholder engagement (e.g., among teachers, students, parents, participating staff) as challenges to ESI implementation. With so many plans and separate efforts in a school, it was sometimes difficult for schools to convince staff to really pay attention to or prioritize ESI. Principals recommended seeking buy-in from multiple stakeholders at the outset so that they feel invested in the program's goals and objectives. One prinicpal said, "When you don't have people staying [in the school], the vision is not shared, and they're not invested in it, and it's not a priority. If people are not invested in it, things are not going to be enacted with integrity." Even schools where personnel were committed to ESI's goals cited the challenge of their staff being spread too thin between ESI, other programs, and their day-to-day responsibilities as teachers. One strategy to increase buy-in and limit the potential for burnout is to diffuse responsibility—from needs assessment to implementation and monitoring—across staff and outside of leadership. This often took the form of a small ESI committee responsible for overseeing initiative-related programs. In Year 2, the Central Team also asked every school to designate an ESI point person and organized regular meetings for those staff members, in addition to regular principal meetings. These point people would not necessarily have to lead programs, but they would act as ESI champions in the building, help create work plans from year to year, monitor changes in data, and disseminate information and training to their colleagues. A principal explained the importance of having a lead person focused on ESI: "You need to have a front person, somebody who can be the go-to. It takes a lot of my time to do that stuff, to manage that." A staff member said that a designated team is especially important given the likelihood of staffing changes. Assigning at least a few staff to oversee an initiative like ESI can help ensure that the institutional knowledge gets passed on over multiple years.

Creating institutional change that outlives the initiative. Though the branding of programs and supports as ESI-related services may have faded over time, many of these changes were institutionalized in ways that outlived or did not require additional funding. These included, for example, changes in curriculum and textbooks, suspension policies, hiring practices, in-house professional development, and partnerships with external organizations. They also included adapting existing structures (e.g., committees and professional learning communities) to focus on the goals of ESI by forming equity teams and utilizing the one-time infusion of resources to create a full-fledged college office and resource room. Approaches such as these make it more likely that changes can persist not only past the life of an initiative but also through the administrative and staff turnover that is inevitable in schools. Even though certain programmatic changes were not sustained past the funding period, our study found that ESI produced a number of important changes in the overall culture of participating schools. It is important to highlight shifts in school culture because they hold promise for creating enduring changes in and across schools. While ESI-supported initiatives, such as afterschool programming or out-of-state college visits, may have ended as schools stopped receiving ESI funds, deeper organizational changes proved to be more durable.

One profound change involved taking responsibility for student learning and success. The idea that the onus of student learning and success in school falls on teachers is embedded in many of the strategies used by ESI schools to shift their school culture. This perspective shifts the conversation from asking why students are disengaged to why teachers are not creating effective classrooms, from why students are not college-ready to how we are failing to prepare students for college. Teachers in schools that primarily serve low-income students of color often adopt deficit perspectives that focus on the disadvantages faced by their students and their communities. By contrast, educators in ESI schools were trained to examine their own limitations and build on the strengths of their students to create improvements.

Another fundamental shift entailed adopting culturally relevant education and a racial equity lens. ESI invested a considerable amount of resources in developing culturally relevant education in schools and an anti-racist or racial equity lens among staff, efforts that were critical to cohesion and sustainability because of their potential to address teacher mind-sets and school culture in ways that cut across individual programs. In schools where CRE was widely embraced, teachers reported the impact of these trainings and resources on their day-to-day practice, their relationships with students, and their entire approach to teaching. These changes included connecting classrooms to students' backgrounds and lived experiences and actively pushing back against the subtle and overt ways schools could uphold color blindness, implicit bias, White supremacy, and racism against boys of color. These frameworks influence curricular choices, approaches to discipline, and relationships with students in general.

An important lasting effect of ESI was viewing teaching as a reflective practice. Changing school culture cannot be accomplished through a district-led policy or mandate alone. Successfully adopting CRE, for example, requires that teachers reflect on their own identities, the biases they may hold about male students of color, and how their worldview informs their teaching practice. While district leadership can mandate CRE or require training around issues of racial equity, the extent to which these approaches take hold or affect change also relies on the teachers' collective capacity to reexamine their own assumptions and push their practice in ways that may be challenging or uncomfortable. Opportunities to practice these reflective stances are important mechanisms for educators to sustain meaningful change.

MAJOR FINDINGS

In designing the initiative, the architects of ESI identified a targeted goal for a specific population, relied on existing research to create a multifaceted intervention, and targeted certain schools based on their capacity for effective implementation. With these strategic decisions came a number of trade-offs. The focus on college-readiness for boys of color raised questions about supporting Black and Latinx girls, while the selection of high-performing schools perhaps limited how far ESI could effect change in a limited amount of time. To some extent, the lack of an explicit theory of action reflected an interest in a research and development approach focused on learning from implementing new ideas. However, not providing a more specific set of expectations about the intervention made it more challenging to implement effectively.

Yet, ESI's broader goals provide a different context by which to measure its impact or influence. Its leaders, for example, while working toward college-readiness, also committed to creating a community of educators with the beliefs and skills to apply reflective practice, CRE, and a racial equity lens to their work. In contrast to previous reforms, ESI seemed to change the conversation by focusing not on the deficit of students but on the responsibility of educators to better serve students who felt marginalized in their own school communities. This aspect of ESI's mission highlights the importance of leaders who embody and practice these approaches and whose love for young people is central to their work. This also speaks to the potential for an initiative and its leaders to engage in courageous conversations internally at the district level and with educators in the field, thereby helping to change a system that typically avoids pointed conversations about racism in schools.

Finally, while reach and sustainability were priorities at the outset and part of ESI's design, sustainability was not operationalized as strongly as it could have been. While we found evidence of shifts in mind-sets, cultures, and practices as a result of ESI, the potential for sustained changes in schools were mitigated by turnover, dwindling resources, and competing priorities from the district itself. Future initiatives would benefit from clearer guidelines about how schools can create policies and infrastructures (versus stand-alone programs) that outlast initiative resources. The areas where educators and students in some ESI schools reported the biggest changes as a result of the initiative—school culture and relationships with students—are examples of the kinds of schoolwide improvements that can live on, even after dedicated funding is exhausted.

RECOMMENDATIONS FOR DISTRICTS

1. *Establish a strong theory of action that closely aligns the interventions with its goals.* In the case of ESI, the district identified a targeted goal for a specific population based on data disaggregated by race and gender. They also relied on prior research related to those goals to create a multifaceted intervention. Yet, it did not create a full-fledged theory of action to capture its assumptions about how the intervention would work and under what conditions. This was partially due to an interest in employing a research and development approach that ultimately limited the district's ability to place tighter parameters on ESI programming and establish stronger connections between the features of the intervention and its intended goals. Engaging in the exercise of establishing a theory of action that draws a clear through line between a specific set of goals and evidenced-based practices will help districts decide how to allocate funding, where to invest resources, and, just as importantly, what *not* to do. Doing so may also expose different assumptions and interpretations about what teachers and students need.

2. *Identify champions who will prioritize love and racial equity.* ESI's leadership serves as an important model for other districts focused on issues of racial equity. By shifting the narrative away from deficit perspectives, prioritizing conversations about systemic racism, and empowering others (both at the district level and in schools) to do the same, ESI's leadership illuminated how the challenges of this work require individuals and teams that are mission oriented and willing to take risks to transform systems. Champions of racial equity work are also driven by a love for young people and a commitment to seeing their full humanity. In this regard, love and caring aren't ancillary to leadership; they are driving forces that motivate inner reflection, empathy, and action even in the face of inertia or resistance. Without such individuals at the helm, initiatives like these may make incremental gains but will be limited in their potential to make systemic change.

3. *Support schools in ways that make sustainability possible.* Educators in many of the ESI schools reported how difficult it was to sustain ESI past the funding period, especially in light of competing priorities and new districtwide mandates. The district could have chosen not to frontload the funding to ensure higher levels of implementation across the four years. Supporting schools to overcome these challenges may also include helping schools address resource constraints by building capacity around grant writing, fund raising, or development. (In Year 4 the ESI team did offer a three-part series on writing grants that was well attended.) But more broadly speaking, it also entails building program cohesion at the school level by supporting efforts to generate buy-in across the school community. For example, one of the ESI team members recommended creating accessible materials that school leaders could use to present this work to teachers, support staff, and families. Finally, to address competing priorities and the risk of compartmentalizing racial equity efforts, districts need to consider ways of integrating an equity lens into other district policies or mandates. The ESI team, for example, created tools for educators to apply a culturally relevant lens on the Danielson Framework and the Great Schools Framework, which were used to evaluate teachers and schools.

4. *Invest in research and evaluation to facilitate learning, not just highlight success.* Though not explicitly discussed in this chapter, NYC DOE prioritized research and evaluation before launching ESI. Though we as evaluators of the initiative were not able to push for random assignment, the program's willingness to subject the initiative to a robust evaluation that included comparison schools was a testament to their interest in learning from ESI, both its successes and its limitations. As a researcher, I have been in more than a few conversations with program leaders who are interested in research only to the extent that it will show that their program works. Had we just examined the outcomes of ESI schools, for example, we would have seen growth on high school graduation rates and college enrollment

patterns and attributed the gains to ESI without noticing similar levels of growth in comparable schools. Districts committed to racial equity goals that can outlive any one initative should maximize opportunities to learn from their policies and programs and consider smaller formative studies of pilot programs before launching larger districtwide efforts.

CHAPTER **3**

Empowering Schools and Educators to Be Agents of Change

> I just really feel indebted to the Team, in that they've given us an opportunity to participate in a program of this caliber because it has helped us to be more purposeful about what we need to do, as a school, for our students.
>
> —*Assistant principal at an ESI school*

EVEN A WELL-FUNDED and carefully designed effort will flounder without the ongoing vision and support of teams dedicated to its success. However, district-level policies and programs are often put in place without a lot of sustained attention to supporting schools and educators in their implementation. We also know that stakeholders on the ground will likely translate policies into practice that fits existing needs, operations, and ethos even if that means deviating from the policy.[1] Even those educators who buy into the goals of a particular initiative and aim to implement it with fidelity may struggle without adequate training and resources, and those policies and programs are less likely to penetrate classrooms and change the experiences of students. ESI was supported by a core group within the district central office that coordinated the distribution of funds and built a network of external partners and collaborators. This ESI Central Team also created a robust infrastructure to support schools in a way that would sustain their efforts beyond the initiative.

First, the team engaged with individual schools in the initial planning phase and replicated this one-on-one support each subsequent year by providing working templates and critical feedback. Second, it provided schools with the opportunity to partner with a curated set of external organizations to supplement and complement school capacity. Third, it provided schools with a number of resources, including ongoing professional development (PD) opportunities, particularly in the area of culturally relevant education but also on other ESI-related topics, such as mentoring and growth mind-set (a belief that abilities can be improved through effort). The team also established a professional learning community (PLC) that met regularly to engage in sustained conversations around educating Black and Latinx males, share best practices, and address challenges that all forty schools faced. Other resources that schools found useful included events and enrichment opportunities for students that the team organized and sponsored. Finally, the ESI team provided individualized support by visiting schools to offer help with, guidance on, or an audience for their programs. Each of these strategies reinforced the others by creating multiple opportunities to communicate the goals of the initiative and expand school capacity to meet them. Moreover, the combination of these efforts helped district leadership develop the kind of deep relationships with schools that are critical to empowering educators as equal partners as well as creating and maintaining buy-in for a multiyear initiative, even in the face of principal and teacher turnover. Throughout the years, educators consistently expressed appreciation for the deep system of support they received from the Central Team. As one principal summarized the team's role, "I don't know how much more supportive they could be."[2] Indeed, it struck many educators that there was nothing the ESI Central Team would not do for them.

At the same time, the support stopped short of prescription or accountability, approaches that may have helped in the implementation of ESI and strengthened its impact on students. At the outset, the NYC DOE decided that schools should drive the improvement process by examining gaps in their own data and allocating ESI resources to close those gaps. The rationale provided by the district for this approach was that educators in schools were in the best position to enact change in their buildings. They also reasoned that letting schools create programmatic changes (rather than being told what to do) would increase educator buy-in and engagement. However, this level of autonomy resulted in wide variation among schools in terms of program "dosage" and quality, and there were no clear benchmarks for levels of student participation. Schools may have needed much stronger guidelines and some system of accountability to ensure that implementation was strong enough to produce an impact on student outcomes, especially those more tangential to the intervention, such as graduation rates or college-going enrollment.

This aspect of the initiative should encourage district leaders to consider ways of leveraging school-level expertise while providing stricter standards of implementation to maximize the potential for results. In addition, the example of ESI should encourage districts to think strategically about the number of schools selected for change. While forty schools represent a small percentage of high schools in NYC, the ESI team, in retrospect, reasoned that a smaller number of schools would have made it more feasible to hold schools accountable to a stronger set of implementation standards that would have ultimately benefited students. The networked system of support ESI used to strengthen this work in schools constituted a unique strength of the initiative, but decision points around how much autonomy to provide schools came with serious challenges and limitations. This chapter describes the trade-offs and presents strategies that may diminish these obstacles for other districts trying to implement similar policies.

USING DATA TO INFORM PROGRAMMING

The initial phase of the program set an important precedent and tone for the remaining four years by providing schools with individualized resources that established relationships among schools and the Central Team and guided educators' thinking about how to meet the goals of ESI. After schools were selected to participate in ESI, the Central Team created "data snapshots" that reported a number of outcomes (e.g., attendance, suspension rates, graduation rates) for their students categorized by race, ethnicity, and gender. The snapshots were designed to help schools take a hard look at their data and use that information to make decisions around the supports and programs that might be most valuable for their Black and Latinx male students. These data were used throughout the initiative. Schools confirmed the usefulness of these data reports in measuring progress, making important comparisons among cohorts, and deciding on necessary changes to their implementation of ESI. A staff member shared: "What I found very beneficial from ESI is that they always provided us with data that we didn't necessarily have at our fingertips about our male students. We used that in our planning and in our actions."

The ESI team also provided direct guidance on how to allocate ESI funds ($250,000 distributed over the two and a half years of the initiative). Though the initial applications captured some of what schools planned to do with the funding, the Central Team created a workplan template that asked schools to list the following information about each program or service that would be funded by ESI: the ESI domain addressed by the program (academics, youth development, or school culture); activity type and description; target audience and frequency of the program; program deliverables; and indicators that would be used to measure the program's success. These work plans, completed in the summer before each year of the initiative, challenged school staff to think about representation across the three domains, remain focused on the target audience of the initiative, and include processes for measuring the efficacy of their programs. The work plan template also included a detailed budget template that helped staff think through the invisible costs of implementing these programs.

Each year the ESI team sat down with each school for a one-hour planning meeting to discuss the work plans. During these meetings, at least two individuals from each school met with members of the Central Team to walk through the school's plan. These were not perfunctory meetings. Rather, the ESI team asked probing questions about how and why proposed programming would support the goals of the initiative and focus on boys of color. Team members asked for clarification as needed and suggested modifications where the purpose of the programming was not clear. ESI director Paul Forbes explained that unlike the applications, the work plans pushed staff to think more concretely about their plans and connect the dots between individual programs and more aspirational outcomes—

> What's your road map? We look at your map that says you're going from New York to California. We get it. But you're not doing that in one stretch in one day. You would break that down to say you're going from here to St. Louis, then stopping here, and then going another 650 miles. You would lay that out. So, the question was, "What's your road map each year to get to the final place you want to see."

These meetings also presented an opportunity for the Central Team to ensure that schools appropriated ESI funds within the initiative's parameters. For example, schools were strongly discouraged from using the funds for additional personnel or technological devices, such as laptops or SMART boards. The district viewed these kinds of expenditures as incompatible with its goals for sustainability (in the case of short-term personnel changes) or with the initiative's focus on targeted programming for boys of color. Following these school planning meetings, all schools were required to make at least one set of revisions to their plans based on the feedback from the ESI team (some required multiple rounds of revisions before approval).

Over the last two decades, terms like *data use* have become prevalent in districts and schools. But the data are not always helpful, and the use is not always strategic. In the case of ESI, the Central Team provided schools with disaggregated data at the school level to inform staff members' thinking about the nature and extent of the challenges they faced in their own buildings and their plans to address them. The team also provided concrete tools and ample support in the planning phase of the initiative, in some cases modifying plans to target young men of color and in other cases steering them away from using funds in ways not aligned with the goals of ESI. Across the board, the team provided the type of support necessary to guide schools in directions consistent with the initiative.

EXPANDING SCHOOL CAPACITY THROUGH EXTERNAL PARTNERSHIPS

The Central Team also facilitated external partnerships with community-based organizations and other nonprofits designed to supplement and/ or complement the skills and capacities residing in schools. Yet, while partnerships can be an important part of implementing innovative programming in schools designed to meet students' physical, socioemotional, and academic needs, they can present their own challenges.

The ESI team provided schools with a list of more than eighty approved vendors that had been vetted through a rigorous application process.[3] That application, which required organizations to provide evidence of prior success in schools and with the target population, was designed to ensure the quality of partners and their added value to ESI schools. Schools that planned to use ESI funding for external partners were required to choose from this list of approved vendors. If schools wanted to partner with an organization that did not appear on the approved list, even if they had worked with the organization previously, that organization had to apply to be added to the list. In many cases, the Central Team encouraged schools to partner with approved vendors to avoid "business as usual" and instead implement new approaches with different partners.

External partners provided a wide range of services to ESI schools, including, but not limited to curricular enhancements across subject areas, mentoring and enrichment programs for students, professional development for teachers, and programs to support college enrollment. The extent of these partnerships ranged from providing curriculaor software to providing much more hands-on support through PD for teachers or enrichment courses for students. Many educators reported their appreciation for the contribution of these external partners. In particular, they valued their expertise in areas lacking in the school, as well as their ability to connect with students—especially programming delivered by males of color. One staff member described how "the way he interacts with the students . . . at the end of the day, it's a bit relaxed, but they talk about issues that are related to them. It's all male. It's their language. That helps." This teacher's statement about the men's group being facilitated in "their language" distances her from the boys, but it also reflects her perception of the partner's contribution as being centered on a collective experience she could not draw on. The most common positive feedback we received about external partners centered on observing students' responses to their programming. Of a mentoring organization, another staff member explained, "I believe that last I checked above 90 percent of the students are emailing their mentors weekly which, again, speaks to the tremendous support that happened within the school . . . and the partnership of [the vendor]."

While many schools reported productive relationships with external partners, others were frustrated by the restrictions placed on the selection process. Some schools reported that limiting the list of potential partners impeded their ability to build on successful programs or to work with vendors that they partnered with in the past. One staff member expressed concern about the barriers to working with existing partners: "The only thing that kind of took me back with the ESI grant was we were looking at bringing people in that may not have been vendors, so we had to find a way to get people in here who we already worked with, because we knew these people, and they knew us. They knew our population. They've been in our building. All of a sudden, it's like, 'Oh, you can only use these people.'" Educators also voiced frustrations about the high price charged by some of the approved external vendors, which they knew would prevent them from partnering with them after the funding period. Compounding the difficulties relating to making these decisions was the short time frame to learn about and select the right partner. One school leader explained, "It would be really great if there was a forum where you could go and check out [the vendors]. You could read about them on this list on the internet, but it was very—'I don't know what this means. I don't know how good this is.'"

Despite the rigorous application process and the high levels of satisfaction among many schools, we also found that the quality of schools' experiences with external vendors varied widely. Interestingly, different schools sometimes reported different experiences with the same vendors, while even educators within the same building reported different levels of satisfaction with the same partner. In several cases, schools that expressed enthusiasm about a particular program found the provider interfacing with the school to be a poor fit for the school community. Educators also reported that they found it difficult to find time to collaborate with and manage partners, while other teachers believed these external programs were needlessly reducing instructional time with students. As one teacher explained, "I have three different programs come in each week, and when you think about that, that takes away from what I actually have to do. It took away from my teaching time with them and what they needed to learn." The intrusion on instructional time became especially frustrating when the perceived value of the program was low. In one case, when a partner implemented a writing program for students, a staff member explained that "the English teachers have been really unimpressed with what they've been seeing. That's probably something that we're just going to say—'You know what, this is not really worth our time.'"

Taken together, these reports suggest that partnerships alone do not guarantee positive outcomes beyond what the school generates on its own. Rather, productive partnerships require several components working simultaneously: alignment between the expertise being offered by the partners and the needs of the school and its students, the time and capacity for a school staff member to manage the partnership, and the pedagogical skills of the partner's representative. To ensure attention to each component, districts should provide accessible and useful information about partners (including brief evaluations from schools that have worked with them in the past), flexibility for schools to choose vendors that best meet their needs, the ability to pilot a partnership for a limited time before committing to a full school year, and mechanisms to document and measure the performance of partners over time to make informed decisions about who they will select to work with their teachers and students.

DEVELOPING TEACHER EXPERTISE THROUGH TARGETED PD

An alternative to some types of partnerships with external organizations is targeted professional development for teachers that develops their capacity to provide a program that a partner might typically provide. This approach may also be more sustainable, as teachers can continue to deliver the programming over a number of years and train other staff to do the same without having to find the resources to pay for the work of an outside organization. In the case of ESI, the Central Team consistently offered a number of wide-ranging but targeted PD opportunities for school staff over the life of the initiative. These opportunities were typically disseminated in the team's newsletter, which functioned as an important resource for participating schools. In addition to publicizing PD sessions, the newsletter included information about ESI-sponsored events for students and opportunities for mini-grants related to the goals of ESI (e.g., funds for summer bridge programs to support incoming ninth graders). It also highlighted successful practices of individual schools to inspire educators and provide practical guidance on how to implement ESI plans and programs.

Professional development was perhaps the most prominent component of the team's resource allocation. The number of these opportunities was rivaled only by their diversity. PDs, workshops, conferences, and events numbered more than one hundred and reflected the team's deep thinking about what schools needed to do to serve young men of color. In the first few years of the initiative, these resources were, to a large extent, focused on providing culturally relevant education and preparing males of color for college. Another broad category focused on ESI's academic domain, including coaching in specific content areas, through organizations like Metamorphosis, STEM-focused PD, and research on adolescent development and academic growth. The Central Team provided schools with opportunities to work with or learn from organizations like the MBK Alliance, the Coalition of Schools Education Boys of Color (COSEBOC), Facing History and Ourselves, the Schomburg Center for Research in Black Culture, the College Board, the State University of New York (SUNY), and CUNY. They invited prominent individuals in the education field to speak to educators in ESI schools, among them Chris Emdin, Geneva Gay, Nikole Hannah-Jones, and José Vilson. Other, less frequently covered, topics for PD included discipline, addressing the needs of LBTQ youth of color, and educating Latinx students. Later in the initiative, the professional development opportunities took on an even more explicit focus on issues of race, power, and politics under two long-standing series of sessions: "Why We Can't Wait: Critical and Courageous Conversations" and "Critically Conscious Educators Rising." The list of these community discussion forums and PD sessions included:

- "Leading Social Justice and Equity"
- "Race, History, and Educational Inequity"
- "Altering Perception and Reducing Implicit Bias"
- "Developing a Critical Consciousness to Address the Impact of Race, Power, and Privilege in Teaching and Learning"
- "Bias Isn't Just a Police Problem, It's a Preschool Problem"
- "Confront Bias and Racism in Schools"
- "Decolonizing Education"
- "Bias, Social Media, and Ourselves"
- "After the Election . . . Now What?"

The titles reflect the racial issues that dominated the airwaves and social media platforms at the time (and still), including the Black Lives Matters movement, the race baiting and xenophobia rampant during after the 2016 presidential campaign, and the escalating outrage over police violence. These sessions were designed to move participants from theory to practice, from talking about issues of equity to applying a racial justice lens to classroom practice and schoolwide policy. While implicit bias training became ubiquitous across the corporate world and organizations, including the NYC DOE, ESI professional development went beyond expanding the critical consciousness of individuals to engaging educators in strategies to raise critical issues affecting students *with* students (e.g., racial profiling, income and wealth gaps by race, school segregation) and to apply a critical lens to school policies that may further alienate boys and young men of color.

While the Central Team could not directly support five thousand Black and Latinx young men across ESI schools, it did support and enable schools to do so by disseminating information about opportunities for students throughout the lifespan of the initiative. Numbering close to one hundred, these opportunities included events hosted by the ESI team and by local and national organizations. Schools reported that this act of curating relevant opportunities for students eliminated the substantial allocation of time staff might typically devote to identifying and sharing these events. Centered on the college-related goals of the initiative, these included information sessions with Historically Black Colleges and Universities (HBCUs), Latinx college expos, CUNY and SUNY recruitment events, and national college fairs for students of color. Addressing the underrepresentation of males of color in STEM careers, many of these activities also focused on science, math, and computer science activities through Code Now, the Summer Hackers program, Google science fairs, and various math tournaments. In addition, they advertised targeted competition programs, including scholarships for undocumented students, scholarships to particular colleges and universities, and other competitions focused on youth service and activism. The ESI team also provided teachers and students with restorative experiences, such as the intergenerational event celebrating MLK Day, film screenings, sports events, artistic showcases featuring males of color, and exposure to important cultural sites in the city, such as the Schomburg or the Smithsonian Latinx Center. Each year the Central Team hosted large gatherings for all male students in ESI schools. These summits, youth empowerment days, and young men's gatherings provided students with a day of relevant programming and generated buy-in, enthusiasm, and reengagement among educators in the ESI schools. Smaller groups of boys attended and participated in the annual COSE-BOC conferences.

To maximize the value of these opportunities for teachers and students, the Central Team considered when, where, and how often these would be offered to accommodate teachers' schedules and demands on their time. Offering the training in different parts of the city, for example, was a priority, recognizing that teachers were far more likely to attend meetings in the same borough as their schools. In addition, participation often required that more than one person from each building attend (to increase the turnkey potential for the relevant learning in a building). As a result of both the depth and breadth of these opportunities, school staff consistently praised the team for this aspect of their support. One staff member explained, "Another thing that I really like about ESI is that every month they bring us different training programs. Some we're able to implement, others not. Just knowing what's out there really helps." The team was able to curate an immense number of experiences and professional development opportunities for ESI communities as a means by which to build on existing school capacity and boost programmatic efforts to better support boys of color.

SUSTAINED LEARNING THROUGH PROFESSIONAL COMMUNITY

After Year 1 of the initiative, the access to professional opportunities and the time with other ESI schools that the PD sessions provided left many teachers wanting to know more about what ESI looked like in other settings—How are schools staffing their programs? How are they dealing with the push and pull of competing priorities? What partners had they selected and were they satisfied with their program services? The sense among the staff was that there was a lot to be learned from other schools confronting the same challenges and focusing on similar approaches through a comparable lens. A consistent recommendation that emerged from interviews with staff in Year 1 was the creation of a structure or forum for schools to learn from one another. One school leader reflected:

> I think there are 40 schools in ESI, and I think they've been saying that we're all trying things, and they're saying there might be some discussion about what's going on and what's going well. I personally would like to try to engage in some of that, because understanding our microcosm—we think we're doing what's best for our school this year with these kids . . . but maybe somebody else down the street is rocking out. And we could flip something and spin it to teachers with one PD and just start doing and adding that. I think that'd be helpful.

The Central Team was responsive to the call for more support—in this case, through the formation of a monthly ESI community meeting (held from 9:00 am to 2:00 pm "because it doesn't make sense to leave and go back to your school for a few hours"). One of the team members described how "schools were going to try things, and they were going to get better at them over time . . . There was always going to be a learning curve, so why not make that learning curve sharper by putting more brains together." Another noted that "professional learning communities among practitioners are essential when you're trying to try to new things." To that end, these meetings served as professional learning communities, where schools could share promising practices from their own sites and tackle common challenges together. Two different types of meetings were held, one for ESI principals and another for ESI liaisons. Until Year 2, school leaders served as the point people for communication about ESI, but it became clear that others in the building might have greater capacity to attend to the details of the program. Thus, the liaison role was established and became a pivotal mechanism by which to disseminate learnings from these ESI community meetings to staff across schools. The role was typically filled by assistant principals or other key staff who coordinated and oversaw the implementation of ESI in their schools. Liaisons were supported by the ESI design team in each school, which included the principal, a group of two to three teachers, two to three other school staff members, and, in some cases, student representatives. The team structure ensured that multiple individuals in a building were committed to seeing this work to fruition, but it also created an in-house system of support for the initiative.

Leveraging the role of the liaison, the Central Team launched ESI meetings as forums for accessing professional development, obtaining individualized data snapshots, and learning about additional opportunities that might be helpful to schools, including calls for small grants and additional funding. Staff who attended these meetings, as well as staff who received the information secondhand, appreciated the Central Team's role as an information resource. They noted the team's ability to provide free or low-cost resources that made a difference for the schools. One staff member said that the team had "provided an unbelievable amount of resources and contacts. For every meeting, [our ESI liaison] comes back with, 'This is available and that's available.' We're really quick. We'll apply." This statement also illustrates the intended chain of information dissemination from the Central Team to principals or liaisons to other staff within the school.

Perhaps more important than having ready access to resources, though, was the role of the meetings in providing a professional learning community for staff across ESI schools. We observed many of these meetings and listened to formal small-group discussions as well as the informal chats during coffee breaks, lunch, and breakout activities. The energy produced by like-minded educators bonded by their commitment to creating more supportive spaces for young men of color was palpable. Principals and liaisons often left the room with best practices, practical strategies to test, and encouragement from colleagues or, at the very least, reassurance that they were not alone in their struggles. One staff member said, "Being part of ESI, I feel, has given us an opportunity to have these open dialogues, to share these best practices and to see how certain strategies have been able to support and move students, in general." It is important to note that the ESI team also provided an online PLC through an ESI wiki page. The online platform provided information about upcoming events, funding opportunities, and relevant resources, as well as a space for ESI educators to interact. While an exhaustive resource, the online community was not used much by ESI school staff; it was the in-person space that they found valuable—the comradery of coming together to share successes and challenges (the same kind of safe spaces that their schools endeavored to create for their young men).

THAT PERSONAL TOUCH:
RELATIONSHIP-DRIVEN SUPPORT

Over the life of the initiative, the Central Team maintained regular contact with schools through weekly emails, an online repository of resources, monthly meetings, and a host of special events for ESI schools and students. Though there was some turnover during those four years, each team member was mission driven, energetic, and enthusiastic about their respective role in supporting schools and empowering teachers to meet the goals of the initiative. The Central Team maintained contact with schools via phone and email, but, providing yet another layer of support, the ESI director engaged in at least one to two visits to each school every year (and to some many more than that). In Year 1, both ESI codirectors engaged in these school visits, but the restructuring shift from two directors to one did not deter Forbes from visiting the schools.

The goals of these visits were to learn more about how programs were progressing at each school, to provide feedback to school leaders and ESI design teams, and to share any relevant resources as needed. Beyond these pragmatic goals, the director used these visits to make personal connections with principals, teachers, and students. Forbes became a familiar figure at some schools, participated in their young men's groups, spoke at their graduations, grieved with communities in tragedy, and celebrated their successes. When one school's college trip was in danger of being canceled due to an unexpected delay in transportation funding, he offered to put the expenses on his personal credit card. The school's design team member said that the trip "wouldn't have happened had he not intervened . . . He really stepped in and took care of that." The work of ESI was personal for Forbes. Investing the time in these school visits helped strengthen the implementation of ESI at some sites; at others it maintained their interest in ESI even through the transition from one principal to another. And at other schools it built relationships that extended beyond the life of the initiative. A handful of schools remained largely unresponsive during the period of the initiative, but it was not for lack of effort. It reached a point where Forbes decided not to return to an empty well and redirected that energy to schools that wanted the help.

Interestingly, many of the participants were unaware that he took the time to visit each school, assuming that he could not have maintained relationships with so many staff spread out across forty schools in four boroughs. One interviewee said, "I don't know if he went to every school, but we were one of the schools he actually came out to visit, and he spoke with my kids. I think that was really helpful." Other staff knew about Forbes's superhuman effort, acknowledging the way he and his staff went "above and beyond" their responsibilities to support ESI schools and the individuals who made up these communities. This type of consistent, personal support and the level of relationship was something many of the school staff we spoke to saw as a unique benefit of being a member of the ESI cohort. A principal shared: "The support of the ESI personnel [was] beautiful . . . magnificent. Paul's here. He comes here on a regular basis, checks in with us. He came one day last week and found out one of my students was—we were having a little reception for him because he got a full scholarship to UConn on signing day for football. He came back the next day to come to the reception. That so impressed me about him. I thought, 'Oh my god, this guy loves kids.'"

During our interviews with Central Team members and in countless interactions with Forbes, the ESI team's deep commitment to the goals of the initiative and to supporting educators in meeting them was unmistakable. This collective commitment was borne out in what they provided schools: multiple resources, points of connection, opportunities to learn from one another, and a bond that comes from forging personal relationships over time.

TOO MUCH FLEXIBILITY, TOO LITTLE OVERSIGHT

Despite this strong system of support, staff in ESI schools often voiced a desire for more direction. Short of requesting that the ESI team tell them what to do, these educators might have preferred a heavier hand in selecting particular programs to implement and allocating resources across the three domains. ESI, however, was not designed to be prescriptive. In part, the hands-off approach reflected the district's emphasis on school autonomy that became a prevalent ethos (and part of the DOE's reorganization efforts) under the administration led by Mayor Bloomberg and Chancellor Joel Klein. The freedom and flexibility given schools to design their own versions of ESI assumed that educators were in the best position to drive improvement in their buildings, to understand the needs of their students, and to support their teachers in meeting these needs. On the face of it, this was also appealing to schools and many experienced school leaders who were accustomed to making decisions about budgeting, staffing, scheduling, etc. One of the members of the Central Team described the rationale for its school-driven approach:

> The message that was sent from the beginning, which I honored and I appreciated, was: You know your school and school communities best. You know your neighborhoods. You should know your parents best. You should know your students. You know where you need to focus and where you need to push harder and where you can pull back . . . The idea was we will give you research and support on what best practices are out there . . . We'll create spaces for you

to come together, for you to learn with and from each other, but we're not going to tell you what it is that you need to do by being prescriptive, saying this curriculum, this number of times.

A hallmark of ESI's implementation was its flexibility to meet the specific needs of individual schools. While informed by a loose theory of action as well as some parameters for selecting partners and creating programs, there was no standardized version of ESI. Schools received a thick network of supports but were granted the autonomy to implement a version of ESI that was responsive to the needs of their students.

This aspect of ESI was perhaps the one that incurred the steepest trade-offs. The level of autonomy granted to schools ensured buy-in at the district and school levels but resulted in wide variation among schools in terms of program "dosage" and quality. A stronger set of guidelines might have been instrumental in helping the Central Team ensure that implementation was strong enough to have an impact on student outcomes. Without establishing an overly narrow version of ESI, the team might have made explicit their expectations about the numbers of students served by each domain, more specific mandates around which academic supports to implement (an area that was relatively weaker than the other domains), and measures for evaluating the quality of common programs like mentoring. Not surprisingly, these issues also complicated efforts to evaluate schools' implementation of ESI.

Our research team helped develop some broad measures of fidelity, intensity, and cohesion, which we shared with the district and schools on a yearly basis. But these rubrics were admittedly and somewhat necessarily blunt measures of implementation (e.g., the presence of ESI programming across the three domains, the target population is being served across all four grades). For example, the sheer variety of ESI programming precluded the possibility of establishing benchmarks for levels of student participation across all forty schools, and more qualitative measures of program effectiveness would have required much more in-depth data collection across the sites that were implementing up to ten different programs, sometimes with several partners. A more constrained vision of ESI, along with some corresponding criteria for its implementation, may have put schools in the strongest position to create new programming (in the face of many time constraints and competing priorities) and implement that programming to a high degree of effectiveness. It may have also made it possible to say with more confidence which schools were strong implementers and measure whether those schools had better outcomes.

The high level of autonomy and the lack of implementation benchmarks also made it difficult for the district to establish a system of accountability. Because each school implemented a somewhat unique version of ESI, the Central Team was unable to uniformly measure schools' participation or the quality of their programs. In interviews during the fourth and final year of the initiative, multiple team members reflected that the initiative might have been more successful had they incorporated accountability measures. One member shared, "I would build in some more accountability . . . It could've been something as simple as . . . for you to get your funding, you need to show four lesson plans [that incorporate CRE], like pre/post CRE training . . . I think a little more creativity about how to keep people accountable would have been good." Her statement suggests that the initiative may have been more impactful if it had developed some mechanism to hold schools accountable, such as tying funding to some set of external benchmarks or set of criteria. The Central Team did provide some important incentives to do the work of ESI, particularly in the area of culturally relevant training for teachers, but there were no consequences for not participating in any liaison meetings, for example, or not taking part in any PD opportunities related to ESI. To be sure, a system of sticks and carrots is not necessarily an effective motivator and can establish perverse incentives that prohibit real change. However, a system that provided even more specific parameters for schools and perhaps a pathway to counsel out schools that no longer wanted to participate in ESI would have likely strengthened implementation and shored up resources in those schools that were actively engaged.

Interestingly, some of the architects of ESI and members of the Central Team conceived of the initiative as a research and development effort rather than an intervention. They envisioned a context in which participating schools would be free to innovate, take informed risks, and make mistakes while refining programming over time as they learned more about its effectiveness. In other words, these ESI leaders did not expect that everything schools tried would work, but they did hope that their efforts would produce valuable lessons about how to improve opportunities and outcomes for boys and young men of color. Explaining this conceptualization of the initiative and how it was communicated to ESI schools, one Central Team member said, "That was one of the first messages that I put out there. The Chancellor, at that time Chancellor Walcott, affirmed [it] by saying, 'We don't expect you to know everything. We don't expect you to succeed in everything. We understand, and . . . we welcome you failing. Because failing is failing upward'—that whole idea that we learn from that [failure]." The research and development approach, however, was not universally agreed on. Some funders and city leaders, in particular, seemed anxious to see results by the end of the initiative. This approach can also present its own set of trade-offs. "Failing upward" takes courage in an environment that rewards success and prizes accountability. It also takes time. Allowing schools to create programming that might need to be abandoned or substantially revamped may have resulted in slower progress toward the intended outcomes, a reality that is politically challenging to sell.

To be fair, putting these approaches in place—measuring the quality of implementation by specific criteria and providing schools with ample time to innovate and abandon or modify plans as they proved ineffective—would have been difficult for the team of four working with forty schools over four years. However, conducting an ESI pilot year with a limited number of schools might have allowed the team (with the support of an internal or external research team) to document the schools' plans and programs, follow how they were implemented and modified over the course of a school year, identify challenges, and measure their effectiveness. Doing so may have uncovered some of the most promising practices and hard-earned lessons that became clear a few years into the initiative, thereby allowing other schools to benefit from the pilot. This tactic may have also empowered the Central Team to draw more specific parameters around what ESI should look like within each of its three domains as well as some criteria to measure and more easily ensure the quality of these plans and programs for students.

MAJOR FINDINGS

Schools that participate in external policies and programs are sometimes provided with initial PD resources, and culminating activities, but not nearly as many touchpoints during the period of implementation. ESI, on the contrary, excelled at creating an infrastructure of support that was designed to increase school and teacher capacity while establishing a professional community among ESI schools. Utilizing a rigorous application process, the district also selected a set of external organizations from which ESI schools could choose partners to assist with the implementation of various programs and services. Each year the Central Team held one-on-one meetings with representatives from each school to discuss the school's workplan and budget, and the director visited schools to establish working relationships and get a first-hand look at ESI on the ground. To increase teacher capacity to serve and engage Black and Latinx young men, the team regularly provided PD opportunities for teachers and enrichment opportunities for young men of color across ESI schools. To provide schools with a forum to share lessons and best practices, it also established monthly meetings for principals and ESI liaisons.

The support structure—including templates for work plans and budgets, individual school planning sessions, professional development, school visits, virtual communication platforms, weekly newsletters, and monthly leadership meetings—required significant planning, coordination, time, and personnel. Grounded in a commitment to empower educators to meet the needs of their students and driven by the passion of the ESI leader and team members, this network of support pushed schools to rethink how they served their young men of color, developed the capacity of individual teachers, and engaged students in meaningful experiences throughout the four-year period. In our interviews with school members, one consistent message was recognition of the efforts and supports provided by the Central Team and, in particular, the director. There were, of course, shortcomings. The partner selection process was frustrating for some (though changes were made to address schools' concerns), and the partnerships themselves were not always successful. Participation ranged widely across schools and waned after Year 2. However, the intense level of district-level support, beginning in the planning phase and extending through the life of the initiative, was an exemplary aspect of the initiative.

But where the initiative was bolstered by support for schools, it suffered from the lack of more prescriptive mandates placed on them. Based on the assumption that educators were in the best position to identify the needs of their students and develop the appropriate plans to support them, the Central Team provided schools with resources but stopped short of indicating how they should be spent. They made available a number of PD opportunities but did not require that teachers attend them. They established three broad domains in which schools could focus their programming but left the specific plans entirely up to schools. As a result, the team could not develop a set of thresholds for participation (e.g., a minimum number of days/hours for programming or a target number of participating students), and our research team's fairly blunt measures of implementation were limited in terms of what we could say about the quality of implementation (let alone specific programs). By prioritizing school autonomy, the initiative avoided any prescription that may have ensured that all schools provided enough support to their Black and Latinx young men and doing so in strategic ways that were more likely to have an impact on their outcomes.

RECOMMENDATIONS FOR DISTRICTS

1. *Align resources with the needs of schools and the goals of the initiative.*
   The resources of any initiative are finite, so it is important to make
   strategic decisions about where to allocate funding, time, and
   human capital. While the Central Team could not individually
   serve forty schools on the ground, it created a robust system of support that was responsive to schools while focusing on the initiative's
   goals. Identifying the needs of ESI schools and educators required
   multiple opportunities to interact with participants and learn about
   their experiences and challenges. Grounding support in the needs
   of the school community can be based on a number of formal and
   informal data collection activities on the part of a program team,
   including listening tours with educators, teacher or student surveys, in-person meetings, smaller focus groups with participants,
   and regular meetings with school leaders and other key staff. That is
   not to say that schools would not benefit from other supports outside of their immediate priorities, but responsiveness to their needs
   helps generate buy-in and ensure long-term participation. Trying
   to meet these needs, however, should not come at the expense of
   the effort's broader goals. In contrast, involvement with schools and
   relationships with individuals can uncover gaps in schools' capacity
   to implement policies on the ground and meet its expectations. In
   the case of ESI, providing professional development on CRE across
   subject matters, for example, was inspired by requests and observations that teachers continued to struggle with moving from theory
   to practice. Beyond that, curating existing resources as well as relying on external organizations can enable a program team to build
   school and teacher capacity in ways that limit undue burden on
   schools and a central program team.

2. *Establish effective partnerships between schools and external organiza-*
   tions. Partners were central to the creation and expansion of programming in ESI schools. The most successful partnerships were

those in which the external organization added expertise or staff not found or fully developed in the building and that fit in well with the culture of the school. Still, ESI schools reported a number of challenges related to external partnerships. Indeed, partnerships can sometimes create problems where none exists. Establishing, developing, and maintaining them can be a burden on schools. To mitigate some of these challenges, it is essential to first provide schools with enough (and the right) information to make a well-informed decision on selecting a partner who can contribute in meaningful ways. Again, an inventory on the needs of schools as well as the capacities of partners can help a program team match partners with schools, especially for those that may lack the capacity to do so on their own. Program teams should also provide clear channels of communication or mechanisms by which schools can provide both real-time and reflective feedback on external partnerships, suggesting changes where needed. Another way to think about partnerships is to promote those that may be short-lived to alleviate schools from having to allocate funds to an external partner in the long term. In schools that were particularly focused on sustainability beyond the ESI funding period, for example, staff reported learning from an outside partner approaches that would allow them to provide for that program or service on their own.

3. *Leverage the power of a professional learning community.* Embarking on transformative work in a school requires a community of learners committed to the same goals who can serve as mentors, confidantes, and creative partners. According to the educators, it was important to have the opportunity to connect with other ESI schools, to share about successes and failures, to think together about problems of practice from the shared perspective of educators and from the unique vantage points of their local contexts, and to codevelop actionable strategies that would work across different settings. Relationships with like-minded individuals who educators may not have the opportunity to work with otherwise combined with the facilitation of the ESI team solidified and strengthened the initiative's

implementation across many ESI schools. Spaces like these can shift the conversation around boys and young men of color, create safe spaces for staff of color, provide a shared vocabulary about naming the harm perpetuated by schools, and empower educators to generate strategies that mitigate those harms.

4. *Balance school-driven improvement with standards and accountability.* Despite the strong centralized support system for schools, educators, and students, the district opted not to be prescriptive on how to implement ESI. Schools were given liberty and autonomy in the creation and development of programming, making it harder to track quality and results. However, the biggest limitation of the relationship between the ESI schools and the district was this lack of explicit guidance on how schools should allocate their resources or what specific supports to offer young men of color. This was based on a logical rationale: schools know best what their own students need and how to meet those needs. There was also a desire on the part of the district to encourage innovation, allow for failure, and learn more about what works. This meant that, left to their own devices, some schools underinvested in certain domains, some tried so many new things that few were ever fully developed, and others implemented strong programs but did not ensure that enough of the target population was participating in them. The mere presence of programs does not indicate saturation. To maximize the effectiveness of a program, districts should provide more guidance on how it should be implemented and on how many students need to be served, how often, and how much. The potential of even the best program will be limited if it is not reaching enough students or delivered enough times to those students. To take a more research and development approach, an initiative would have to be structured in such a way that the district is obtaining timely feedback or data about outcomes and using that data as formative feedback to modify or abandon programs as needed. Of course, this is more feasible with a smaller number of schools, considering the time and resources it takes to implement such an approach. A smaller

PART II

Transforming School Culture
for Black and Latinx Boys

CHAPTER 4

Engaging Teachers in Culturally Responsive Approaches

> Schools have been perceived as this "neutral zone" where there's no politics; we just focus on academics. But ESI has allowed the political dimension to be acknowledged . . . There's now a language that people can use to talk about these things . . . Now there's at least some comfort level with people using a word like racism where usually you can't even say that word . . . It's part of a proactive way that we can include all our students and fight for them in this world that is not so friendly to African American and Latino students.
>
> —*Ninth-grade teacher at an ESI school*

TOO MANY EDUCATORS in K–12 schools assume they cannot openly talk about race or racism in the workplace. And those who want to confront these topics do not always have the vocabulary to do so or the support of their colleagues and/or administrators. ESI created a unique opportunity to educate and empower teachers, school leaders, and other school staff with the language and skills to identify how racial biases may work against male students of color in the hallways and in their classrooms.

Rather than concentrating solely on how students might improve their behaviors, ESI invested much of its resources and training in changing teacher beliefs and pedagogy. In particular, the initiative and its leaders committed themselves to raising critical questions about how teachers perceive the Black and Latinx boys they serve, their expectations around college and academic success, and the extent to which their instruction reflects or ignores the cultural backgrounds and everyday realities of their students. These aims and their impact on teachers and students stand out as a mark of success in ESI and suggest important lessons for the broader effort to address racial and gender inequities.

ESI programming was organized into the three domains—academics, youth development, and college-focused school culture, with culturally relevant education informing all three. Several scholars have written extensively about culturally *relevant, responsive,* and *sustaining* pedagogies.[1] Gloria Ladson-Billings introduced culturally relevant pedagogy in 1995, calling it a "a theoretical model that not only addresses student achievement but also helps students to accept and affirm their cultural identities while developing critical perspectives that challenge inequities that schools (and other institutions) perpetuate."[2] More squarely focused on practice, Geneva Gay defines culturally responsive teaching as "using the cultural knowledge, prior experiences, frames of reference, and performance styles of ethnically diverse students to make learning encounters more relevant to and effective for them."[3] Taken together, these concepts advance our understanding of what it takes to be an effective educator. Attending to academic material alone—without consciousness of and responsiveness to students' cultures, identities, and experiences—is insufficient. This responsiveness not only promotes student learning but also empowers young people to challenge inequitable systems in their schools and in society at large.

In their review of research on culturally relevant education, Brittany Aronson and Judson Laughter align the frameworks proposed by Ladson-Billings and Gay with four critical dimensions of CRE: connecting students' cultural references to academic skills and concepts; engaging students in critical reflection about their own lives and societies;

facilitating students' competence and pride about their own cultures and those of others; and unmasking oppressive systems through the critique of discourses of power.[4] With the aim of providing some important guideposts for other districts and schools, this chapter explores how ESI expanded teacher competency along these dimensions of CRE and the difference it made in the ESI schools.

Under the umbrella of culturally relevant education, ESI provided schools with professional development opportunities throughout (and beyond) the lifetime of the initiative that focused on understanding the role of race and racism in education, questioning one's own biases, making both instruction and curriculum relevant to students, and using the classroom to raise critical questions about race and power.[5] As a result of these trainings, educators reported important shifts in their mind-sets and beliefs as well as in their instructional practices. Largely positive, the CRE story that emerges from these schools provides insight into the promise of this work and its limitations. There is much other districts and schools can learn from the implementation of this aspect of ESI and some of the barriers that schools face when they commit to these efforts. Still, as many scholars have shown, CRE remains an essential approach to addressing gaps in educational opportunity and outcomes.[6] To that end, this chapter also showcases the implementation of CRE in two ESI schools, and ends with recommendations for practitioners in schools.[7]

PROFESSIONAL DEVELOPMENT GROUNDED IN CRE

In New York City, nearly 70 percent of public school students are Black or Latinx, while 59 percent of teachers are White, mirroring the demographics of other large urban districts across the country.[8] In addition to this racial and ethnic mismatch, many of the teachers we interviewed over the four years of the study did not recall engaging in discussions about race when they were students themselves. Many teacher education programs limit their discussions of race to one or two required courses on multicultural education or diverse populations, and even these courses largely deal with issues of linguistic and cognitive diversity as opposed to race. This explains why many educators feel both reluctant and ill-equipped to address issues of race in their schools with colleagues or students. Several educators indicated that at the outset of the initiative they felt uncomfortable with discussing students' racial or ethnic backgrounds. Some thought talking about race might get them in trouble with their leadership. One teacher admitted that, prior to CRE training, he felt "afraid of those topics." Others asked us to turn off the recorder when asked how their school used ESI to target Black and Latinx young boys. While few educators made overtly racist comments, many espoused color blindness, asserting that race does not or should not matter in educating students.[9] One teacher said, "To be honest, I've worked in multiple schools of all different demographics. There's maybe some needs or issues that are different depending on [student demographics] . . . but I found that at the end of the day, kids are kids." Some statements also revealed a more nuanced reluctance to target students based on their gender. A principal at one school reported, "When we approached our design proposal, we made a decision to implement programs that would not be targeted exclusively to boys. We just felt like it was a wiser and more comprehensive approach to spread things across the entire ninth grade, and not just to boys." While these educators applied to participate in an initiative designed for young men of color, they resisted the idea of targeting particular groups of students. In fairness, some of the resistance reflected a reluctance to pathologize boys of color or to exclude female students from receiving additional resources. But these reservations were expressed infrequently as compared with the more commonly conveyed general discomfort with targeting supports at students because of their race or ethnicity. Statements made early in the implementation of the initiative highlighted an inability—or outright reluctance—on the part of many educators to identify specific ways schools underserved male students of color. It was, in part, this perspective that ESI made a commitment to challenge through CRE.

Other teachers and staff, especially educators of color, expressed awareness of the disconnect between the teachers and students in their schools and how that affected boys of color in particular. As one teacher explained, "A lot of the young men, we feel like they're on the periphery of what's being taught. These students come in sometimes with very—not necessarily negative, just very different experiences. Often times the classroom is an alien place." Some staff acknowledged that many of their Black and Brown boys encountered painful situations in their current schools or in previous schools. When explaining some of the disparities in her own school, for example, one school leader said, "Many of our students come in with either negative or scarred experiences with teachers that didn't necessarily give them the support that they needed." While these educators could articulate "problems," they struggled to identify solutions. One teacher's response to this question summarizes a lot of what we heard at the outset of the initiative: "I guess we don't know . . . [about] special strategies for Black and Latinx boys . . . I'm really not sure what strategies are separate and apart from other kids? What special strategy is there just for Latinx and Black males?"

To help teachers and other staff in participating schools address issues of race and gender and become more comfortable doing so, ESI devoted substantial time, effort, and resources to training teachers in culturally relevant approaches to teaching and learning. In fact, ESI's professional development focused on CRE over any other topic or theme. Even in workshops dedicated to academic topics (e.g., STEM, writing a college essay), CRE remained a central principal around which to organize and deliver that PD. ESI schools utilized a wide range of CRE training, resources, and experts (see table 4.1). During Year 1 (in fact, within a few weeks of the start of the school year), the Central Team facilitated a three-hour CRE symposium for all forty schools during which schools met with external providers in smaller groups. Beyond that initial training, and based on an interest expressed by some schools, ESI provided an intensive training course—"College Readiness Through a Culturally Relevant Approach," led by Michelle Knight of Columbia's Teachers College—to a group of ten ESI schools. Throughout the life of the initiative, the ESI team generated a list of individuals and organizations that could provide schools with CRE training and also invited staff in ESI schools to attend additional week-long sessions on CRE, including "Creating a

Culturally Responsive, College-Going Culture" (2013–14 and 2014–15) and "CRE Immersion Week" (summers of 2014 and 2015), as well as the more in-depth, action-based sessions "CRE Institute" and "CRE Fellowship" in the last year of the initiative.

The initiative's design paid considerable attention to which organizations schools could allocate their ESI resources. Through a lengthy application process (separate from the application to be a vendor with the DOE), the ESI team required that external partners describe their cultural relevance approach. While all the organizations were labeled as providing CRE, the focus of their training fell into four strands that sometimes overlapped:

TABLE 4.1   External organizations offering CRE professional development in Year 1

ORGANIZATION	MISSION STATEMENT
Advancement via Individual Determination (AVID)	Provide schools with professional development, a suite of resources, and ongoing support to shift to a more equitable, student-centered approach.
Brotherhood/Sister Sol	Provide workshops and training to educators to deepen their understanding of social issues facing Black and Latinx youth as well as pedagogical strategies for supporting students' academic and social development.
Coalition for Schools Educating Boys of Color (COSEBOC)	Connect, inspire, support, and strengthen school leaders dedicated to the social, emotional, and academic development of boys and young men of color.
The Efficacy Institute	Rooted in a fundamental transformation of the way adults—teachers, administrators, and parents—think about intelligence and development to produce positive outcomes and sets the foundation to accelerate the change.
The Metropolitan Center for Research on Equity and the Transformation of Schools	Advance equity and excellence in education by connecting to legacies of justice work through critical inquiry and research, professional development and technical assistance, and community action and collaboration.
Umoja Community	Actively serve and promote student success for all students through a curriculum and pedagogy responsive to the legacy of the African and African American diasporas.
Undoing Racism: The People's Institute for Survival Beyond	A national and international collective of antiracist, multicultural community organizers and educators dedicated to building an effective movement for social transformation.

- *increasing academic expectations* among teachers and students by offering rigorous coursework (e.g., AP and honors classes) to young men of color and adopting a college-going culture in school;
- *developing culturally responsive curriculum and instruction* informed by students' cultures, backgrounds, and prior experiences;
- *promoting critical consciousness among students* by providing them with opportunities to study examples of and participate in social action and community-led movements; and
- *challenging teachers to come to terms with their own privilege and bias* and how those might collectively shape policy, practice, and relationships in school.

Reinforcing this external training, the ESI team held workshops within their principal and ESI liaison meetings with schools that challenged how educators perceived their male students of color, which educational opportunities they made available to which students, and how their discipline policies disproportionately affected Black and Brown students. The PD also provided school staff with common terminology (e.g., color blindness, microaggressions, interpersonal versus institutionalized racism) or shared language that enabled teachers to identify and name examples of racism in their schools.

Providing PD opportunities does not guarantee that schools or educators will take advantage of them. In the case of ESI, however, school participation proved to be as robust as the offerings. As displayed in table 4.2, the number of schools that participated in CRE was consistent across the years, and the number of schools putting CRE into practice increased over time. This level of participation speaks to the case the ESI team made about its importance and its potential impact on student experiences and outcomes. In particular, the ESI team communicated the value of CRE by drawing on literature that demonstrated how building connections from the classroom to students' identities and the issues that matter to them can increase student engagement and improve student performance.[10] CRE training affected the educators in two stages. First, it provided teachers and staff with a new set of knowledge and

TABLE 4.2 CRE participation among ESI schools

	NUMBER OF SCHOOLS THAT PARTICIPATED IN CRE TRAINING	NUMBER OF SCHOOLS THAT IMPLEMENTED CRE
Year 1	37	22
Year 2	36	26
Year 3	34	35
Year 4	34	37

expanded (or challenged) existing belief systems. Second, these shifts in mind-sets and beliefs translated into changes in practice. This process is somewhat parallel to what Chezare A. Warren describes as the movement from acquiring new knowledge (Phase 1) to the "negotiation of that knowledge and interpretation to make pedagogic adjustments" (Phase 2).[11] In the case of ESI, teachers often returned to Phase 1 over the lifetime of the initiative as changes in their practice generated new understandings about their students and inspired an interest in deepening their knowledge through ongoing professional development.

CHANGING MIND-SETS: REFRAMING THE PROBLEM

The assumption driving the CRE training was that it would, in the words of ESI director Paul Forbes, "change the hearts and minds" of participating educators (and eventually teachers across the system): "ESI for me is, again, about a mind-set paradigm shift of how we think about our youngsters, our Black and Latino youngsters, in particular our young men. Yeah, there are operational things we're talking about, but for me ESI is about a social change, a change movement, a mind-set paradigm shift of adults and how they think and see the youngsters in front of them." To that end, as a by-product of the CRE training, educators began to acknowledge and articulate the root causes of disparities in educational outcomes as well as their own complicity in perpetuating those inequities in schools. These explanations stood in contrast to those that attributed underachievement to deficiencies among the students, their motivation, their families, and/or their "cultures." One principal shared, "CRE just exposed a great deal of the staff to some preconceived notions that they have of Black and Latino males that they might not be quite aware of. That was brought out a lot in the CRE training." In particular, the staff members we spoke to expressed a deeper understanding of the impact of pervasive structural inequities, such as neighborhood unemployment, intergenerational poverty deepened by American policy, and the stress or anxiety created by the threat of police violence. One principal said of the boys in his school, "I believe [they are] constantly being harassed by the police. That people looking at them as a no good—won't amount to nothing—has to change." Explicitly identifying and naming the experiences of his students and the biases they faced daily provided evidence of the ways CRE training had shifted the perspectives of educators in ESI schools.

CRE training also created opportunities for school staff to examine how their own backgrounds and biases could be shaping their perceptions of and relationships with Black and Brown boys. As one principal described it, prioritizing CRE training helped teachers think about who they are, to "step to the table in terms of our background and our experiences and the impact that has and how we relate to the kids." An ESI liaison echoed:

We made CRE a centerpiece and involved everybody in the movement. It's a movement. It's not a program . . . We asked ESI to do a presentation on the data relating to the achievement gap, because we really felt like there was a lack of awareness. What we'd hear from staff all the time was that we don't treat our students differently depending on gender, race, background, anything. Everybody's equal. Everybody's the same. What we knew, in fact, was that the data was not showing that the boys were doing as well as the girls, for example. That needed to be clear to everybody. It couldn't just be clear to the small group of people creating the plan design. We asked him to do the presentation, which I think had an impact, because now there's an awareness. This is not just nationwide, citywide. This is in our actual school. We have this happening here.

This statement highlights the use of a CRE lens in making the case to teachers that the problems affecting young boys of color do not just exist "out there" on citywide graphs but are true of their own schools and classrooms.

Another principal described how CRE directly challenge the color-blind narratives many educators felt most comfortable championing:

> I think that the introduction of the CRE team has aided in that conversation a lot over the last two years. One, just being able to bring it to the forefront, this idea that color blindness is not serving our Black and Latino male population in the way that maybe teachers have thought that it was. This feeling that, "I'm a teacher and I teach all of my students and I don't see their color and I don't distinguish between them as a student versus anybody else in my classroom," and how that is not necessarily the best approach.

The language of these school leaders begins to frame teachers' "good intentions" to be unbiased as a potential source of the disparity in outcomes between Black and Latinx boys and other segments of their student population. Their statements also show a new level of comfort among principals and teachers willing to engage in this type of self-reflection, to think about their own impact on the success of their students rather than resort to blaming the young people they aim to serve.

In particular, educators across ESI schools identified discipline policies as one area that was particularly vulnerable to teacher bias. School approaches to discipline and behavior have historically and systemically disadvantaged Black male and female students.[12] The New York Civil Liberties Union found that Black students accounted for 53 percent of suspensions while only representing 33 percent of all students.[13] As a result of ESI-related PD, educators began to acknowledge how they contributed to disproportionality in their schools. One principal explained:

We, like the city . . . and the nation, have had a disproportionate number of suspensions that impact Black and Latinx boys and a disproportionate number of the students who are suspended frequently being Black and Latinx boys. Now, a lot these boys are engaging in some really problematic behaviors. We haven't necessarily had a set of practices to help us shift behaviors, right? . . . We recognize that as an issue, and it's something that both we had to do something structurally about. But also we needed to start, as the adults in the building, having different conversations among ourselves and with kids and families about what is happening, how we fix it, and how we come to a place of respect in the school and in the classroom.

While this principal still communicates some deficit language, the awareness of their role in perpetuating the very disparities they wished to disrupt seemed to help many school leaders and teachers think differently about their own practices. One teacher explained that participating in a PD about disproportionality "contributed to the staff thinking more creatively about how we do discipline, not just suspending kids without them fully understanding what's going on or having conversations [but] figuring [out] how best to repair the harm that was done."

Beyond discipline and suspensions, the greatest shift in mind-set related to CRE training could be characterized as moving from passive acceptance of an intractable problem to taking responsibility for creating potential solutions. This perspective seemed to permeate all aspects of schooling, from the academic success of boys of color to their relationships with adults in the building. How responsible teachers deemed themselves marked a profound shift in their thinking. One principal explained:

I think that in some ways there's an attitude that permeates the culture that these kids are at such a low level that we can't do a lot. I think that attitude puts so much of the emphasis on the students. Like, "They came to us like this. It's not our fault. Look how low level they are" versus "Well, what can we do to impact that?"

I think that this emphasis on culturally relevant education has the potential to do that. Because then all of a sudden you're trying to look at these students not as this group that are low level, but rather as individuals who have this range of experiences that are coming into your classroom. Well, how do you use that to your advantage? How can you reach these young people who need to be reached and who could show tremendous growth if we tried to address those issues the right way?

Documenting this shift in thinking led us to raise questions about the extent to which these perspectives made a difference in teacher practice.

CHANGING PRACTICE: CONNECTING CLASSROOMS TO STUDENTS' LIVES

Central to the initiative's mission was changing the mind-sets and beliefs of educators in ESI schools to motivate action that would improve the experiences and outcomes of boys and young men of color. During the launch and Year 1, the ESI team managed to make a compelling case for CRE and the broader need for educators to examine how their perspectives and practices might be contributing to the outcomes of their students. While many educators reported changes in their thinking that first year, they struggled with how to make these ideas concrete. One teacher admitted, "I really am struggling with CRE stuff, and we're talking about how we have this population. We're all aware of that, but that's not really changing what can we do. That's what I need . . . I think we're walking away with a theory behind it and not the practical application."

By Year 2, however, there was ample evidence of schools adapting to or adopting new practices to increase the cultural responsiveness of their pedagogical approaches. The changes fell into four broad areas: implementing strategies to better understand their student population; modifying curriculum to affirm students' racial and cultural backgrounds; incorporating current events that were most relevant to their students' lives; and utilizing new instructional strategies to engage students. Based on the feedback from principals and teachers on support in this area, subsequent CRE trainings were able to provide teachers with specific tools to use in their classrooms and daily interactions with students. The Central team also created tools that incorporated these practices into existing accountability frameworks to further reinforce these lessons across the school building. In direct contrast to the teacher who struggled with "practical application" of CRE, one principal said that "when we do PD, it's not only just about theory. It's about the actual practice, and how you embed these different strategies into your practice."

First, the ESI schools introduced specific approaches aimed at helping their staff understand the lives of their students and their experiences in school. These efforts assumed empathy in adopting the "cultural points of view of diverse youth and families" and resulted in new knowledge that ultimately changed teacher practice.[14] Teachers in a handful of the schools conducted home visits before the start of the year to establish relationships with students and their families. In one school, students led a video project that chronicled how Black and Latinx students felt attending their schools. In other schools, staff—many of whom never resided in the communities they worked in—engaged in efforts to familiarize themselves with the neighborhood. One teacher recounted:

> Just from my personal experience, I'd never really walked the Bronx, but in the morning, I got together with two other people who were on my team—because we had teams of three—and we just kind of took public transportation, took buses, took trains, and walked the Bronx—looked at the surroundings that we have. We also brought in a few of our upperclassmen—our juniors and seniors—and had them talk to our new staff about . . . [their] neighborhood. "Let's just talk about what is it like to come to school here, and what is it like to live in this neighborhood? What is it like to come to school in this neighborhood if you don't live here?"

For these educators, a culturally responsive approach to teaching included improving their understanding of the lives of their students, becoming familiar with their communities, and developing relationships with their families. Recognizing their outsider status in the communities they served, these teachers made efforts to bridge the gaps between themselves and their students. At the same time, these efforts to develop understanding and empathy must avoid interpreting students' home lives or communities through a cultural deficit lens.[15] One teacher reflected, "I've learned . . . how to affirm—and how not to negate—my male students' identities. What I got out of it most is understanding how I can improve my communication, how I can improve my teaching and interactions with the students."

Many schools initially responded to CRE training by modifying their curricula This included introducing new authors and texts that served as the "windows and mirrors" reflecting and affirming students' multiple identities. One Latinx teacher explained the way decision-making around ordering books changed with ESI: "We have a certain amount of budget for getting more books each year. Having us shift away from Walt Whitman to Ernesto Quiñonez . . . The variety in our bookroom here is something I've not seen before. I'm used to the dead White men. I mean, I was brought up on the canon. I studied the canon. I know the canon. It's refreshing to see authors that reflect people who look like me." This teacher, and others, selected texts written by people of color and featuring male protagonists of color to engage their male students in ways they may have overlooked before. Another teacher offered:

> I didn't realize that all the literature I was teaching in my class was so much focused on the female's perspective and experience. I didn't realize how tuned-out my boys were . . . I was able to see that I was singling out the boys. That was causing them to withdraw from the curriculum. They weren't as motivated. They weren't being as successful as they could. With that, I was able to reflect and re-create my curriculum to make it more balanced. I started looking at more books and novels and short stories and articles that will not only be successful and interesting for my girls, but also include the boys.

These teacher statements reflect how ESI challenged educators to examine their own practice and take concrete action to serve their Black and Latinx male students. In addition to expanding the curricula teachers provided students with learning opportunities centered on their identities and backgrounds. In one such project, they required students to explore their family histories and cultural ancestors. As the principal described it, "[Students] do family trees; they do research with their parents, parent interviews . . . 'Who are our ancestors and what are the really powerful things that happened that have allowed us to be here today?' There's this sense, and that's all intentional, a part of this healing process, of 'before we were slaves, we were kings and queens.'"

Teachers also discussed the importance of incorporating current events into classroom instruction, including the police killings of Michael Brown and Eric Garner, broader policies like stop-and-frisk, and the criminal justice system in New York City. One principal said, "If you know that the Eric Garner issue is burning in the community, how can we take a current and relevant event into the classroom and apply it [to] what we're doing?" I sat in on one class applying the Socratic seminar method to discuss Tamir Rice, the twelve-year old Black boy who was shot by a White police officer in Cleveland. It was clear that students were anxious to talk about what had happened and that providing them an opportunity to do so in class centered their voices and honored their emotions. One teacher said:

> I think that when opportunities present themselves through the law classes and through the history classes, we seize those moments. They're teachable moments. You can't get them back. For example, when the indictment—well, lack of indictment [in Ferguson]— came back, I set aside whatever I had planned because the idea was whatever I taught them that day, in twenty years they'll forget. If I took the time to talk about what had happened and actually let them talk about what had happened and ask questions that they didn't know who to ask or where to get the answers. That's something that they were going to walk away with and that was going be

something meaningful to them that they were going to carry much further than the causes of the Civil War.

Overall, teachers began to think about leveraging students' existing interests and expertise to imbue classrooms with meaning and relevance. One principal noted, "I see teachers really trying to make connections to student lives and to current events that make that a little bit more tangible, and the curriculum more tangible, to students." By Years 3 and 4 of the initiative, a few schools also implemented learning experiences outside of the classroom to address the fourth dimension of CRE, "unmasking oppressive systems through the critique of discourses of power." Whether by becoming politically active in the Black Lives Matter movement, organizing around local issues, or participating in protests around the city, these students engaged with the curriculum in ways that could be applied to their lives long after high school.

Because of its focus on engaging students authentically, CRE training inspired teachers in ESI schools to modify their curriculum and their instructional approaches For example, many teachers reported moving away from traditional lectures to experiential learning, storytelling, and collaborative project-based student work and assessments. In response to youth culture and students' pervasive use of social media platforms, teachers also shared creative ways of incorporating social media into their classrooms. One teacher advised, "Instead of saying, 'Oh, I hate Facebook. All you guys do is just go on Facebook all the time,' learn to use it." We also saw a shift in the emphasis on pedagogical approaches that centered student voice and student ownership of their learning. One teacher shared:

> [I use] student-centered learning where children are accountable and responsible for their own learning. They're leading class discussion. They're doing the group presentation, and they're working off what each other's research is and what they have found. [It's about] getting them to sort of monitor themselves as far as how a classroom should run and how a discussion should run. The key push from [our teachers] has been [to show students that]

when you go to college and you find yourself as one of two or three Brown or Black individuals in a room, that you're capable of competing, if not outperforming, those around, and not be reluctant or reticent to participate.

It is important to note that while this strategy can simply be described as "good teaching," the way she frames it as being particularly important for students of color speaks to the core principles of CRE. Similarly, another staff member described implementing "roundtables" in their classrooms, a structure that provides students an opportunity to present to a small group of peers a topic they are passionate about or have some expertise in. The roundtable focuses on presentation skills required in academic and professional environments, communicates high expectations on the part of teachers, and instills a sense of confidence among students—"How do we put our students in a position where they can be successful, but they do feel challenged and they do feel accomplished after they've completed it?"

Overall, CRE pushed educators to consider multiple approaches for better serving Black and Latinx boys and young men through their curricular and instructional choices. These approaches also reflected the larger shift among educators away from perceiving students' performance as a lack of motivation and toward taking direct responsibility for engaging them in their classrooms. As one principal said, "It's incumbent on our teachers to find ways to make the curriculum connect to our students, to communicate with our students in such a way that they understand and take an interest in it." A teacher echoed, "We're starting to change the mind-set where it's not the student's job to engage. It's our job to plan activities and lessons that engage students."

The impact of CRE training on teachers' perspectives and practices in ESI schools was robust. By focusing professional development on CRE, vetting providers for a CRE lens, providing various CRE training opportunities, and reinforcing this training through ESI meetings and materials, the Central Team shifted the thinking of many educators across the forty participating schools and eventually shifting teacher practice toward a more culturally responsive approach. One teacher's reflection shows how far-reaching a CRE orientation to teaching and learning can be:

> [CRE] changed the way I interact with my students. It changed my instruction, my relationship with my students. It changed how my classroom looked on a daily basis. Both on a personal level and a schoolwide level, I think the CRE is the most meaningful, and I think it's something every school—every school that has teachers that are different from their students and teachers that are the same as their students in terms of their background, and every school in New York—should [implement].

At the same time, the training was limited in two important ways. First, while the ESI team made these PD sessions available to all schools throughout the life of the initiative, only a small number of teachers from each could attend. We found that the teachers who were involved in the planning and implementation of ESI were often fully engaged in CRE training, while other teachers in the building remained unaware of culturally relevant education. Second, attendance at a single training in any given year did not necessarily lead to this kind of meaningful change without the ongoing support of the school leader, other teachers, and schoolwide policies to sustain the commitment, including school-based accountability tools that reinforced the use of CRE across classrooms. Despite the number of schools and teachers that applied their CRE training in policy and practice, questions remain about how to institutionalize these approaches and make them sustainable beyond the lifetime of an initiative and beyond the individual teachers who attend a given PD.

CRE IN PRACTICE: CASE STUDIES FROM THE FIELD

Beginning in Year 2 of the initiative, the Research Alliance team conducted a series of case studies in seven schools that were particularly strong models of ESI based on their implementation scores.[16] The first portrait here looks at a school's creation of a professional learning community focused on CRE. A second illustrates how an ESI school applies the principles of CRE to serve its large population of immigrant students.

High School for Law and Public Service: Institutionalizing CRE

The High School for Law and Public Service is a small high school in Manhattan. While the principal at Law and Public Service was committed to the vision of ESI, the assistant principal made that vision a reality. Not only did she actively engage in the ESI community, but her school was often cited as exemplary in multiple aspects of the model, including providing early college supports, establishing adult-student mentorships, and training teachers in culturally relevant education.

Embedding CRE into an existing school structure. In Year 1, six staff members participated in a ten-week CRE training course led by Michelle Knight. After the training, the school decided to devote one of its PLCs to CRE, which allowed the school to extend the PD to more than those six teachers while also applying it to schoolwide policy and practice. All teachers joined one of five PLCs of their choice—small groups of five to seven staff members that met once a week for one class period during the school day to discuss a particular topic related to serving students more effectively (e.g., college- and career-readiness, social-emotional support). In its meetings, the CRE group used an inquiry process to examine teachers' practices and look for ways they could make their curriculum and instruction more culturally relevant. PLC members also shared CRE resources and strategies with other teachers at staff PD sessions. The existence of a PLC devoted to CRE reflected a commitment to institutionalizing CRE as a schoolwide approach, not restricting it to just those who received external PD. One school leader explained, "[The PLC] kind of gave us time to talk together and understand the importance of having the school invested [in CRE]; it can't just be a small pocket activity." The structure of the PLC can be powerful in other ways: it sets aside time to discuss topics that may otherwise be overlooked, helps ensure sustainability of strategies or an ethos in the face of staff turnover, and, because it is led by teachers, helps promote buy-in among staff.

Using data strategically. School leaders reported that some staff challenged the focus on Black and Latinx boys and young men; they did not see a need to focus on their male students. One strategy they used to confront this resistance was to provide staff with school-generated data reports about the graduation rates, grades, and credit accumulation of their male students. When teachers saw the clear discrepancies between the performance of their female and male students, they understood the importance of being intentional about addressing the needs of an underserved population.

Incorporating CRE into teacher observations. When school leaders conducted classroom observations, they looked for evidence of CRE, particularly as it related to making instruction relevant and engaging for boys and young men. School leaders asked teachers to think about how often they participated and whether they engaged their male students as frequently as their female students. This came in response to PD that highlighted the subtle ways teachers can engage female students more frequently than their male peers. As a result, teachers focused on using certain questioning techniques (e.g., posting sentence starters on the walls) for students who were more apprehensive to share in class, ensuring that all students had a voice. They also rearranged the desks in classrooms, moving from traditional rows to clusters, which further facilitated student-led discussion. One teacher reported that while these techniques were born out of their focus on male students, all students benefited from this approach.

Manhattan Bridges High School: Serving Newcomers and English Language Learners

Manhattan Bridges High School predominantly serves English Learners (ELs) or emergent bilingual students. Fifty percent of its students are designated as ELs, while another 30 percent are either former ELs or students whose home language is Spanish. In addition, 41 percent of students are also students with interrupted formal education, a group that faces unique obstacles to high school graduation. The staff approached CRE in terms of serving ELs and recent immigrants as well as their families.

Offering targeted language training. Teachers received PD and certifications related to supporting ELs and bilingual students. Nearly all ninth- and tenth-grade teachers had bilingual extension certifications (some obtained before they were hired) or were in the process of receiving them, which prepared *all* educators to teach the school's EL students in a bilingual setting. Teachers were also trained in Quality Teaching of the English Language, a program offered by the district. In addition, teachers participated in PD led by Ofelia Garcia of the CUNY Graduate Center on translanguaging, a bilingual person's flexible and sometimes simultaneous use of both languages to interpret their everyday lives and experiences. While some teachers said that their classes already incorporated translingual methods, they found it helpful to formalize their practices through research, teaching guidelines, and benchmarks.

Celebrating students' native language. Teachers used Spanish to scaffold content for native speakers. They provided materials, including exams, in both Spanish and English. Some content classes (e.g., history, science) provided instruction primarily in Spanish. One teacher described how conversations in Spanish provided a foundation for learning English:

> [When] I was realizing that some students felt better off expressing themselves in Spanish, I let them do that. They would express themselves in Spanish, and then we would go back to the English. I wouldn't force them and say, "No. You have to say it in English." Then they're stuttering and nervous and everything else. At first, they go with their strength. Articulate their thoughts. Then we strategically summarize it in English or something. It's purposefully

switching from the language that the student feels strong in back to the other language as necessary.

These approaches enabled staff to think of students' Spanish as a linguistic resource, not a limitation holding them back. As one teacher said, "Our EL population is very talented. I personally believe ELs are gifted. Just the fact that you could read García Márquez and you could also read Steinbeck—Hey, not everybody could do that, and they could actually tap into those two worlds." Some parents expressed concern that speaking Spanish in class would prevent their children from developing English skills. In response, teachers described reinforcing Spanish language skills as a resource: "We want them to be good at both [languages]." Sometimes teachers also convinced students—especially those who were more comfortable in English—that speaking Spanish will be a valuable resource in the future." Moreover, celebrating Spanish encouraged students to be proud of their background. As one teacher noted, "We don't have students, especially boys, feeling, 'Oh, I'm less than.' [Instead they feel like,] 'It's okay for me to celebrate my language and be proud of who I am.'"

Recognizing diversity within and across cultures. The staff were committed to recognizing the differences within cultures that are often painted with one broad brush. The principal said, "Assuming that because they're all Latino, they're all from the same culture, is a big error." Students and their families not only hailed from different countries—the Dominican Republic, Mexico, Puerto Rico, Nicaragua, etc.—but also had diverse experiences. The school sought to ensure that all students and families established at least one point of connection in the building by hiring teachers from diverse Latinx backgrounds. The school also chose not to commemorate national holidays from particular countries in favor of hosting schoolwide celebrations that honored all the cultures of their students. Finally, the school emphasized the importance of cultural and racial diversity within the Latinx diaspora to new teachers so they became conscientious about including all students.

Supporting immigrant families and undocumented students. Staff worked to address the challenges faced by students new to the United States so that they could participate more fully in their education. Many students had missed a year or more of school or had received limited formal education in their home countries. Thus, the school emphasized the delivery of academic content and helped students develop skills they needed to adjust to school and their new environments. Staff explained that many of their immigrant students—a large proportion of whom were separated from their families or living in multifamily homes—lacked some basic resources. To alleviate any financial burden associated with attending school, the school purchased students' uniforms and supplies and subsidized school events and trips. Staff also reported that some students deemed academically ready for college lacked documentation needed to enroll. One teacher recalled how a school handout used "American," which immediately alienated many students from considering that university as an option. In the face of growing xenophobia, the staff made it a priority to provide ample outreach to and develop relationships with families so they could feel safe and welcome to take advantage of the school's college services and supports. To that end, the school partnered with college support organizations that provide students and families with information about scholarships and financial aid packages available to undocumented students. Also, through meetings and other events, staff advised parents about paying for college and provided information to students about organizations that would support them in securing required documentation.

MAJOR FINDINGS

While ESI programming focused on academics, youth development, and school culture, culturally relevant education became central to how the initiative was envisioned, communicated to educators, and implemented at the school level. As a result of robust professional development in CRE, educators began to infuse their curricula with texts and conversations relevant to boys and young men of color and applied instructional approaches to better engage them across the curricula. However, CRE goes beyond textbooks and pedagogy; it also represents a "firm commitment to social justice education and seeing the classroom as a site for social change."[17] We found fewer opportunities for students to engage in social justice education, suggesting perhaps that more sophisticated applications of CRE require further time and development among teachers implementing CRE in schools.

Overall, educators in ESI schools were more likely to articulate their own roles in improving the learning experiences and outcomes for young men of color, departing from both color-blind and deficit perspectives. While these shifts in beliefs and practices were an important dimension of ESI, it is important to recognize the difficulty of implementing and sustaining this kind of effort. Even in schools where CRE was relatively strong, one or two active detractors potentially limited the impact of this work. After a year of commitment to CRE from the school leader and their teachers, the next year might have seen staffing changes that could derail previous efforts. Consider the statement of a teacher attempting to explain the disparities in student outcomes: "They're way behind, and they're very, very apathetic. There's nothing that we could do that could make them care about their own education and their own grades." Or this comment from a teacher in one of the case study schools: "I know it sounds bad, but just like thug culture, like, 'I don't have to go to school. I'm going to make money. I'm going to make dirty money. I don't need to follow this path.' I think a lot of them really don't see themselves—and the other thing to point out is that they are fourteen. They're not twenty-five. They're probably going to realize how silly they're acting right now because they are not thinking long term. They're living in the moment." It's not clear whether this teacher actively opposed the measures being taken in their school or simply held these beliefs while never espousing them publicly. But considering the relationship between teacher beliefs and their actions toward students, their words provide a potent reminder that this work is not only sorely needed but may always be aspirational.

RECOMMENDATIONS FOR PRACTICE

1. *Formally assess the level of racial equity in your school.* A benefit of the ESI application process was that schools were required to provide data on the Black and Latinx males in a number of different outcomes (e.g., attendance, suspensions, honors or AP classes) to identify priority areas for allocating the grant money. This exercise can be expanded to understand the performance of different student groups and to get a sense of students' experiences in classrooms and in the school community. Schools can use a number of tools to assess how they are serving marginalized students, including Black and Latinx young men, special education students, and English learners (and how these student demographic data may overlap in ways that reveal teacher bias). Identifying important gaps and areas for improvement—instructional materials, access to high-level courses, discipline policies, racial makeup of leadership and staff—and using shared terminology is an important first step toward transformational change.[18]

2. *Embed CRE in classroom observations and other accountability measures.* When staff in ESI schools reported frustration that their evaluation tool did not align with the CRE frameworks they studied, the Central Team developed a rubric with practical examples from real classrooms. Principals and teachers incorporated this tool into their observations of classrooms and intervisitations. Another tool some schools found useful related to this work is the Equitable Classroom Practice Observation Checklist.[19] Embedding CRE into a school's expectations of an effective classroom empowered school actors by providing tangible actions toward developing a culturally responsive approach, communicated its importance to the school community, and helped institutionalize CRE in schoolwide policy.

3. *Provide all adults in a school building with ongoing PD.* As with other areas of professional development in education, a one-off PD in

CRE will never be sufficient to change teachers' mind-sets and beliefs, let alone practices. Teachers should deepen their knowledge of CRE—its concepts and practices—over time and learn from different experts and organizations as well as provide turnkey training to other staff. ESI highlighted the role that other staff (e.g., school safety officers, guidance counselors, paraprofessionals) could play in this work. Including additional members of the school community in these professional development opportunities can ensure that CRE is not limited to a few individuals who are already engaged in these issues.

4. *Hire teachers of color.* In 2015, the NYC DOE launched the NYC Men Teach program under the umbrella of the Young Men's Initiative. Its goal was to recruit men of color to teach in the city by providing early career support, professional development, and mentoring. While the progress has been slow, the aspirations were motivated by a growing body of research showing that students of color (and White students) benefit from having teachers of color.[20] This "role model effect" is especially powerful for Black male students.[21] Though the Research Alliance team did not systematically analyze our data by the race or ethnicity of the individuals interviewed, we did hear from principals and teachers about both the lack of teachers of color and their importance for students. One teacher said, "Another big challenge, they don't have role models in our school and I guess in many schools. Last week, one of the girls in the class asked me, 'I'm in the tenth grade, but I've never had a Black teacher.'" Though not a solution by itself, hiring teachers of color can strengthen schools' efforts to successfully implement CRE and improve the experiences and outcomes of males of color.

CHAPTER 5

Creating Safe Spaces and Communities of Care for Students

I think that's what I loved. I think that this program teaches you how to be compassionate for other people and to create something that you can't get anywhere else . . . To have these guys every day that I came to school just made me want to come to school that much more, because I got to be with my brothers in a sense. I got to be with my family.

—*Eleventh-grade student at an ESI school*

YOUNG PEOPLE NEED a sense of safety and belonging to learn and thrive. In the realm of child psychology and human development, social capital is defined by healthy relationships, feelings of trust and safety, and a sense of belonging within a community.[1] Other scholars have applied these models to schools, arguing that relationships and interactions with other individuals in the school community play a critical role in the well-being and success of students: "In order to develop, a child needs the enduring, irrational involvement of one or more adults in care and joint activity with the child. Somebody has to be crazy about that kid."[2] Many schools participating in ESI embodied this ethos via

programs and spaces that facilitated the development of positive relationships between students and their teachers as well as among their
peers. These programs engendered feelings of safety and belonging
among participating students. An important dimension of these efforts
included restorative approaches to discipline in addition to mentorship
programs and dedicated spaces for boys and young men.

Research underpinning ESI's youth development domain shows
that strong teacher-student relationships are associated with a range
of positive student outcomes, including increased student participation, satisfaction, attendance, and college-going rates.[3] The initiative's
focus on mentoring was similarly informed by evidence of the promise of mentorship and mentoring programs for improving student outcomes.[4] ESI also drew on literature that established differences between
male and female students in terms of relationships with teachers and
academically oriented relationships with peers.[5] Research focused
on Black and Latinx boys and young men in particular highlights the
impact of relationships on academic success.[6] Oscar Barbarin contends
that "a mentally healthy and safe school is a prerequisite to successful
learning and advancement, and key to addressing the achievement gap
affecting African American boys and young men," citing three essential features: relationships and connectedness to school, student safety
and school discipline, and mentally healthy students, staff, and school
environments.[7]

Informed by this research and recognizing the sense of alienation
many boys and young men of color feel in their own schools, educators
in ESI schools went to great lengths to create supportive environments
for Black and Latinx male students. They did so primarily through a
variety of mentoring opportunities and by creating formalized spaces
for smaller groups of boys to come together under the facilitation of
teachers invested in getting to know students as individuals. These programs amplified student voices and promoted student leadership while
providing a safe space for boys to share with one another, care for each
other during difficult times, and celebrate each other's accomplishments. In addition, some ESI schools placed students' safety, trust, and

well-being at the center of their approaches to discipline, an aspect of school that tends to marginalize boys of color.

As a result of these efforts, ESI's influence improved relationships in schools and positively impacted students' feelings of belonging and of sense fair treatment. Considering the historical marginalization of boys and young men of color in schools, ESI's ability to improve schools in these ways is noteworthy.[8] Though these outcomes alone may not have improved college-readiness for the young Black and Latinx boys in this study, they were nonetheless meaningful and served as an essential first step to serving students holistically and addressing their academic success more directly. The promotion of relationships and the use of restorative justice were hallmark of ESI's influence on the culture and communities of ESI schools.

DEVELOPING RELATIONSHIPS THROUGH COMMUNITIES OF CARE

In each year of the initiative, under the auspices of ESI's youth development domain, a majority of the participating schools developed or enhanced programming to address students' socioemotional needs. Many of these schools established mentorship programs, advisories (small non-subject-specific classes that met regularly), and other student groups in a "single-gender" context. Though the form, function, and goals of these programs varied widely, the educators framed these as opportunities to create welcoming, supportive spaces for Black and Latinx males in schools and to promote a stronger sense of community and belonging among students.[9]

Adult-Student Mentorship

More than half of the ESI schools provided some type of mentorship opportunity in all four years of the initiative (table 5.1). These included more traditional forms of adult-student mentorship involving staff in the building or mentors from external organizations. In one ESI school, every teacher was assigned to coach a small group of students who

TABLE 5.1   Number of ESI schools implementing mentorship and advisory
periods

	MENTORSHIP	ADVISORY
Year 1	24	9
Year 2	29	12
Year 3	31	11
Year 4	23	12

struggled academically. These coaching sessions, conducted during the school day, were initially used to check on academic progress and provide additional support; but over time, the period provided an opportunity for teachers to learn more about their students and connect to them as individuals.

One of the teachers involved in the coaching program said, "This mentor program, I think, is fantastic. It gives us a chance to get really personal with [students] and kind of break that wall down . . . In their minds, there's a huge gap between staff and them. Once they get a chance to really interact with us, they realize we've gone through many of the same things they've gone through." The principal of this school spoke extensively about the benefits of the program, including how it created "deep relationships" among teachers and students while also adding an important layer of academic support for struggling students: "Nothing warms my heart more than when I see students across the hall and students' faces glow when they see their coach. They're excited to see their coach. They're excited to see the progress they've made in their academics." Implemented in groups, these sessions also facilitated deeper relationships among the participating students. Referencing the boys in the coaching program, one teacher said, "I think that the connections and the bond . . . have been really great for these guys. They spend a lot of time together even outside of school. They've established bonds where they do things with each other without staff members . . . They're really proud of this collective that they're part of." In this case, the mentoring program allowed school to be a place where young men who might otherwise be written off as unmotviated could find care and community along with personal, academic support from an adult in the building.

In a few ESI schools, adult-student mentoring primarily involved male staff of color. These staff reported the benefits of pairing students with staff who looked like them, who could relate to the boys and young men more easily, and who sometimes came from the very neighborhoods they served. There's no question that these mentors were particularly effective; but given the dearth of male teachers of color in NYC, this was not a feasible model for all of the ESI schools. Additionally, these male staff often served in roles (e.g., deans, coaches) that allowed them to build nurturing relationships with students beyond the classroom, but these roles may also pigeonhole males of color and limit how they are perceived by other adults in the building, as a few male deans of color reported. Moreover, it could be argued that delegating this type of mentorship to Black and Latinx male staff may signal that other teachers and staff do not share in the responsibility of mentoring boys and young men of color and may reinforce the idea that they need "heroes" and "saviors."[10] As with many programmatic efforts related to a race- and gender-focused initiative like ESI, making decisions about how to serve students raises important questions about the assumptions underlying school norms and practices.

Though these adult-student mentoring opportunities played an important role in the efforts of some schools to create protective spaces, they were less typical than others that focused on peer mentoring. Many schools preferred peer mentoring programs and student-led advisories because they were more widespread and could be offered during the school day. They also depended less on the capacity of any individual teacher and more on a structured program facilitated by a few staff and led largely by other students. These programs did not focus solely on males of color; yet educators framed these efforts as having the most impact on their boys while also being beneficial to the larger school community.

Peer Mentoring

Advisory programs, common among ESI schools, were classes of ten to twenty students who met once or twice a week. Schools that implemented advisory programs utilized a diverse set of curricula (both created in-house and externally provided) that most often allowed students to discuss a number of academic topics, such as time management and graduation requirements, as well as nonacademic topics, including personal experiences and future aspirations. A particularly effective example was a peer-led advisory program called Peer Group Connect (PGC), which has shown to have had positive effects on the graduation rates of Latinx males.[11] In PGC, juniors and seniors served as peer advisers for incoming ninth graders. Guided by an existing curriculum focused on relationship building, identity formation, and goal setting, the older students met daily and worked with a teacher to prepare weekly sessions. Together with a teacher, two of these students facilitated a class of approximately ten ninth-grade students. Staff and students spoke at length about the wide-reaching benefits of the program. One principal called PGC "a phenomenal experience . . . something that's helped transform the culture of our school" and emphasized that its most salient characteristic was its capacity to build relationships: "It's about relationship building; it's about giving kids a space to talk about things outside of the context of adult-kid relationships. And it's about building community in a sense of kind of collective responsibility for the upper-grade students to take care of the ninth-grade students. And kind of vice versa, like this sense of accountability." A teacher in the same school shared a similar reflection:

> The advisory—that was the first big change that came about through the [ESI] grant. I feel that it went from there being some resistance [among students]—"Why are we doing these workbooks, these success goals," and whatnot—to a real conversation, not just with their peers but really having a real conversation, asking questions, wanting to learn more about themselves, their peers. I feel that there was interest, and I feel that the lines of communication were

definitely open . . . It's really building a relationship. I feel that we had more of that than we had before.

These observations capture how leveraging the formalized time and space of the peer mentoring program created opportunities for students to discuss the things that mattered to them and in so doing to form relationships that the ninth-grade students in particular could rely on outside of the program.

While many of the advisory periods were provided to all students, some schools offered these programs only to males as part of ESI or placed male and female students in separate groups, believing that they might be more open among peers of the same gender (a strategy that doesn't work for students who identify as non-binary). One school offered a peer mentoring group similar to PGC, in which ninth- and tenth-grade male students were matched with and mentored by eleventh- and twelfth-grade male students. The peer mentoring classes met twice a week for one class period during the school day. Though three teachers oversaw and facilitated the program, the student mentors met a few days before the class to select a topic of discussion and develop a presentation and short activity related to the topic. The shared responsibility to plan lessons from week to week provided these mentors with an opportunity to be student leaders and to create welcoming spaces for other students in the building. The program included experiences outside of the classroom as well, including visits to HBCUs, which staff said allowed them to get to know their students in ways that may not have otherwise.

I would just say from my personal experience, having the ability to have a class with boys or young men, it's affected the way I view them. I just joined the school back in September, and I think through meeting with them twice a week I get to connect and communicate with them on a more candid level. It's not just simply academic. We actually get to talk about a lot of things that they probably wouldn't talk to a teacher about on a normal basis. I think it's affected how quickly I've been able to immerse myself and to feel comfortable with the students.

This peer mentoring program thus worked in tandem with the CRE training to address teachers' perceptions of and improve their relationships with boys and young men of color in their schools in situations that might not arise in a regular classroom.

The mentoring and advisory programs benefited both mentees and mentors. The mentees engaged with a built-in network of individuals who knew them and could provide them with needed supports as they transitioned into a new school. The mentors took the opportunity to serve as leaders and mentors in their schools. Teachers also benefited from getting to interact with their students in more informal settings. In our focus groups with students, many in the peer mentoring class also openly shared about the relationships they had built over the course of the semester and the care they had received from their teachers and peers. One ninth-grade student said, "[In my] sophomore year I had to get surgery on my back, and all three of those staff members always called me and rooted for me. I was out for a month of school. They would constantly check up on me and see how I was doing. It just goes to show that these guys cared about me because of what this program did for us." Another young man described "meeting different people that turned out to be like family, turned out to be really close relationships. I recommend this program to all of my friends . . . I feel like when you join, you meet people, and you learn about people from their experiences, and you use it as yours. You grow as a person with this program . . . I think we grew as a brotherhood. I think it goes for everybody that we grew a friendship that can last for a lifetime."

In addition to the relationships developed, teachers and students reported the positive influence these programs had on students' engagement in school overall. For one student we spoke to, the comfort he found in the mentoring program motivated him enough to show up even on days it would have been easier to stay home: "When things like that [mentoring] happen, you feel comfortable actually coming to school . . . You actually want to come to school, because you feel comfortable around the people. You'll be like, 'Oh, I'm just going to go today because I want to see my friends.' Some days I be waking up, I be like, 'I don't want to go to school today.' I be like, 'Let me just go, because I know it's gonna be fun, so let me just go today."' According to this student, and consistent with the literature, the connectedness promoted by the peer mentoring program established school as a place he felt comfortable in, a place he wanted to be in.

The program activities also seemed to improve students' engagement with their classes. Early each marking period, both mentees and mentors set specific goals (e.g., get a B average in all core classes, apply to four colleges). They and the staff then tracked progress toward these goals and publicly acknowledged the students who met or exceeded them. I witnessed this on my way to observe the mentoring group one day, when I heard roaring applause emanating from the classroom down the hall. The young men stood, cheered, and clapped as if their teachers had just announced a week off school. They were actually celebrating each student who had either earned the highest GPA that semester or whose GPA had improved the most, calling out their names one by one. After that meeting, a staff member spoke about a sense of collective responsibility for one another: "I saw with the seniors—the guys that left last year—and the juniors study groups evolve just on their own . . . [They're] holding each other accountable. 'We gotta graduate. We're going to meet, and we're going to check in with each other. We're going to meet in the library.' I just saw things happen. We gave some pushes, but for the most part things just evolved and grew on their own." Another teacher similarly recounted how "there definitely was an impact, because they were holding each other accountable, pushing each other . . . 'You gotta get your homework done, what about this, what are you doing for the test?' There was this pulling, pulling, pulling." This pushing and pulling by peers continued as past mentees began to serve as mentors to new students over the lifetime of the mentoring group.

Fostering Brotherhood

Even without formal advisory or mentoring programs, other ESI schools established all-male spaces and forums designed to build and strengthen personal relationships among their Black and Latinx young men. It should be noted that some educators and students took issue with these single-gender spaces, feeling that they excluded female students or did not afford them the same opportunities as male students, that some of the content or conversation of these forums might reinforce heteronormative views of masculinity, and that students who identified as nonbinary, non–gender conforming, or transgender may have felt excluded from these spaces. Other educators argued that these spaces allowed students to explore aspects of their shared experiences and issues that pertain to how Black and Brown boys are perceived in schools and by the outside world. And some described the benefits of programming that specifically challenged harmful norms related to men and masculinity. One teacher explained that the all-male program in his school allowed older students to communicate to ninth-grade students "that it's okay to be 'soft' sometimes. It's okay to have some type of emotion. That's another thing that I discuss . . . that as a male and especially a Latino or an African American male, it's [often seen as] not okay to be like, 'Oh, this is wonderful and this is great.' The emotions that we can express are anger or frustration . . . Even just showing fear is seen as something that's weak. [So, we emphasize that] it's okay to show these emotions and to be compassionate."

As part of ESI, most schools offered special events and gatherings targeted at boys and young men. One of these was a day-long seminar featuring Black and Latinx male speakers on different socioemotional issues, historical and current events, relationships, and postsecondary options. One of the sessions, "Know Your Rights," was promoted with the following description:

> As Black and Brown young men growing up in Brooklyn, New York, knowing your rights is crucial. With 'Stop-and-Frisk' being so prevalent in our city and our young brothers being the target of it, it is important that we equip them with knowledge that will prevent them from being victims of the judicial system and becoming part of the prison-industrial complex. This panel discussion will inform students of their rights under the law; it will also deal with racial profiling.

Students spoke positively about these forums and events, citing the opportunity to see men of color from different professional fields and the opportunity to talk with other male students about issues that might not come up in their classrooms.

A few ESI schools also utilized rituals and ceremonies to provide an opportunity for male students to affirm their commitment to academic success and to engage in a shared experience centered on fellowship and joy. One school held a formal ring and sweater ceremony, to which all ninth- and tenth-grade boys received invitations to participate, that involved students making a public pledge to another person—usually a family member, but sometimes to themselves or even a teacher—to achieve a personal goal. It also included the gifting of ceremonial rings and personalized sweaters. The ceremony mirrored the rituals of a fraternity (Latin for *brotherhood*) and reinforced a sense of brotherhood; the ring and sweaters served as ongoing reminders of the ceremony and the goals students articulated to each other, their families, and their teachers. One student said, "I could say these guys are [my brothers], because I never really had a brother, and I guess I learned brotherhood from these people who share close bonds with each other."

One particularly powerful program focused on brotherhood is the Umoja Network for Young Men, or UMOJA (*unity* in Swahili). An ESI school implemented UMOJA by establishing a male-empowerment group targeted to serve the lowest performing boys in each grade (based on attendance, lateness, disciplinary incidents, and credit accumulation). While these students are typically isolated or remove themselves from the school community, the educator who designed the program believed strongly that these young men should be "pulled in" rather than "pushed out," reasoning that through trust and relationships these young men would be more likely to attend school and reengage with school. UMOJA participants (about twenty young men) met twice a week for bonding opportunities and academic support. One study of UMOJA in this school described the program in terms of the ethos of love and culturally responsive care exhibited by the mentors and mentees, generating collective responsibility, trust and open dialogue, and broadened aspirations.[12] The Research Alliance team also observed that the prosocial bonding experiences of the program, including trips off campus, created a unique space for these young men to share their lives and to express vulnerability and emotions within a close-knit community. In addition, a school leader explained, "Our young men [have learned] that brotherhood includes [being responsible] to one another. During the school year, the young men now hold each other accountable for coming to school on time; submitting work and homework on time; and consistently demonstrating the qualities of an UMOJA leader." While academic improvement is not the primary thrust of UMOJA or the other mentoring programs, greater school engagement, especially as a result of peer support, seemed to be a consistent by-product of creating these affirming spaces.

Tragically, in 2016 one of the original UMOJA students was murdered over mistaken identity just over a year after he graduated from high school. Students had the opportunity to meet with grief counselors from the district office, but ESI director Paul Forbes recalled sitting with the UMOJA students as they mourned together and comforted each other with memories of their friend and brother and being struck by their sense of "love, community, and brotherhood . . . in the ways that they held and supported one another."

> These young men, brothers and Kings, truly embodied the quality of *umoja*—unity—even in the face of loss and tragedy. There is no program that can compensate for the death of a young man like JJ or that can single-handedly eradicate the appalling injustices young men of color face every day of their lives. But the enduring solidarity and leadership that these young men have developed in the UMOJA program fills us with hope for the future—not only for our individual Kings, but for our schools and our communities.[13]

Together, these approaches and programs reflected a commitment to transforming the experiences of young men in ways that outlived the initiative. One school leader summarized, "It is our belief that through authentic relationships with adult mentors ... peer mentorship, and brotherhood, and a fierce sense of belonging, we can transform these boys' experiences of high school and, in turn, their futures."

RESTORATIVE APPROACHES TO DISCIPLINE

An extensive body of research demonstrates that male students of color are much more likely to be suspended, expelled, or otherwise removed from class than are their white peers.[14] And given the relationship between learning time and academic achievement, frequent removals from classrooms and school can be detrimental to student outcomes.[15] Suspensions correlate with being held back, dropping out of high school, and becoming caught up in the juvenile and criminal justice systems, and the negative long-term impacts of suspensions can have economic ramifications.[16] A study out of California found that suspensions translated into a "statewide economic burden of $2.7 billion dollars in lifetime costs from just one graduating class."[17]

As an initiative, ESI challenged school staff to understand more about the disproportionate rates of suspension among Black and Latinx young men and to examine disciplinary actions taken against boys in their own schools. For most schools, this involved systematically collecting data about which students were referred for disciplinary action or suspensions and by which teachers, examining this data, and making decisions or modifying practice accordingly. One principal shared that after engaging in this form of self-assessment for two years, the school learned that 60 percent of the classroom removals came from two teachers. After working with these teachers, he reported, student removals numbered fewer than five. Another ESI school principal shared that "the effect of going to these trainings and thinking about restorative justice—[that] if you look at the list of the kids who get kicked out of class and never get asked back, those tend to be predominantly Black boys. We need to think about that as a school and what is happening."

To combat these patterns and to approach discipline in a way that does not further alienate male students from school, ten to twelve ESI schools each year reported implementing alternatives to suspension models or restorative approaches to discipline. Per the NYC DOE,

> A restorative approach can be used as both a prevention and intervention measure. Restorative processes can help schools build relationships and empower community members to take responsibility for the wellbeing of others; prevent or deal with conflict before it escalates; address underlying factors that lead youth to engage in inappropriate behavior and build resiliency; increase the pro-social skills of those who have harmed others; and provide wrong doers with the opportunity to be accountable to those they have harmed and enable them to repair the harm to the extent possible.[18]

Restorative approaches can thus refer to a wide range of practices and programs, including conflict resolution, peer mediation, youth courts, and broader efforts to improve relationships in the school building. To that end, the programmatic data on these approaches in ESI schools is less clear than that of other youth development programs because some of these efforts were a set of practices or strategies rather than particular programs that could be counted. Overall, however, these approaches sought to reduce suspensions and create environments that were more protective and less punitive than many males of color typically experience in school.

To that end, some of the specific mechanisms ESI schools employed included peer mediation and conflict prevention programs. These approaches empowered students with a specialized set of skills to help each other repair and restore relationships. One school incorporated conflict prevention into the curriculum of their advisory program while also providing formal training in conflict mediation to a dozen or so students to run a peer mediation program. The principal of the school discussed the benefits of an approach that allows students to work out their conflicts without adult intervention, saying, "The basis of [peer mediation] is allowing students to handle conflicts or things that could lead to bigger conflicts amongst themselves. They are trained by staff, but it gives them an alternative to just having adults in the school tell them what to do, which I think is pretty interesting." A handful of schools implemented youth court programs, another student-centered approach to addressing disciplinary issues. These were typically led by students in the upper grades who received training in how to examine "cases" and make constructive recommendations to their peers. The program stipulated that students with infractions could choose to participate in youth court. In one school, the youth court program became a formalized strategy for understanding the root causes of students' behavior and generating ways of restoring the individual to the community. As the youth court coordinator explained, "We really try to get into the shoes of the student who has committed the infraction. The way that I train the students is to no matter what the student did, we really try to deep dive. So when we ask questions we really want to find out what is going on with the student and how to rehabilitate them . . . We focus on the infraction, but we try to get them to understand the consequences of the infraction on themselves and the community."

Beyond the features or structures of these programs, it is important to note the adult mind-sets that informed the efforts: students can be trusted and empowered to negotiate and deescalate conflict, understanding motivations behind student infractions is important, and rehabilitation, not punishment, is the ultimate goal.

Other schools opted to train staff in restorative justice strategies and implement formal restorative justice programs not only to reduce suspensions but to understand how educators can either perpetuate or mitigate harm in this area. One teacher explained, "We've really invested in restorative justice, which is a program where it's less about punishing . . . bad behavior and more about addressing bad behavior and figuring out how to remedy [it], and thinking about how it affects the community. I think that it's much more—it's been much more responsive to our Black and Latino males because, [with] restorative justice, we asked them to become a part of the solution." Restorative approaches can include informal practices that help students feel like valued members of their school and classroom communities. For example, as one teacher explained, rather than saying, "Hurry up! You are late!" if a student is running behind, an alternative reaction might be, "We need you. The class is not complete without you." The shift in language also reflects the way the educators in these schools shifted their priorities from maintaining "order" to developing more positive relationships with their students. In this vein, rather than removing students from class, teachers held impromptu one-on-one conferences to deescalate disruptive behavior and attempt to reconnect with the students. Teachers in ESI schools were also trained to evaluate how their own curriculum and instruction may disengage students or how their misinterpretation of normal student behavior as antagonistic may contribute to a greater number of avoidable conflicts. Though we did not measure how many individual teachers meaningfully changed their practices in this way, this CRE PD indicated a broader commitment on the part of ESI schools to improving the environment rather than resorting to removing students from classrooms.

As an example of a more formalized approach to restorative justice, one school used ESI funds to hire a restorative justice coordinator. This coordinator recruited and trained approximately twenty students to join the school's Restorative Justice League. The students selected had several past infractions and held a more informed perspective when it came to working with their peers who were asked to participate in "restorative circles." The restorative circles, facilitated by trained staff but run largely by students, were guided by a line of questioning that allowed staff and students to describe the situation, state who was affected, and propose how the harm could be repaired. Restorative circles were utilized any time a student was removed from class but were also employed to address conflicts between students or to repair fractious relationships between teachers and students. Notably, the Research Alliance team found that ESI schools did not eliminate the use of suspensions, but many did opt to develop skills and tools for addressing issues of discipline in ways that leveraged student voices and centered repair over punishment.

Alternative approaches to suspension and discipline were used in fewer ESI schools than were other youth development programs, and because they were diffuse, they were more difficult to capture than other programmatic shifts. In addition, restorative justice programs can be challenging to implement well and can sometimes reinforce traditional forces of power.[19] However, according to the educators using restorative approaches, they substantially shifted the culture of their schools in ways that deescalated incidents, improved relationships between teachers and students, and created less hostile school environments for males of color. These approaches also provided students the opportunities to be leaders and take responsibility for this aspect of the school community.

COMMUNITIES OF CARE: CASE STUDIES FROM THE FIELD

Here I draw on case studies of two schools that implemented ESI in exemplary ways.[20] The first school created a student group focused on gender, sexuality, and other aspects of student identity to push back and expand on narrow definitions of masculinity. The second school developed an alternative-to-suspension program called Social Justice Panels. The examples illustrate particular programs and practices in detail to help other schools and educators imagine what similar approaches and commitments to students' mental health and well-being might look like in their own environments.

Academy for Young Writers: Gender Sexuality Alliance

The Gender Sexuality Alliance (GSA) at the Academy for Young Writers provided students a safe space to openly address together issues of social identity with the goal of promoting student leadership and creating a safe school environment, especially for marginalized students. The GSA was launched in Year 2 by two teachers who knew that students were talking to each other about identity-related issues and wanted to create a space for structured conversations about these topics with adult guidance. In contrast to the single-gender spaces commonly implemented in many ESI schools, the GSA in part reflected the resistance among some students to "single-gender" spaces. In fact, the students changed the name from the Gay Straight Alliance to the Gender Sexuality Alliance to ensure that all students felt included even if they did not identify as gay or straight. GSA provided a forum for students to engage in conversations with each other and with adults about the intersection of race, gender, and sexuality and about how students engage with these aspects of their identities in everyday life and in relation to current events. School staff and GSA students believed that creating a formal structure for GSA, encouraging students to take leadership roles, and holding regular meetings allowed students to help shape the school community in positive ways.

A typical meeting. Supported by two teachers and the principal, GSA met twice a week during lunchtime in a designated classroom. About fifteen students attended each meeting, but they could attend as infrequently or as often as they liked. Student leaders and staff arranged the seating in the room in a circle, with the goal of making all students feel equal and included. A student facilitator led a check-in, where everyone was asked to introduce themselves with their name, preferred gender pronoun, and how they were feeling on a scale of 1 to 10. Students were allowed to expand on why they felt that way but were not required to do so. If the check-in revealed that students wanted to talk about a current event or a particular topic, the student and teacher coleaders gave the group the option of continuing that discussion. Otherwise, the session focused on planning for any upcoming schoolwide GSA initiative. At least once a year, members in grades 10–12 visited all ninth-grade classes and shared their club experiences.

Establishing a safe space. Students practiced "one mic," which meant that only one person spoke at a time. At the beginning of each meeting, a student leader wrote on the board a list of students who wanted to speak. This student leader was also responsible for making sure that students who decided to speak later in the conversation were given a chance to participate without cutting off other students. During and between meetings, students checked in with each other to see how they were feeling in general and about GSA and to make sure they felt safe and secure. Students alerted a staff member if there was any concern about a peer's sense of safety. Staff noted that schools played an important role by offering a safe space for students who were not able to hold conversations with their families or home communities. They believed that exposing students to role models who share aspects of their identity could empower students to express their own. The norms of communication modeled by the group kept this space safe and inviting and spilled into other classrooms and interactions in the school.

Milestones. During the year of our research team's observation, the GSA coordinated schoolwide events as well as members-only activities designed to promote an inclusive community and to address discrimination against the LGBTQ community. Students led and/or designed many of the activities, including:

- *Pronoun Awareness Day.* Students passed out stickers to the school community that said, "Hello my name is _____" with a space for individuals to indicate their gender pronoun. Students and staff members were encouraged to wear the name tags all day.
- *Day of Silence.* Approximately two hundred students committed to remaining silent for the first four periods of the day, both inside and outside the classroom, to represent the impact of bullying and silencing LGBTQ students.
- *Bullying awareness and prevention.* Club members posted flyers around the school featuring the #StandUpAgainstBullying hashtag. Students also created signed pledges, such as "I pledge to not be afraid to be myself/stand out" or "I pledge to be considerate of other people's feelings." Pledges appeared around the school on bulletin boards.
- *"Safe Space" stickers.* Small square stickers with the LGBTQ rainbow flag and the words "Safe Space" were placed in every room in

the building to remind students to reject discriminatory language against other members of the school community.

- *LGBT Pride Month.* Throughout June, GSA members (students and staff) took field trips to locations across NYC with relevance to LGBTQ history and pride. Past trips included a trip to the Stonewall Inn (considered to be the birthplace of the gay rights movement), a tour of Manhattan's West Village that traced the development of the gay rights movement in Manhattan, and a visit to the Hetrick-Martin Institute, a direct service and advocacy organization for LGBTQ rights.

In their own words. Comments from students capture the importance of this space:

- "I think having a GSA is as important as having any kind of after-school activity, because it's a place where we can go and feel accepted and important. We can confide in each other about our difficulties and problems and help each other as a family, and that brings us closer together."
- "The GSA for me is a place where not just LGBT students can come and are able to express themselves. All are welcomed and never judged. We work on trying to help educate our school and creating a safe environment for all."
- "GSA to me means a place I can feel safe. We've always been an open community and accepting of students and/or staff regardless of gender identity, sexuality, religion, etc."
- "I'm the only trans male here [in the school], and I go to GSA to connect to others who are for the LGBTQ community and who are part of the community, so I feel like I'm not alone in this."

Brooklyn Preparatory High School: Social Justice Panels

Brooklyn Preparatory High School's Social Justice Panels provided alternatives to suspension by having students play a role in deciding disciplinary outcomes for their peers. Students who were believed to have committed an infraction, and who were willing, came before the Social Justice Panel to discuss their behavior and its impact on the school community. The student-led panel held the power to decide the consequences that their peers would face, with a focus on preventing repeat infractions. Students who sat on the Social Justice Panel class received elective credit, but the facilitators tried to ensure that the class was comprised of students who expressed interest in the process. In fact, some of the students who enrolled in the Social Justice Panel class did so because of prior involvement in incidents reviewed by the Panel. As one student said, "It's like you get a good feeling when you know that you've helped a person choose a different path in this way—this can affect their life not only in school but outside of school." The Panel encouraged students to learn from the experiences of their peers; for high school students in particular, peers can be a powerful force for improving the broader school environment. Staff also reported that the Panel empowered students by giving them ownership over a process typically managed by adults.

Student training. Students spent the first few weeks of each semester preparing for their role. This included facilitator-led team-building activities to develop rapport among the panelists. Students then received formal training for several weeks, during which they discussed sample cases on topics like chronic absences or skipping class, disrupting class-room instruction, and ongoing conflicts with teachers and other students. The case studies provided panelists with the opportunity to work as a group and think through decisions they would likely face. They also received conflict resolution trainings where facilitators provided tools for addressing disagreements among the panelists. General preparation included discussion of sample questions to ask during cases and a fact sheet detailing the program's underlying principles, how cases would be referred to the panel, etc.

A typical session. Approximately fifteen to twenty students served as panelists in two different Social Justice Panel classes, which met during school for a full class period four days a week and were facilitated by two guidance counselors (one per class). Throughout the term, when students were accused of committing an in-school infraction, they were referred to a Panel by a teacher or administrator (some infractions, such as fighting, were not eligible for a referral). Many students opted to have their case heard by a Panel rather than receive discipline from an administrator. On average, each Panel reviewed six to eight cases per term.

At the beginning of each session, the staff facilitator recorded attendance and greeted panelists as they entered. Students and the staff facilitator discussed upcoming cases by reading a document with the name of the student involved, the name of the person who brought the case forward, and the date and time of the incident. The referred student then entered the room and sat in the circle with the panelists. Panelists asked the student the types of questions they learned about in their training (e.g., whether they agree with the charge, what they would have done differently if they could change the situation, what they learned from the behavior they were being asked to correct). Without a formal protocol, student panelists held the authority to decide which questions to ask. Certain panelists were designated to take notes.

After hearing from all individuals involved in the case, panelists deliberated in consultation with the guidance counselor. Next, they decided how the accused student would be "restored" to good standing in the school community. Typical consequences included requiring that the student ask each teacher to sign an attendance sheet (to confirm they went to class) or develop a plan to document positive behavior. When the conflict involved students, the Panel provided an opportunity for students to address their disagreements in a nonthreatening space. Through these conversations, the Panel sought to restore broken trust and communication among members of the school community. Finally, all participating students signed the Social Justice Logbook, a record of all cases brought before the Panel. Panelists completed an in-school "sanction" sheet that summarized the type of infraction and recorded whether the student appearing before the panel was receptive to both the discussion and the suggested sanction (indicated by the student's signature). Panelists also completed a survey to self-evaluate their individual contribution to each case.

MAJOR FINDINGS

There is a large body of literature—in the fields of psychology, child development, and education—that demonstrates the importance of relationships to the well-being and long-term success of young people. While schools can provide these nurturing relationships for students through friendships with peers, the support of teachers, and mentorships with other adults, for boys and young men of color schools are often places of alienation, neglect, or harm. ESI attempted to disrupt this pattern by creating protective spaces for male students to be seen, heard, and cared for. The creation of these spaces across ESI schools communicated their value to their school communities and provided young men with opportunities to be leaders and contribute to the school environment in meaningful ways, while offering targeted socioemotional and academic support from teachers who cared about more than their test scores.

As a result of these efforts, the most prominent change reported each year of the initiative was improvement in relationships between students and staff and among students. Over and over, we heard how mentorship, advisories, and male groups fostered a sense of community, brotherhood, and family. Restorative approaches to discipline, though not as widely implemented, reinforced these dimensions by heightening teachers' sensitivity to their own biases, the challenges faced by their students, and the tools with which to practice repair over punishment. Together, these efforts made a positive impact on boys and young men of color. Relative to their counterparts in similar schools, male students in ESI schools reported a greater sense of belonging and of fair treatment and were more likely to report engaging in positive conversations with adults. On the ground, we heard from students about the care they received from teachers and mentors and about the love they experienced in places and groups designed for them and their peers. We observed how young people and teachers served as collaborators in creating positive experiences for Black and Brown boys in their classrooms and schools.

The efforts to create exclusive spaces for boys raised fair questions about the message sent to young female students of color, gender nonconforming students, or students who may have found the heteronormative dynamics of these groups challenging. To address these concerns, some schools created more intimate spaces, such as advisories, but offered them to all students, reasoning that young men of color would also reap the benefits. In other cases, the creation of these spaces led staff and students to think in new ways about how to serve their most marginalized students. The impact of the GSA in particular was such that a young person who transitioned into their male identity became confident enough to assume male pronouns and was embraced by male students involved in ESI. This example also demonstrates how schools should be mindful and attend to the multiple identities of students in terms of race, ethnicity, sexuality, and gender expression. By placing race and gender at the forefront, an initiative like ESI can generate conversations that change students' experiences in ways that might not otherwise be possible.

RECOMMENDATIONS FOR PRACTICE

1. *Create spaces centered on love, care, and joy.* Too often schools present Black and Brown young men with harmful messages (spoken and unspoken) about who they are as students and as individuals. Too few classrooms affirm their multiple identities or forms of self-expression. ESI schools created a number of different formalized spaces and structures for boys and young men of color grounded in love and communities of care. Protective spaces like these, established over time with attention to building trust and modeling vulnerability, can help schools develop meaningful relationships among teachers and students while generating a sense of brotherhood and of family among students. These programs enabled

students to talk about difficult issues but were, at the same time, joyful gatherings of young people. To understand more about students' lives, their families, and communities, educators might focus too much on the challenges that they face instead of the joys they create and experience. Broadly speaking, a school's focus on relationships and protective spaces as well as the mechanisms to sustain both over time can ensure that students have a solid network of academic and socioemotional support within their school buildings.

2. *Examine root causes and levels of disproportionality.* To address the overuse and/or racially disproportionate use of suspensions and other disciplinary measures in schools, staff should first investigate these data to identify patterns that could be useful when creating solutions. Are specific teachers more likely to remove students from class? Does the period after lunch pose special challenges for teachers and students? Are the students repeatedly called to the dean's or disciplinary office because they struggle with other issues that the school can address? Alternative-to-suspension approaches should include attention to classrooms, including the presence of engaging curriculum and instruction, expanded notions of what productive or disruptive environments look like, and a set of tools to deescalate conflict and to restore relationships. More formal approaches, including restorative justice programs, cannot address disproportionality without taking into account the role of teachers and other staff members in mitigating or exacerbating issues of discipline.

3. *Let students lead.* Many of the most successful and enduring practices around improving school culture across ESI schools involved student-led efforts to shape their own school environments. When students hold agency and voice—for example, in the ESI schools' peer mentoring, peer mediation, youth court, the GSA, and Social Justice Panels—they can utilize their insights and perspectives to address issues better than staff might do on their own. In addition, positioning students as leaders also generates multiple opportunities to develop the types of skills and tools that will allow them to engage with other systems in their schools and in society at large.

CHAPTER 6

Promoting Academic Rigor and a College-Going Culture

Does everyone in the school believe that you are going to go to college or a positive career path? All the young people and all the adults have to believe that and they have to promote that.

—*Paul Forbes, ESI director*

IN ADDITION TO ACADEMICS and youth development, ESI's initial design required that participating schools also invest resources and effort in the college-going goals of the initiative.[1] It is important to consider ESI's emphasis on college in the context of district performance indicators at the time. The funders and designers of the initiative often stated that "while the nation was focused on graduation rates, the city was focused on college."[2] This focus on college was deemed especially critical for young men of color.[3] Despite rising high school graduation rates for Black and Latinx males in New York City at the time, data from the district showed that of those who were not proficient in the state's eighth-grade ELA exam (Level 1 or 2), only 4 percent graduated college-ready four years later. Even among Black and Latinx males who met the highest level of proficiency on the same exam (Level 4), only about 10 percent were college-ready by the time they graduated high school.

What does it mean to be college-ready? In New York State, "college-readiness" is a somewhat blunt measure. It is the equivalent of scoring an 80 percent on the Regents exam in English language arts and a 75 percent on the math exam. But this "definition," however limited, is meaningful. When students do not meet these thresholds, the city's college system requires them to take remedial courses prior to taking credit-bearing classes. In addition to being an added financial burden for students who struggle to pay for college, less than a quarter of students who enroll in remedial college coursework graduate within eight years of enrollment.[4] With roughly 40 percent of NYC high school graduates (and more than half of NYC students who enroll in college) entering the CUNY system, its benchmarks have profound implications for the city's high school students.[5] Even without the CUNY requirement, it stands to reason that a diploma alone may not be sufficient if it means students are leaving high school without the requisite skills to succeed in college when they get there.

These patterns of performance and their relationship to college access were used to motivate an urgent call by the district to "raise the bar" and focus not just on graduating from high school but on graduating college-ready. In an early promotional video for ESI, Shawn Dove from the Open Society Foundation, one of ESI's major funders, stated, "Before we were saying, 'Let's graduate them.' Now we're saying, 'Let's graduate them at a certain level of performance at a certain standard to be able to move on.'"[6] To that end, the designers of ESI challenged participating schools to implement a number of evidence-based strategies for designing and redesigning academic practices, including requiring four years of math and science (especially completing Algebra II), offering rigorous coursework in other subjects, devising summer bridge programs to support the transition to high school and college, supporting digital literacy, and teaching academic behaviors (e.g., study skills and time management). The initiative also called on schools to provide more resources related to postsecondary planning, college exposure, and college enrollment through the work of teachers, college counselors, and partnerships with higher education institutions.

This chapter highlights some of what it takes to academically support students on the pathway to college, especially those who are underrepresented in higher education and those who may have college aspirations but lack the information to apply and enroll. It specifically describes efforts that are responsive to students' academic needs and gaps upon entering high school, strategies for increasing academic rigor, and resources targeted at introducing students to college and promoting a college-going identity. Detailed portraits of two schools illustrate efforts to reimagine academic support and college access for their Black and Latinx male students.

WHERE ESI FELL SHORT

While a number of promising practices emerged from ESI's academic domain, the efforts ultimately fell short of the intended goal. Schools were responsive to the call of the ESI Design Challenge and adopted academic supports and resources, especially related to preparation for college. Yet, these efforts were not applied across the target population, nor were they as widespread or sustained (with a few exceptions) over the course of the four years as those that focused on youth development. In fact, of the three domains, academic programming came up the least in our interviews and focus groups with educators in ESI schools. ESI schools were also more likely to tweak academic services and supports rather than create new structures or programs. And while schools participated in ample training around culturally relevant education over the lifetime of the initiative, far fewer teachers participated in training around specific subjects. Finally, aside from partnerships with higher education institutions and other college-focused organizations, more of the partnering organizations provided youth development services as opposed to academic services.

While educators believed that academic outcomes would improve as a result of students' deeper engagement with the school, the staff, and their peers, the relative dearth of academic programming should have tempered the evaluation team's expectations for improved academic outcomes, such as GPA and credit accumulation. Attention to students' lived experiences and their socioemotional outcomes was necessary but insufficient on its own to effect the type of change the ESI designers intended.

To be fair, ESI schools invested substantial effort and resources in college-related supports, and certain student outcomes reflect this, including the degree to which students engaged in conversations with adults about postsecondary plans and the number of colleges applications among Black and Latinx male students. However, intermediary outcomes on the path to college—earning credits, maintaining a strong GPA, and graduating high school—were no more prevalent at ESI schools than they were at comparison schools. Addressing college-readiness for students who have likely been underserved for years prior to high school requires making up for previous years while simultaneously preparing them for the future.

FILLING THE GAPS

Under the academic domain, ESI challenged schools to increase the rigor of their academic offerings, provide access to higher-level coursework and courses, modify their curriculum and instruction to be more culturally responsive, and give students direct academic support. In this last category, the most common academic strategies schools employed were tutoring and summer bridge programs, both of which helped fill important gaps in students' learning or experiences.

While tutoring may seem far less innovative than some of the other programs instituted by ESI schools, it played an important role for students who participated in these programs. Many educators reported that even while some of their young men of color could perform sophisticated tasks like literary analysis or the application of complex mathematical concepts, gaps in more basic skills around writing and computation limited the extent to which they could engage in and demonstrate success in more advanced coursework. It was critical to address these needs by providing targeted support outside of what might be provided in a specific course.

Tutoring in ESI schools ranged from small-group gatherings before or after school to targeted one-on-one sessions during the school day. In the initiative's first two years, it also included the use of external organizations to support students in core subjects or in developing metacognitive skills that could be applied across courses. These supports were also made available through added staff or coaches who could provide supplementary instruction in classrooms or afterschool sessions. Tutoring is a common support across all NYC schools, but it is often offered outside of regular school hours, thereby decreasing the number of students who take advantage of these services. As a result, the ESI team encouraged schools to offer tutoring during the school day. Doing so, however, required a restructuring of students' programming. And though there was evidence that some schools provided tutoring, the exposure within schools was limited and not delivered in a sustained way that filled in critical gaps. Nor was it necessarily focused on Black and Latinx males. So in effect, the tutoring that occurred in ESI schools may have matched what was offered in most non-ESI schools.

Another approach commonly used across ESI schools was the introduction of summer bridge programs designed to help incoming ninth graders make a more successful transition to high school by combining an academic component (often a math course to prepare them for Algebra I) with youth development elements (e.g., leadership training to increase student confidence and agency, sports programs to build relationships and increase belonging). The Central Team provided training around creating summer bridge programs and offered a mini-grant program for schools implementing them. As a result, three quarters of ESI schools offered a summer bridge program for at least one summer during the life of the initiative.

Both educators and students reported that summer programs provided meaningful support for those who attended. Teachers described that the attendees acclimated themselves to the particular school's environment on day one of ninth grade, that they already formed positive relationships with the teacher facilitators, and that the academic portions of the program helped teachers make important decisions about ways to support struggling students from the beginning of the school year. Students felt that the bridge programs gave them an advantage during the school year, though they still expressed nervousness about attending a new school and starting high school. Teachers admitted that attendance in these programs was low, that it is difficult to attract students to school in the summer. Without the additional funding that was provided in the first two years, many schools struggled in the last two years to justify a practice that would only reach a handful of students.

While tutoring and summer bridge programs can be important means of addressing students' academic needs, their effectiveness hinges on the school's ability to design them in a way that ensures widespread and sustained participation. In the case of ESI, staff were to focus on the target population. Though these supports may have been beneficial for all students, it was less clear how schools were aiming these supports to benefit Black and Latinx males

INCREASING ACADEMIC RIGOR

Those who serve struggling students and students who may not have been exposed to challenging curriculum in prior years hold the dual responsibility of filling in gaps in students' learning through additional services and resources while providing access to the types of learning experiences that will prepare them to succeed in college. This includes attending to both a broad base of content knowledge as well as college-readiness skills, such as writing research papers, making public presentations, and working collaboratively in groups. However, Black and Latinx boys and young men are often subject to lower expectations, which may water down curricula, thereby reducing learning opportunities to do college-level work. Additionally, these students tended to be in schools that did not offer higher-level courses or that may have limited these opportunities to a small number of students. This is parallel to the documented lack of access to more advanced math and science classes among Black and Latinx students nationwide.[7]

The ESI schools that succeeded in addressing these issues designed creative solutions around course programming and schedules, trained teachers in the delivery of advanced coursework to students who struggled academically, and raised expectations across the curricula. For example, noting that not all students took Algebra II, despite its connection to college success, a few schools restructured students' programming (the classes they were expected to take within a given year) to ensure that they could complete at least four years of math and science.[8] One principal said, "The school is moving in the direction of making sure all of our kids have four years of math and science, making sure that all of our students have a wide variety of courses by the time that they leave. ESI affirmed what we were doing and really pushed us further to make that happen." Another school made substantial changes to the school day to offer additional opportunities for advanced coursework. One staff member described how "freshmen now have to stay until 4:36. They receive additional supports in terms of two math [courses]. They take two math courses during the day, two English courses during the day. Then after school, Tuesdays, Wednesdays, and Thursdays, they have an extended day where they will be in a STEM class where they do the robotics, heavy emphasis on math and science." This robotics class was also intended to engage students who might not have been otherwise interested in STEM. Offering multiple math and English courses also provided an opportunity to address concrete learning gaps in both subject areas while exposing students to higher-level coursework.

A more commonly employed strategy to increase academic rigor among ESI schools was the addition of Advanced Placement (AP) courses, with measures to ensure that existing or new AP classes were being offered to and taken by male students. Many schools that offered one or two AP courses to a small group of self-selecting students prior to ESI expanded the number of offerings as well as the number of students who could enroll in them. (This shift overlapped with the district's launch of the AP for All initiative in 2015.) AP courses enable students to earn college credits, but in ESI schools AP courses were framed as an integral part of a larger effort to ensure that students were prepared to enroll in and be successful in college. As one principal said, the goal "is that Black and Latino boys not just get into college, but to come out through the door with a degree."

In addition to adding specific classes or courses to the academic program, about a quarter of ESI schools incorporated what they deemed to be college-ready curriculum and assignments into existing courses by focusing on the skills that students need for college. These typically included conducting research and writing research reports, presenting completed work to peers and other members of the school community, and engaging in long-term projects, especially in collaboration with other students. A related effort increased academic rigor within exist-ing courses by raising critical benchmarks in grades 9–12. Some schools prioritized getting all ninth graders through Algebra I and passing the Regents exam in Algebra. Other schools raised cut-off scores to deter-mine if students should be passed on to the next course in a sequence. One principal explained, "We're not going to accept a 65 as a passing or whatever in moving students on to geometry. We made a concerted effort in saying, 'No, you have to repeat the exam. You have to continue the course. Yes, you took algebra in middle school. Yes, you got a passing grade, but if it wasn't a college and career benchmark, then you're going to repeat the course until you can get that grade and 80 or better.' In the past, we would not have done this." The school leader did not intend for this strategy to be punitive but, rather, to provide struggling students a second (and sometimes third) opportunity to take a course they would likely need to thrive in college later on.

Even while some schools did not determine consequences related to GPAs and other benchmarks, there was a greater sense that teachers should be transparent with students about the "numbers" that would be impor-tant for college entrance, including GPA, AP scores, and SAT/ACT scores. This transparency empowered students with critical information about the benchmarks associated with college enrollment. As one staff member said:

> It was acceptable initially for a student, and they would argue with you. "I passed the Regents; I got a 65." Now with the emphasis in ESI on that college- and career-readiness . . . they are more attuned to the fact of, "I know I'm going to graduate, but now I want to graduate and be prepared and to be successful in college, so that 65 or 55—it's not acceptable anymore." They'll tell you, "I got a 70, I failed. I have to retake it." It's kind of amusing to outsiders to hear that, because they're saying, "70 isn't failing!" But our kids know that if you don't get a certain score, you're not as likely to be college- and career-ready. That was definitely a cultural shift.

Overall, educators reported a greater awareness among students about the importance of course grades, diploma type, and standardized tests scores in determining access to certain postsecondary options.

The most strategic schools used a combination of approaches to fundamentally transform teaching and learning. But, again, the evaluation team found relatively few of these examples across the forty ESI schools, especially in ways that were sustained over the four years—a missed opportunity to target the skills, outcomes, and experiences that served as important prerequisites to college-readiness, enrollment, and success. As one of the architects of ESI noted during the last year of the initiative,

> there was a sort of notion that if you just stay in school, or if you're in school more, it will lead to the level of rigor required to be successful after higher school . . . If you could just maximize the dosage of school—meaning the dosage of school as it is currently set up—then college- and career-readiness will materialize. And I actually don't believe that's true at all. I believe there has to be a fundamentally different thing that has to happen inside of school once kids are there . . . If you don't focus on the academic piece of that learning environment, then you can't get to rigor . . . all these parts have to work simultaneously.

CULTIVATING A COLLEGE-GOING CULTURE AND IDENTITY

While labeled "school culture," ESI's third domain referred more specifically to a set of priorities that infused college- and career-readiness throughout all aspects of the school environment and student experience. In response, a majority of schools substantially expanded college supports, though many fewer provided career supports. Perhaps more critical to these efforts, however, were two major shifts related to how ESI educators regarded and implemented college preparation for young men of color. First, educators reported making the decision to raise the bar from graduating high school to attending college. As a result of ESI, school missions focused on college, with principals and teachers shifting their expectations, coursework, and conversations to be about what students needed to enroll in and succeed in college. Second, while most ESI schools were providing a number of college supports and services prior to the initiative, these were largely dedicated to serve eleventh and twelfth graders. The shift under ESI meant they offered a robust set of college supports to incoming ninth graders, not just eleventh and twelfth graders. These included college trips, workshops related to the college application process, and college-level classes in partnership with higher education institutions.

From Preventing Drop Out to Increasing College-Readiness

ESI was implemented in schools with relatively high graduation rates among their Black and Latinx male students (compared to those of the district) with the intention of pushing schools to raise the bar of achievement from high school graduation to college-readiness. Notably, this shift occurred citywide as college- and career-readiness became a metric on each school's "Quality Report." ESI schools enjoyed the benefit of additional resources, much of which they invested in preparing students for college. Like the emphasis on CRE, the prioritization of college was embedded in messaging to ESI educators, ESI materials, and professional development opportunities. Even after the first few months of the initiative, principals, design team members, and teachers described a notable schoolwide culture shift that elevated college-going.

Beyond verbalizing college-readiness as a priority, several schools actually changed their school's mission to explicitly state it as a focus. Staff in these schools said that while college had always been an implicit goal, ESI had pushed them to frame college-readiness and enrollment, rather than high school graduation, as the objective for staff and students to meet. This required a shifting of responsibility. While schools' guidance counselors always played an outsized role in supporting students with college aspirations, ESI created an expectation that everyone on staff shared this responsibility and that college was not just for students who may have shown the most promise but also for those who had not pictured themselves there. As part of this culture shift, there was a shared realization that the assumptions teachers held about their students' college knowledge were limited. One teacher said, "As a faculty, we're more on the same page. We definitely understand the importance of promoting a college-going culture, which was not the case three years ago. As much as we wanted kids to go to college, we didn't understand how little they knew about college. Now I think as a faculty we're very clear. Our kids need more college talk to get them ready to go."

The collective responsibility around establishing college as a goal translated into frequent and regular communication ("college talk") about the mission through both formal events (e.g., college days) and informal conversations about college. A principal explained, "It's always a conversation. '*When* you go to college. *When* you go to college.' Really drilling in for students that the goal is college." An essential part of this college talk made it transparent to students which classes, test scores, and forms they needed to apply to and enroll in college. These efforts in part responded to previous years when students sometimes found out too late in the process that they were missing credits and/or other requirements. Through ongoing communication from multiple staff across multiple classes, ESI schools demystified the college enrollment process and positioned students to take active roles in tracking their own progress. One student said, "Nearly all of our classes at some point, whether it be freshman, sophomore, junior, or senior year, whether it be science, math, or English—all of our teachers understand that we are on the journey to go to college . . . [and] the goal is somewhere out of high school. They all share that knowledge with us so that we can go further to the best of our ability."

The Four-Year Runway

The second shift changed the orientation toward the college prep timeline. College supports for eleventh and twelfth graders, including access to a guidance counselor, were common in ESI schools prior to the initiative and present in most high schools in the city. However, explicitly shifting the target from high school graduation to college-readiness necessitated that schools invest in college-related resources for students much earlier in their high school careers. This approach was critical for students who may not have had the benefit of college funds, college-educated parents, or personal connections to a higher education institution.

For many ninth graders, college seems like a distant goal. But waiting until they are halfway through high school makes for too short a runway for students aspiring to attend a four-year college after graduation. Just as a plane needs a sufficiently long runway to generate enough speed to take off, a student needs a sufficient amount of time to accumulate the academic credits and skills needed to graduate and prepare for college. In most states, students need to successfully complete a required number of courses, and in some cases pass exit exams, to earn a high school diploma. Some might even argue that four years is too short, as some students and families begin planning for college long before high school.

ESI educators felt strongly about the importance and potential impact of expanding college supports to earlier grades. As a reflection of their conscious decisions to avoid waiting until it might be too late, more than half of the ESI schools described an expansion of college supports to ninth graders. One principal said:

> I think getting everybody to realize that if we start planting those seeds early, that then it becomes part of the whole school culture.

Rather than just suddenly eleventh and twelfth [grades], now you start working on it. So many of us have worked with eleventh graders who, in the second semester, are like, "Oh, I want to go to this school," and they think that they're going to pull their GPA up by twelfth grade, and it's heartbreaking to have those conversations. I think when we all, as a staff, talk about everything like that, it helps everybody realize that we'd have to start at an earlier grade.

Staff in about a quarter of the ESI schools reported that elevating the topic of college earlier resulted in greater awareness and curiosity among ninth graders. One design team member said, "This group, I have to say, is the most aware of college. We started talking about it from, like, day one." Another teacher said that previously, when a ninth-grade student came in for a one-one-one conference, "I wasn't thinking . . . 'What do you want to be?' I wasn't necessarily doing that goal planning with them, the goal setting. Now, we're more conscious of it. I meet with a ninth grader . . . [and] in addition to going over credit accumulation, I'll start that dialogue and get that child thinking, 'What do you want to be?' Then it forces them to do some goal setting and see what's happening now, how that's going to relate to what they want to do and where they want to go."

These comments show an evolution from thinking about short-term goals based on performance in one grade level to assisting students in setting and planning for long-term goals after high school. Teachers also reported a greater awareness among incoming ninth graders about the importance of maintaining strong academic performance throughout high school. One teacher said, "Before kids would say, 'Oh, freshman year doesn't matter.' Now other people are telling them, 'You need to really work on your GPA from freshman year. You don't blow it off and wait until eleventh grade.'"

Removing Barriers

One way to support students' aspirations to enroll in college is to remove barriers along the path to higher education, including a lack of knowledge about the requirements and process for getting there. Importantly, this is not about addressing motivation. Staff said that many of their Black and Latinx male students were vocal about their desire to go to college but were unaware of the specific steps they needed to take to apply and enroll. Most schools addressed these gaps internally through mandatory classes or workshops about college requirements and the application process, while others partnered with organizations like College Now and College Access: Research and Action (CARA). Increasing students' knowledge of the steps involved in applying for college included focusing on a number of different college-related topics, including preparing for the PSAT/SAT/ACT, filling out the FAFSA, applying for CUNY, obtaining recommendation letters, selecting colleges based on GPA and SAT/ACT scores, and applying for scholarships. Demystifying the college application process and providing the one-on-one guidance and support to meet these requirements was helpful for all students but especially so for those who were unfamiliar with what it entails. One teacher said, "We get kids comfortable and used to the fact that applying for college is a process and that teachers are there to help implement it." Breaking that process into specific, smaller steps also helped make the college application less intimidating for students: "They need a lot of hand-holding . . . It's not familiar to them. They're often the first in their families to go to college, and it's a Byzantine process. For the best of students with the best of support, it's overwhelming. [For] a lot of them, it's too hard. They just kind of crumple in denial. We try to keep them away from denial and say, 'Let's just get it done.'"

Another element of the strategy of raising academic benchmarks included creating systems for teachers and students to assess progress toward college. For example, one school created a visual display of college-related benchmarks by grade level, which helped staff and students become deeply familiar with college requirements and expectations. The school's ESI liaison said, "We identified a theme for each grade, so then it's really clear as to what they should be doing, and no one is in the dark. I think that was a big piece, because previously kids knew it was just college. It was a big deal. 'How do I fund this?' 'How do I go about applying?' They were kind of lost, but I think that we've created this culture where the students feel comfortable that they have some guidance in that area." Another school created a database that tracked college-readiness levels of individual students based on course credit and exam scores, which provided them with a user-friendly tool to track their own progress.

Creating a College-Going Identity Through Targeted Exposure

Another perceived barrier for some students is a limited sense of belonging in a higher education institution. Even students who are confident about wanting to attend college may feel apprehension about their abilities to fit in. ESI schools addressed this by offering an array of college trips, particularly to schools outside of New York City, and even outside the state, including to HBCUs (opportunities that were virtually impossible prior to ESI funding). ESI staff found that visiting a college or attending a college class on a real campus made it easier for students to picture themselves there. Staff reported that the visits not only helped students envision themselves on these campuses but also motivated some to stay on track for college. One principal reported how a college visit "makes it very real. Most of our kids have never had that kind of exposure. Being able to offer that then changes the conversation about college. They can picture it better. They have an idea of what they're working for. It's not this nebulous concept that you're supposed to go to college . . . It has already started to change things, but I think it's going to continue to change things."

The number of college supports offered by the ESI schools as well as the college trips resulted in multiple opportunities to develop knowledge about college, thus helping make college a viable choice. One design team member noted that

> when we're teaching "College and Career," it's like, "I need you to look at two public and two private universities, and I want you to tell me how you're going to get there, and what are the steps

that you need." Then, when they go to iMentor, they talk to them about the same thing—"Let's talk about college."[9] [Students] are like, "Whoa, we're talking about college so much" that eventually it's already something that they expect to do. It's not something that is out there that I might not be able to do. It is something that's very reachable.

Staff reported that college trips, especially those to HBCUs (e.g., Howard University, Morgan State), were "eye openers" for students, especially for those who had not spent much time outside of the city (or, for some, their own borough). The goal of these trips was not necessarily to push students toward enrolling in HBCUs (though that might have been an added benefit); it was to enable students to see themselves as part of a larger community of Black college students. One principal recalled a student saying after a trip to a college outside of NYC, "Wow, I never knew we could go there." Another principal explained:

> I think if you don't grow up in an environment where that is a reality, you don't know what to imagine . . . You don't know what it looks like. Being able to go on college tours, being able to speak with people that look like them, that still have swag, that are still cool, but are successful out there making money and doing something productive, I think gives them an idea of, "Oh, okay so that's what it looks like." . . . They know that "Oh, okay, so that's what life after high school, if I can make it out of high school, is going to look like."

Educators also found it useful for their students to discuss college with near-peers, namely alumni from their high schools who were attending or had recently graduated from HBCUs and other colleges. These near-peers served as tour guides on college visits and answered candidly students' questions about campus life, college-level coursework, and balancing college classes with other responsibilities. One teacher offered, "I think the biggest success were the college tours . . . A lot of students, especially when they go as freshmen and sophomores, come back to school ready to start working because they get to see the larger picture. They see themselves able to reach other places and want to go to other places."

Students also said that college trips offered through ESI were particularly effective in terms of making college seem like a reality. One twelfth-grade student reflected on how college trips he took in the ninth and tenth grades motivated his college pursuits, describing those visits as "a visual aid, how college life would be from the early-on stage . . . My first college trip was . . . to Upstate New York, when we visited SUNY Cortland . . . and Mercy College. We visited a bunch of different schools, and it was really interesting just to see lecture halls and to see dorms and all of that . . . That's where it made me start thinking about where I wanted to go."

Collectively, these efforts helped students envision themselves in college by providing them with concrete experiences on college campuses. Moreover, as some educators described, college preparation involved efforts to address nonacademic barriers students might face on their path toward or experience in college. One school leader explained that his students wouldn't be college-ready if they didn't "have the social/emotional aspect of that . . . That's the piece that we're trying to focus on in [our college program]—those implicit, less-tangible aspects of college prep and college success." One ESI design team member explained that college "takes an understanding of the challenges that are out there, not just the academics but the social challenges. That you're going to be away from home, that you are going to have to work on your own . . . You have to be able to manage your own time; you have to prioritize your own time. That is taught in schools but not very explicitly." Some of these less-tangible aspects might include anxieties about fitting into an environment that is unfamiliar or potentially alienating. For many of the students we spoke to, the idea of being away from home and feeling isolated from family and friends also introduced a degree of uncertainty and fear around college-going. Educators who were aware of these sometimes-unspoken barriers acknowledged that providing college supports was not merely about ensuring students meet academic requirement but also about addressing the challenges students might face even when they meet their academic goals.

COLLEGE *AND* CAREERS?

ESI was designed to increase college- and career-readiness, but career-related supports and programming were much less prominent across ESI schools. The most commonly reported career support reported in ESI schools was the coordination of internship opportunities, career days, and presentations by representatives of certain industries. Less frequently reported career supports included technical education, visits to workplaces/job shadowing, and the presence of a career office.

In fewer than five ESI schools, teachers and students reported that internships were especially powerful because they provided real-life experiences (that could be listed on their resumes) and opportunities to practice time management and become familiar with the norms of a workplace. These schools established paid and unpaid internships for their students across a broad swath of organizations and agencies, including city offices managing parks and public gardens, residences for the elderly, museums, and law offices. Internships took place both during the academic year and over the summer; summer internships typically required a commitment of thirty to thirty-five hours a week, while school-year internships usually took place on weekends.

Aside from the handful of schools offering robust internship programs, fewer than ten schools each year provided any kind of career programming. At some level, this reflects a need to manage competing priorities and limited resources. However, it also reveals a belief among ESI educators that the pull to work might divert attention from the college pathway or that emphasizing careers over college might be feeding into stereotypes about which students are fit for college. At the same time, a minority of voices raised questions about the appropriateness of college for all students. Their concerns stemmed in part from observing that many incoming ninth graders were several years behind grade level, struggling to read or to perform basic math operations—barriers they believed no amount of college prep could remediate in four years. According to these educators, the "college for all" expectation was unfair or unreasonable and set up students for failure without exposing or preparing them for pathways other than college. One teacher explained: "You know, there are some males who are on third- and fourth-grade reading levels who may not go to a four-year college. They may not even go to a two-year college. That doesn't mean they're not going to be successful. They might get a trade in culinary arts and become a sous chef and still be able to provide for a family and to contribute to society. It's just in terms of how we look at what success really means." According to these staff members, expanding the definition of success after high school to include full-time employment, trade schools, and other alternatives to four-year colleges would help schools meet the needs of students while providing multiple options for students to consider for their futures after high school.

However, concern that a focus on careers would move students away from college or that an exclusive focus on college limits student options misses an important and established connection between college and careers as well as other long-term outcomes that matter. The growing emphasis on college- and career-readiness has focused on preparing students for college *versus* supporting students toward a successful transition to work and careers.[10] Yet, training in the skills and capacities that come along with workplace experiences—in addition to industry-specific training or experiences—can affect opprotunities for success in both college and long-term careers. A longitudinal study of career academies, for example, showed positive impacts on the labor market prospects, sustained earnings, and overall stability in young adulthood for young men, especially for those at risk of dropping out of high school.[11] Thus, the dearth of career-focused programs marks another missed opportunity to support young men of color in ways that may have affected meaningful change in their postsecondary plans and outcomes.

EARLY COLLEGE PREP IN PRACTICE: CASE STUDIES FROM THE FIELD

The following case studies feature two schools that took two different approaches to supporting students' academic success and their readiness for college.[12] While the first school invested resources, time, and effort in revamping curriculum and student programming in math and science, the second established a grade-by-grade ladder of college supports for students and families.

Manhattan Bridges High School: Reenvisioning Math and Science

Manhattan Bridges was a model for how to rethink instruction and curricular practices that schools often consider "business as usual." After the first year of ESI, a core group of experienced teachers at the school made a concerted effort to improve math and science offerings and instruction. They sought to increase the rigor of coursework, align the curriculum with the Common Core State Standards, and prepare students for more advanced math and science, including AP courses. The staff viewed rigorous math and science instruction as a gateway to college and as a vehicle for preparing students to succeed in college courses. Manhattan Bridges also aimed to improve students' academic readiness through a range of differentiated supports designed to meet the needs of the diverse student body, allowing staff to tailor academic experiences to each student. Together, these teachers

- *redesigned the curriculum.* A group of eight math and science teachers spanning grades 9–12 used the summer as an opportunity to examine, and then redesign, their curricula. They developed units that aligned with Common Core standards, incorporated elements of the CARA curriculum (which maps the college landscape and provides guidance on applying to and paying for college), and provided more scaffolding to help students prepare for AP coursework. They also created an additional course for the lowest performing students to help them advance toward grade-level work.

- *improved the alignment and functionality of assessments.* The redesigned curriculum also focused on utilizing a greater number of formative and summative assessments as well as ensuring that there was strong alignment among learning activities and relevant standards and exams. Assessments emphasized high-order thinking and use of academic vocabulary across both math and science. Moreover, instructional strategies promoted opportunities for peer and self-assessment.

- *targeted essential skills across subjects and grade levels.* Teachers worked to develop and reinforce critical skills (e.g., writing based on research, public presentation) across subject areas and grades, with the goal of building horizontal and vertical ladders. For example, they asked themselves which skills students should demonstrate proficiency or mastery in each year of high school and then created standard rubrics for teachers to support and assess the development of these skills across subjects.

- *offered more advanced classes.* The school increased the number of AP, honors, and accelerated math classes offered. Importantly, it has also increased the number of students taking the courses, doing so, in part, by "opening up a pipeline" so students can enter advanced courses at different points in their high school careers. One staff member explained, "If a student who starts here is not doing so well, that doesn't mean that's where they're going to stay."

- *provided targeted supports for struggling students.* The school offered a semester-long Saturday math prep course as well as tutoring sessions before and after school for struggling students. They also piloted Reading Plus, a computerized reading program for students unable to read on grade level. In addition, each year the school identified ten to twenty students not on track to graduate or who were struggling and had teachers meet with them weekly in one-on-one meetings to discuss their needs and progress.

- *modified course sequencing to provide more math.* To ensure that more students had the opportunity to take higher-level math during high school, Manhattan Bridges started allowing students to take

Algebra I in a single semester by taking it for two periods each day. It applied the same tactic with geometry. These changes allowed students to take Algebra II, trigonometry, and statistics before graduating.

El Puente Academy for Peace and Justice: Involving Families in the College Process

As part of its implementation of ESI, El Puente Academy established the Early College Awareness and Preparation Program (ECAPP) to increase college-readiness for all students in grades 9–12 *and* their parents/guardians through comprehensive college prep activities. Managed by one full-time staff member with assistance from other school staff, ECAPP provided college advising, application support, and connections to EL Puente alumni attending college. According to the ECAPP coordinator, "planning early is key," especially for students who will be the first in their family to attend college. ECAPP offered a series of college-related workshops to all students in each grade, slowly building their understanding of the college-going process. Some were integrated into existing classes, and others were stand-alone credit-bearing courses. For classes that included English learners, the workshops were also offered in Spanish.

ECAPP also involved families out of a belief that "a college-going culture cannot be just in the [school's] four walls. It has to spread out to home." The school held two afterschool workshops for parents in each grade in both English and Spanish. To encourage attendance, staff asked students to invite their parents and asked family members who participated in past workshops to help recruit others. El Puente also made it easier for families to attend the parent workshops by providing a structured activity for younger siblings of ECAPP students.

MAJOR FINDINGS

The multiple approaches, strategies, and practices that ESI schools created or expanded to create a college-going culture for Black and Latinx

TABLE 6.1   Grade-by-grade college supports for students and families

	STUDENTS	FAMILIES
9th grade	Twice a year, a regular class period was cancelled so that students could participate in college workshops. Workshops focused on: *Building college expectations.* The ECAPP coordinator talked to students about their current college-going goals and shared statistics about where recent El Puente alumni went to college. They also discussed different postsecondary options (e.g., two- and four-year colleges, vocational and trade schools, etc.). (October) *Transcripts.* Students were shown real transcripts (with names and other personally identifying information removed) and talked about how to evaluate transcripts and grades. (Spring) In addition to the workshops, the school's part-time guidance counselor held individual meetings with students to remind them of how many credits they needed to earn in the 9th grade. (Spring)	The ECAPP coordinator checked in with parents/guardians, sometimes along with the school's part-time parent facilitator, about how they thought their child was adjusting to high school and offered tips on supporting the transition. The ECAPP coordinator shared information about services and key personnel at the school and suggested ways parents could help their children develop study skills. (October) Staff provided parents with copies of their child's grades, as well as information about internship opportunities and a list of colleges and universities in NYC or within 20 miles of the city. (May)
10th grade	Twice a year, a regular class period was cancelled so that sophomores could participate in college workshops. Workshops focused on: *PSATs.* The ECAPP coordinator led a workshop about the PSAT's purpose, why it is important, and logistics of taking the test. Students also received sample PSAT questions. (October) *Transcripts and college goals.* Students examined their transcripts and had one-on-one consultations with the guidance counselor about whether they were on track to graduate. The ECAPP coordinator also shared information about a specific set of 2- and 4-year colleges, which included schools in NYC or less than 20 miles outside of the city as well as schools where El Puente alumni were enrolled or where the school had a contact. Students had a chance to discuss their interest in these schools. (May)	Staff introduced parents to the PSAT and discussed the school's expectations for student preparation. (Fall) Staff helped parents interpret PSAT scores and provided information on tutoring services, such as Kaplan and the El Puente Leadership Center. (January)

(continued)

male students throughout their high school careers included addressing important gaps in students' skills, increasing the rigor of instruction, and removing barriers to college access and enrollment by attending to both the application process and students' sense of belonging. Schools

TABLE 6.1 Grade-by-grade college supports for students and families, *continued*

	STUDENTS	FAMILIES
11th grade	The ECAPP coordinator led a half-credit class for juniors that met 2 or 3 times a week. The course was designed so that students entered 12th grade with the knowledge they needed to begin the college application process. The class covered, for example: *SAT preparation.* The school had a partnership with Khan Academy that helped students register for the SATs (by creating a College Board account) and access SAT test prep materials. *Majors and career options.* Students researched different career options based on their potential major and/or examples of majors provided by the ECAPP coordinator. This project encouraged students to consider how their choice of a college major might influence their career options. *Scholarships.* Students learned about online scholarship search and application tools and used case studies to consider which type of financial aid students should receive. For instance, the ECAPP coordinator provided examples of fictitious students with different GPAs and asked the class to decide who should receive financial aid and which kind (e.g., merit, institutional, private scholarships). The ECAPP coordinator also encouraged students to look at online databases of scholarships (e.g., Fastweb).	Staff encouraged parents to envision their child in college, regardless of their academic performance. The ECAPP coordinator also discussed the importance of emphasizing study skills at home, preparing for the SATs, and starting to think about the college application process. (Early fall) The ECAPP coordinator helped parents and families understand their child's academic standing and provided information about summer academic programs, internships (e.g., Summer Youth and Employment Program), and 2- and 4-year colleges. (May)

(continued)

invested a good portion of their ESI resources in supports they believed were critical to college preparation. These were grounded in two shifts within schools: raising the bar from high school graduation to college-readiness and building a four-year runway to college beginning in the ninth grade instead of waiting until the eleventh or twelfth grade. Leaders, teachers, and students talked extensively about the ways these culture shifts helped establish a college environment, made college talk pervasive, and set a schoolwide expectation that all students could not only enroll in college but succeed once there. By addressing common barriers to college, ESI schools made important strides toward ensuring that their young men of color could envision themselves in college and be empowered with the tools to get there. These efforts are borne out in the data, which shows that males of color in ESI schools were more

TABLE 6.1   Grade-by-grade college supports for students and families, *continued*

	STUDENTS	FAMILIES
12th grade	ECAPP provided: *College application support.* The ECAPP coordinator, along with a few 12th-grade teachers, met with students 3 times a week in a half-credit class for the entire year. The course focused on completing the Common Application, CUNY and SUNY applications, financial aid applications, and using scholarship databases. Drafts of students' college essays were reviewed in English classes, and the ECAPP coordinator conducted a final review. *College advising.* Supplemental, individual college advising sessions with the ECAPP coordinator were available on an as-needed basis (as often as weekly). During these sessions, the coordinator helped the student select a list of colleges to apply to. The coordinator also worked with students to collect documents needed for financial aid application and the state's Higher Education Opportunity Program (designed to support academically and economically disadvantaged students in attending college). *Help navigating racial bias on campus.* Staff worked to prepare students for meeting others from a variety of sociocultural backgrounds at college and potentially facing microaggressions, biases, and racist practices/policies. El Puente staff believed that these challenges could hinder students' transition to college and therefore talked with students about privileges that White students may enjoy on college campuses that students of color do not, uncomfortable experiences that El Puente alumni of color have had and how to challenge false assumptions they may encounter.	The school invited recent alumni and the parents of alumni who participated in ECAPP workshops in recent years to attend the workshop and share tips with current 12th-grade students and families. The ECAPP coordinator talked to families and students about the paperwork their children would need for college applications (e.g., application fee waiver requests, tax documents, child support documentation). Parents received a timeline for when paperwork was due, including college application deadlines. (September) In addition, parents and students were encouraged to meet directly with the ECAPP coordinator to share any sensitive or private information relevant to financial aid or any challenge to college enrollment. As students approached graduation and the beginning of college, the school offered tips to families about how to support their children through this exciting and potentially challenging transition.

likely to be exposed to college supports earlier, have conversations about postsecondary planning with adults in their school building, and apply to a greater number of colleges.

While all ESI schools addressed college access and enrollment, few of them invested the resources into making academic changes that might have had an impact on other outcomes related to college readiness and success. Those that did modified their course sequencing and programming so that students could take four years of math and science, expanded access to higher-level courses and coursework to Black and Latinx males, and integrated college-level writing and research across the curriculum, while providing targeted support for students who struggled academically. This attention to what students were learning in classrooms was designed to increase students' skills and ensure that they were on track to earn the credits and test scores required to be college-ready per state standards. Exposing students to college and providing support on tasks like filling out applications and financial aid materials are essential, but they should not be confused with academic preparation. As one principal said, the goal was not merely to help students enroll in college but to make sure they were adequately prepared to succeed there.

It is possible that ESI's odds of success would have been bolstered by ensuring that participating schools were attending more to the academic domain specifically and the nature of teaching and learning more broadly. In addition, schools might have made more of an impact if they had used ESI to improve outcomes related to high school graduation, including attendance and credit recovery. And finally, incorporating career supports into schools' college preparation plans, in particular for boys of color, may have boosted student engagement and the types of skills that are important for succeeding in college and the workplace. These gaps highlight important lessons for other schools and districts committed to establishing college as an achievable goal for students who are underrepresented or first-generation college-goers. While socioemotional supports were emphasized, the schools' targeted academic supports were limited. Schools need to consider how to do both.

RECOMMENDATIONS FOR PRACTICE

- *Target gaps in skills without compromising access to advanced coursework.* While several schools took steps to increase the rigor of their offerings and/or the access to advanced coursework, those efforts may have been limited by an inattention to existing gaps in essential skills. Though tutoring was common in both ESI and comparison schools, this add-on was likely insufficient to make substantial improvement for those students reading well below grade level, for example. Ensuring that students are appropriately supported during the school day by staff with targeted expertise and additional resources is an important first step toward supporting students to succeed in high school and college. (This will be especially important in the aftermath of the learning loss associated with the pandemic.[13]) At the same time, struggling students should not be denied the opportunity to engage in higher-level coursework, especially those courses that provide important foundations for college. Struggling with skills in one area doesn't necessarily mean students lack skills in other potentially more challenging areas. In essence, these are double-pronged priorities that require systematic programming, professional coaching, and collaboration among teachers to identify students who need support and address areas of need while maintaining high expectations and opportunities for academic rigor.

- *Maximize efforts in the ninth grade.* One of the by-products of ESI's college focus was the shift from targeting college preparation at eleventh and twelfth graders to beginning with ninth graders, acknowledging that, for some, serious attention in the eleventh grade is far too late to intervene or correct course. College exposure and increasing college knowledge early in the ninth grade provides students a long enough runway to meet the requirements for college enrollment and allows them to make the connections on their own between their high school coursework and their post–high school aspirations. The benefits of starting early can also help schools keep students on track for graduation. Research shows that earning ten or more credits and passing at least one state exam is a reliable predictor of graduation among NYC high school students across subgroups.[14] These types of indicators can be used to identify students who are at most at risk and who require additional support.

- *Address the multiple dimensions of college preparation.* ESI schools excelled at acknowledging and addressing the multiple dimensions of preparing students for college. A multipronged effort can include "college talk" with peers, teachers, and alumni; increasing college knowledge and exposure starting in the ninth grade; infusing

CHAPTER 7

A Vision of Equity, Justice, and Hope for Our Nation's Schools

> We didn't get here overnight. When we think about these
> disparities, this is a generational challenge.
>
> —*ESI funder*

THE AIM OF THIS BOOK is to tell the story of ESI—its origins, its design, the lives it changed, and the trade-offs inherent in its execution. Throughout the chapters, I focus on multiple roles—the funders who invested in this enterprise, the district leaders who served as the architects of the initiative, the dedicated program team running its daily operations, and the principals and teachers implementing ESI in their schools and classrooms.[1] I describe multiple dimensions of ESI, including its underlying assumptions about how change happens, the numerous supports provided to help educators realize its goals, and the experiences of boys and young men of color from the rocky cliffs of northern Bronx to the seashore of Brooklyn.

In an effort to document, narrate, and understand the life of ESI, I lay out a number of specific recommendations and raise critical questions for other districts and schools. I argue that both the accomplishments and limitations of ESI provide opportunities for other policy makers around the country to think strategically about how they design and implement their efforts to address the systemic inequalities faced by young men of color and other marginalized students. What can we learn from the story of ESI? Which elements of the initiative were deemed successful or distinctive and may be worth replicating or building on in other districts? Which aspects seem to have limited ESI's ability to improve the performance of students on key indicators? How can we evaluate these efforts in a way that focuses our attention on the outcomes that we want to see and on the underlying inequities perpetuated by schools?

New York City's enormity—with 1.1 million students—presented some unique challenges for improving outcomes. However, the lessons from this book can be even more powerful in smaller districts, where disrupting existing systems might be accomplished more efficiently, where trying innovative approaches can be achieved on a smaller scale, and where replication across an entire system may be feasible.

Overall, the Research Alliance's assessment of ESI's "results" was mixed. We found the initiative to be successful in getting schools to create or expand programming in academic supports, youth development, college-focused school culture, and culturally relevant education. Most schools implemented programming activities aligned with ESI's theory of change, especially in the first two years of the initiative. And many of the Black and Latinx young men indicated that they participated in activities in one or more of the ESI domains, talked to adults about college with some regularity, and felt a sense of belonging and fair treatment in their schools. However, as funding levels declined, so did the alignment of activities with ESI's core principles. Only a handful of schools sustained a high level of programming alignment during the four-year measurement period. In addition, ESI fell short of its ambitious goal of improving college enrollment rates. Although 40 percent of Black and Latinx young men in ESI schools enrolled in college, this figure did not differ significantly from the cohort of non-ESI comparison schools that we evaluated (though outcomes were higher in both sets of schools than the city averages).

ESI aspired to improve relationships and perceptions of the school environment and to raise college-readiness rates (and other academic outcomes) among Black and Latinx males. However, the changes we documented among schools, educators, and students did not, by themselves, prove to be enough to increase Black and Latinx young men's academic outcomes, college-readiness, or college enrollment. What accounted for the lack of success in this area, and how might other districts focused on college-readiness design and implement efforts that achieve the desired results?

WHAT ESI ACCOMPLISHED

ESI represented an unprecedented investment in the educational outcomes of young males of color. Thoughtfully designed and implemented with some success (particularly in its early years), it provided the impetus for some positive outcomes. While ESI did not increase college-readiness and enrollment for Black and Latinx male students, it changed elements of school culture and students' experiences in school. For districts seeking to improve school culture for Black and Latinx young men, an investment in ESI-type supports aligns with those goals.

Shifting the Conversation

Designed to confront racial, ethnic, and gender disparities, ESI became a means for addressing the racism inherent in our systems of education. It asked schools to think about push-outs instead of dropouts. It asked educators to consider not only who gets suspended but how teachers contribute to harmful dynamics in their classrooms. It laid bare the reality that achieving in school depends not only on individual motivation but on providing equitable learning opportunities for students. ESI also created spaces for teachers and students from across the system to engage in critical conversations about racism and the numerous ways it manifests in schools. It gave teachers a vocabulary for discussing these truths with each other and with their students and emboldened them to talk about things like White supremacy without the fear of being fired.

ESI also challenged deficit narratives by focusing on the successes of boys and young men of color and the historical contributions of Black and brown people.[2] At the same time, it looked unflinchingly at painful current events and considered how the deaths of Michael Brown and Tamir Rice affected the lives of the young men the initiative aimed to reach and teach. Social justice and youth action were not ancillary to the work but a core part of how ESI was translated in the field. Some of the seeds of this work remain in the district in the Critical and Courageous Conversations series, the substantial investment in implicit bias training for teachers, and the work to recruit and retain male teachers of color. Though some contend these efforts do not go far enough, they lay the foundation for paying more sustained attention to issues of systemic racism and the ways that schools can either disrupt them or perpetuate them on a daily basis—an important legacy that may influence policy and practice at both the district level and within individual schools. It also provides a model for other districts that want to ground their work in race-conscious policies and support their educators in doing the same.

Changing Teachers' Mind-Sets, Beliefs, and Practices

Under the auspices of ESI, teachers across participating schools (and later in other schools) could select from a number of professional development opportunities around culturally relevant curriculum. These took different forms, including one-off workshops, ten-week programs focused on college-readiness for young men of color, summer institutes guiding teachers in how to apply CRE across the core subjects, and CRE showcases that featured student work and celebrated their voices as agents of change. All of the ESI schools participated in this work, and some engaged in it over a number of years. While focused on instruction and pedagogy, these PD opportunities sought to shift practice by changing hearts and minds. They challenged teachers to consider their biases against boys and young men of color when they perceived their behavior as disruptive, when they did not recommend them for AP classes, when they assumed a lack of parental involvement, and/or when the classroom texts did not include a single protagonist who looked like them. ESI's emphasis on CRE training provided a mechanism for shifting the conversation in ways that changed the look and feel of classroom practices, teacher decisions, and student experiences.

Improving School Culture and Relationships

Embedded in the work of ESI's CRE training was a commitment to creating welcoming, safe environments for boys and young men of color and providing opportunities for them to build supportive relationships with adults and other students. Programming included adult-student mentoring (especially with adult males of color), peer mentoring groups, small advisory classes that facilitated authentic sharing and emotional connection, and restorative practices and other alternative approaches to suspension designed to transform a culture of punishment into one rooted in healing and restoration. Observing these spaces and talking to the young men involved made clear the importance of these programs in the lives of participating students. In particular, students spoke about the sense of brotherhood they felt in school, the practical ways adults in the building guided them through the transition to college, how their peers and young alumni inspired their own future aspirations, the affirmation they received in gatherings of their peers, and the messages of empowerment about achieving academically and changing the world around them. It is no wonder Black and Latinx males in ESI schools reported a strong sense of belonging and connection in their schools. The initiative's ability to improve school culture and relationships was both notable and meaningful, especially considering the historical disenfranchisement of Black and Latinx students. Other districts may consider building on ESI's strategies to achieve this goal as an important first step in addressing students' needs and serving them holistically.

Building Capacity in Schools with Ongoing Support

Another strong feature of the ESI model was the robust infrastructure of support provided by the program team and its emphasis on professional learning through relationships and community. The Central Team invested considerable time, effort, and resources to support the planning and implementation of ESI in schools. It provided individual feedback on schools' yearly plans, regular PD opportunities focused on the initiative's goals, and external partnerships with community-based organizations that served Black and Latinx boys and young men. Perhaps most important, the team established a professional learning community by facilitating regular working sessions for both principals and ESI liaisons. These full-day professional meetings supported the aims of ESI and responded to the real-time requests of the participating school leaders, thereby increasing buy-in and maximizing the potential for the initiative to take root in these schools. Educators attributed many of the positive changes in their schools to the insights they gained from these meetings and the opportunities to collaborate with other educators committed to the same goals. Moreover, they were struck by the commitment of the program team and the director to going above and beyond in their service to and support of ESI schools and students. Other districts should consider that even the most thoughtful plans cannot realize their aims without the dedication and skills of the individuals leading on the ground and their building-capacity role among the teachers who interact with students daily.

WHY DIDN'T WE SEE IMPROVEMENTS IN COLLEGE OUTCOMES?

Even though ESI students engaged in a range of positive activities, reported a stronger sense of fair treatment and belonging, and spoke more frequently with adults about college and careers than did students in comparison schools, these positive outcomes did not bring about the desired increases in college-readiness or enrollment numbers for Black and Latinx males. This suggests that we cannot assume that greater participation in these activities, more college-focused support, and a greater sense of belonging in high school will necessarily promote college access and success—at least not on their own. While the Research Alliance study provided evidence that ESI improved socioemotional outcomes, the path to improved college-readiness requires more sustained and targeted effort than the initiative provided. ESI's design might have also overlooked mediating factors, including that some of the comparison schools also provided a set of interventions (or policy mandates) related to the work of the initiative during the same period. I focus here on those factors that districts are more likely to control.

A Diffuse Intervention Not Focused Enough on Academics

Previous research suggests that a diffuse set of interventions may not be as meaningful as a single targeted intervention.[3] ESI's focus on teacher practice, in-school relationships, and school culture moved schools to support Black and Latinx male students on a number of different fronts, often through multiple stand-alone programs. Some participating schools, for example, created up to seven different ESI programs, with a number of these changing from year to year. The diffuseness of the intervention meant that many schools could not focus on certain aspects of the school's culture or build expertise that might have had more of an impact on students. Moreover, while ESI increased students' exposure to activities in all three domains—academics, youth development, and college-going culture, as well as culturally relevant education—the difference between ESI and comparison schools proved to be smaller for activities in the academic domain.

Broadly speaking, ESI did not substantially change schools' approaches to teaching and learning beyond the adoption of CRE. Most schools did not use ESI as an opportunity to revamp curriculum or to improve teacher mastery in particular subjects, for example. Perhaps a clearer focus on supports tied directly to high school graduation, college-readiness, and enrollment (e.g., credit accumulation to remain on track to graduate and pass Regents exams) would have enhanced ESI's ability to improve college-related outcomes.

Improving students' academic trajectories in the face of long-standing educational disparities will likely require a robust set of supports to meet students' academic needs before they enter high school. If districts want to focus on improving college-readiness and enrollment rates, the study of ESI suggests that there may be ways to improve on this model, particularly by creating targeted interventions that more closely align with the intended outcomes.

Widespread Participation over Deep Engagement

At the outset, the district and the Central Team emphasized the importance of schools driving the improvement process by identifying gaps among their students and deciding how to use ESI resources to close them. The rationale behind this strategy was that schools best know the needs of their students and how to effect change within their buildings.

This decision also ensured a level of buy-in and engagement among schools that might not have existed with a more prescriptive approach. At the same time, this level of autonomy resulted in wide variation among schools in terms of program design, dosage, and quality and no clear benchmarks for school, teacher, or student participation. Beyond the varying degrees of participation among schools, data also showed that levels of implementation declined across the board after Year 2 as funding decreased. Moreover, within schools that appeared to be fully engaged, it may be the case that the engagement was less widespread or only concentrated among a small number of teachers. A district report about ESI noted that "over the lifetime of the initiative, almost all ESI schools participated in one form of training or another, but deep engagement was limited to a handful of individuals."[4] In terms of student participation, only about a quarter of the schools engaged 50 percent or more of their Black and Latinx male students in activities in all three domains across grades 9–12. Schools may have needed to reach many more students more consistently to make progress on outcomes like attendance, graduation rates, or college-going.

This aspect of the initiative should encourage policy makers to consider means of leveraging school-level expertise while providing direct guidelines or standards for implementing high-quality programs, such as evidence-based rubrics for assessing and improving program quality and concrete goals for evaluating program dosage and student participation. Future initiatives might benefit from clearer guidance about how to create policies and structures that can outlast initiative resources, including setting stricter parameters about using funding to build staff capacity in targeted areas rather than relying on costly external partners to implement new programs. These tracking and measurement strategies may have been more feasible in a smaller set of schools.

Substantial Change Takes More Time

Whole-school models and programs do not often result in significant increases in student achievement, and when they do, it may take more than five or six years to have an impact.[5] As one of the architects of ESI stated, "In the school change timeline, four years is not very long . . . Change is hard and takes a while. If you're going to do it, you've got to be in it for the long game."

ESI was conceived as a research and development effort that encouraged schools to develop new approaches and then modify them as they learned more about their effectiveness with students. Consequently, much of what ESI schools implemented in the first year evolved or completely changed over time. Perhaps some schools participating in ESI needed more time to strengthen their programs, and maybe a more mature version of ESI would have had a greater impact on student outcomes.

It would have been illuminating to track outcomes for both future cohorts of students in ESI schools, given that some ESI programs were sustained, as well as long-term outcomes for ESI students, including college completion and employment. Indeed, disappointing results may be followed by positive outcomes later in a young person's life, especially those associated with overall well-being, such as job stability, labor earnings, and healthy relationships.[6] The possibility of long-term improvements highlights the importance of persistence in the face of ever-shifting policies and initiatives.

District leaders should consider giving their own policies—and the schools that implement them—sufficient time to demonstrate progress before giving up and turning their attention to new plans all together. This is especially true when the problems have gone unattended for too long and the interventions are complex and thus require time for effective implementation. As one ESI funder reasoned, "We didn't get here over night. When we think about these disparities, this is a generational challenge."

SUSTAINING THE MOVEMENT: THE LEGACY OF ESI

ESI evolved from being an initiative located in forty schools to a series of conversations, supports, and frameworks that reached schools and offices across the district and the city. After the initiative ended, ESI director Paul Forbes shared the work with additional NYC schools— "Now there are no silos or borders. Now it's for anyone who's interested: school folks, community-based organizations, central folks. If you are interested, then are you invited to participate in our discussion, training, and professional development." CRE now plays a prominent role in the district's mission and vision statements, over fifty thousand teachers across the city (even in the midst of the pandemic) have enrolled in implicit bias training sessions, "equity teams" exist across twenty-nine community school districts, and conversations about segregation and the lack of Black and Latinx students in specialized high schools take place on a regular basis.

Many forces helped bring about this sea change in the NYC district, among them the social movements across the country during and since that the initiative. But ESI played an important role in helping shape these movements in the district and in readying hundreds of educators across the five boroughs to engage in the work of racial equity and justice. This development harkens back to the broader goals of ESI, highlighting how it evolved into something more enduring than a single initiative.

SHOULD WE BE ASKING DIFFERENT QUESTIONS?

While the empirical questions investigated by the study of ESI are important, and their answers can help identify important considerations for other districts and schools, they overlook other aspects of addressing equitable opportunities for Black and Latinx boys and other communities of students and families historically underserved by the American education system. These questions, which are by no means comprehensive, emerged from conversations with hundreds of policy makers, researchers, parents, educators, and students about how we as a nation should be thinking about change and what it will take to achieve educational equity.

How Can We Learn from Success and Failure?

Districts and policy makers have a vested interest in being able to say that a particular initiative "worked." But in trying to validate the success of a policy or program, we can miss an opportunity to examine what we learn from failure. While efforts should focus on how to achieve the aims of policies, considering that so many of them fall short of their intended targets, perhaps a secondary goal should be learning what can be applied in the future and in other contexts.

One method for doing this work involves implementing a research and development design in which failure is not feared but expected and, in the process of experimenting, small innovations produce gains that can be tested or replicated. There are serious constraints to this model, however, when trying to garner political favor or obtain substantial funding. As one of ESI's program team members said, "When central folks were trying to sell this to their funder, it's not like funders want to hear we're expecting a 95 percent failure rate, so they would sell hard numbers: 'We're graduating every Black and Latinx male student in four years.' But that's not what we're saying we're doing. That's now what we're telling schools. We're trying to be different from that, but when we talk to a funder it becomes very explicitly about that." In fact, a few of ESI's designers always saw the initiative as a way of testing particular approaches and then focusing on implementing those concepts across more schools. But as one ESI leader noted, "People don't want to hear that. It's not sexy. It's sexier to say you're going to address racial inequity. You get people emotionally invested."

In addition to framing goals around learning, policy makers should show some courage when things do fail. As John Duval, one of the architects of ESI put it, "We didn't have a culture that was like, 'It's okay if you fail, just contribute to the learning of our field.' That's not what we were. The culture then was if you're successful, then you're lauded. If you're not, then there are ramifications. Our field is very cowardly when it comes to talking about success and failure. We just never want to talk about things that didn't work. But I personally don't think you can learn authentically any other way." In practical terms, this kind of courage requires district and program leaders to be open to rigorous study, to be transparent about what has and has not been achieved, and to recognize and accept misguided assumptions. At the same time, this approach allows policy makers to be bolder in their actions, to listen to a wider range of voices, and to take informed risks while empowering educators to adopt the same stance toward learning.

How Do We Define Success?

The things that we measure can become what we value the most. Passing Regents exams and accumulating credits are important in that they allow students to progress to the next level of education, should that be their aspiration. But as proxies for authentic learning, critical consciousness, or the capacity to contribute to and collaborate with one's community, these metrics do not tell the full story.

What, then, is "success" for a young person? If students graduate from college and engage in work that exploits others, did we educate them in the truest sense? If schools focus on developing grit and resilience but never mention mental health or well-being (let alone activism or resistance), have they served their students well? Do the traditional metrics for evaluating schools and districts reflect White, hegemonic norms that overlook other ways of seeing and being that would undercut a system that continues to widen inequalities? Can we look through a more holistic lens to consider what schools should be doing? Should a good education include racial and ethnic identity formation, the generation of joy, the identification of social injustice, and the capacity to lead and participate in social action? And if we evaluate schools based on their ability to achieve these goals, what would their hallways and classrooms look and sound like, how would the young people in those buildings feel, and what type of adults would they grow up to be? How might our communities, systems, and societies operate differently if led by individuals who possess these dispositions and skills?

What Is the Role of the Broader Community in Effecting Change?

Parent activists and youth-led movements play an important role in demanding justice and pushing policy makers to enact changes in schools and other segments of our unequal society. Meanwhile, top-down approaches to policy making are not typically motivated or informed by the voices and concerns of the communities they serve, thereby limiting their impact. Activist groups remind us of the necessity and power of grassroots organizing to call attention to the lived experiences of constituents that may be otherwise overlooked. Through storytelling, lobbying, and direct action, parent, youth, and community-led groups like the Alliance for Quality Education, United We Dream, Black Visions Collective, Mijente, and the Sunrise Movement (to name a few) have fought and won important battles related to NYC schools, LGBTQ rights, support for undocumented young people, and climate justice.

This work pushes us to recognize that racial equity efforts in schools cannot be achieved through district leadership alone. There are methods by which municipalities and school districts can engage with the community and be responsive to the demands of parents and students, creating multiple channels to work hand-in-hand with direct action groups, collect their stories to inform decision-making, and empower multiple stakeholders in decisions that will affect the system. At the same time, parents and youth do not wait around to be invited to the table; they are active now and will continue to push the conversation and move policy forward. Their efforts can serve as a reminder to school districts and systems that a culture of collective action and coalition building can be applied to their work as well. Districts can work together to share promising approaches and lessons from their work that contribute to an understanding of how geographical, political, and cultural dynamics influence the implementation and outcomes of similar efforts across the country.

Can We Find Hope in a Crisis?

Improving opportunities for low-income students of color has been at the center of national conversations and education policy for decades. But it has not been implemented in a way that considers the historical and systemic racism that intentionally excluded minoritized groups from meaningful education and how these systems of exclusion manifest in schools today. Compounding these long-standing disparities, school districts must contend with a public health crisis that is disproportionately affecting these students and their families.

As I write, the United States is in the midst of what has been described as "dual pandemics," a term that acknowledges both the steady devastation of COVID-19 and police brutality as health crises of epic proportions.[7] The public health community also described the physical, mental, and emotional tolls of being disproportionately affected by the disease and potential police violence.[8] National data show that Black and Latinx individuals are three times as likely to become infected and twice as likely to die from the virus. While early analysis focused on underlying conditions that might be contributing to these disparities, evidence shows that the better explanation lies in structural elements—the fact that Black and Latinx individuals are less likely to have jobs that come with adequate health care or that allow them to work from home and are more likely to take public transportation and live in tighter quarters.[9] In this context, school districts must undertake emergency remote learning, face difficult decisions around the opening and closing of schools, and recognize how these instabilities will disproportionately affect their most vulnerable populations for years to come. Policy makers' responses must attend to the dual crises for all and consider whether their actions will widen existing disparities.

Addressing some of the underlying opportunity gaps even in pandemic-free times will require investing earlier in students' lives as well as in systems outside of the schools. Educators continue to argue that schools and districts alone cannot fix the deep inequities created by intentional segregation or the remedy systematic neglect of certain communities over generations. The current crises, however, raise questions about the role of systems beyond education to address disparities in mental health, the technology divide, and housing and food insecurity that continue to widen. We confront a larger question: *How can we reimagine the systems we take for granted?* We must ask why we would want our schools to "go back to normal" after the pandemic when "normal" conditions have proven to be toxic for so many of our students.

Acknowledging that it may not be enough to "tinker toward utopia" or make changes at the margins, Black, Latinx, and Indigenous thinkers, writers, and shapers of political discourse call for radically different approaches to educating students, keeping cities safe, ensuring economic justice, and formulating immigration policy.[10] Calls for abolitionist teaching, defunding the police, or working toward a carbon-free future do not merely demand changes in policy and practice; they present a different vision for the world.[11] While just a year ago these movements—many of them in conversation with each other—may have represented the perspectives of a vocal minority, shifting public polls and growing participation in protests suggest a widening embrace for this reinvention of our systems.[12] Creating equitable education systems may thus require us to imagine beyond the constraints of the policy making we have become accustomed to. It will also require those in positions of power give something up. It will require an unbroken demand for justice. As Frederick Douglass reminds us,

If there is no struggle, there is no progress. Those who profess to favor freedom and yet deprecate agitation are men who want crops without plowing up the ground; they want rain without thunder and lightning. They want the ocean without the awful roar of its many waters. This struggle may be a moral one, or it may be a physical one, and it may be both moral and physical, but it must be a struggle. Power concedes nothing without a demand. It never did and it never will.[13]

MY BROTHER'S KEEPER

While I was writing about the educational journey of Black and Brown boys and young men, our nation witnessed the murders of too many Black men and women. The deaths of Ahmaud Arbery, Breonna Taylor, and George Floyd sparked protests in every major American city in the spring and summer of 2020. And then as I prepared to submit the manuscript another video emerged, that of Jacob Blake being shot repeatedly in the back by a police officer while his three young sons watched. By the time I see these pages again, what names will we be chanting in the streets? Which stolen lives will families be grieving that don't make national headlines?

This book focuses on education, but it is motivated by love for Black and Brown lives, an appeal for justice, and a desire to frame the question *Am I my brother's keeper?* not rhetorically but as a clarion call that each of us must answer. May the words of Letetra Widman, Jacob Blake's sister, be a final call for these pages:

I am my brother's keeper. And when you say the name Jacob Blake, make sure you say father. Make sure you say cousin. Make sure you say son. Make sure you say uncle. But most importantly, make sure you say human . . . I don't want your pity. I want change.

Data Sources and Analytic Methods

The ESI evaluation was designed with two overlapping and interacting components: a study of the initiative's implementation in the participating high schools and a study of its impact on student experiences and other outcomes. This appendix provides an overview of the data sources and analytic methods that were used to address the research questions for the implementation and impact studies.

SCHOOL-LEVEL IMPLEMENTATION STUDY: DATA AND METHODS

The implementation study draws on interviews we conducted with key members of the district's ESI Central Team, as well as our review of key district-generated documents, including the ESI Design Challenge, the

This appendix is wholly reproduced from Adriana Villavicencio, Sarah Klevan, and James Kemple, "The Expanded Success Initiative Challenges and Progress in the Pursuit of College and Career Readiness for Black and Latino Young Men" (report, Research Alliance for New York City, New York, 2013). More detailed information can be found in the report's Technical Appendix, https://research.steinhardt.nyu.edu/scmsAdmin/media/users/ks191/ESI_progress_challenges/ESI_Challenges_and_Progress_Appendices.pdf. Used with permission.

rubric used for scoring schools' applications to be part of ESI, and ESI's yearly planning templates. The assessment of ESI implementation in each of the participating schools was conducted through three related sets of research activities:

- Documenting programming activities and support schools provided,
- Assessing alignment with the ESI goals and theory of action, and
- Assessing student participation in ESI-related activities.

Table 1 provides a list of the key data sources related to each of these research efforts. It also shows the samples of respondents who provided the data and role of the data in the evaluation. Following the table is a discussion of the measures and analytic methods that we used to carry out each of the implementation study components.

Documenting Programming Activities and Supports

The first component of the implementation study sought to document the activities and student supports that each school planned and implemented in accordance with ESI's three core domains—academic supports, youth development, and college-going culture—as well as culturally relevant education. Each year, members of the research team completed an in-person questionnaire by interviewing the principal or ESI coordinator in each ESI school. The questionnaire began with an inventory of all programming activities in the areas of academic support, youth development, college readiness, and culturally relevant education. It is important to note that ESI was designed both to enhance existing activities and supports and to create new ones in these areas if the schools felt there were gaps. With this in mind, the research team attempted to compile a full inventory of all programming activities and supports in these areas, not just those that were funded or enhanced with ESI resources and technical support. These activity inventories were used both as part of our effort to assess implementation alignment and in the design of the student surveys (which asked about participation in ESI-related activities, among other topics).

TABLE 1   Data Sources for the ESI Implementation Study

DATA SOURCE	SAMPLE	PURPOSE
Structured program activity questionnaire	ESI Liaison or School Principal or Assistant Principal	Compile a list of ESI-related programming activities
Semi-structured 60-minute interview	ESI liaison or school principal or assistant principal	Capture the perspectives of school leaders about ESI's implementation and its influence on the school
45-minute semi-structured focus group interview with teachers	Three to five teachers who volunteered for the interviewed after being selected by the ESI liaison or principal	Capture the perspectives of teachers about ESI's implementation and its influence on the school
45-minute semi-structured focus group interview with students	Three to five 10th grade students who volunteered for the interview after being selected by the ESI Liaison or Principal (Spring 2014, Spring 2015 and Spring 2016)	Capture the perspectives of students on ESI's implementation and its influence on the school
35-minute student survey	All 9th grade students (Spring 2013 and Spring 2014) All 10th grade students (Spring 2014 and 2015) All 11th grade students (Spring 2015 and 2016) All 12th grade students (Spring 2016)	Measure student participation in ESI-related activities, capture their perspectives on self and school, and document involvement in future planning activities
60–90 minute semi-structured interview with ESI Central Team	Three members of the NYCDOE's ESI Central Team (in 2012 and again in 2016)	Capture the Central Team's perspectives on ESI's design and implementation.
Document review	Select documents identified by research team.	Enhance our understanding of ESI's goals and strategies.

Source: The Research Alliance for New York City Schools

Assessing Alignment with ESI Goals and Theory of Action

The second component of the implementation study sought to assess the degree to which the implementation and overall support of these activities were aligned with ESI's goals and theory of action over the four years for which ESI funding was available. The assessment of implementation alignment also surfaced information about the challenges that schools confronted throughout the funding period. In addition to the questionnaire, the research team also conducted annual semi-structured interviews with the ESI Liaison or Principal in each school. The interview included a range of questions that aimed to generate information about the overall quality and intensity of ESI implementation. It is important to note that ESI was not designed as a "model" that each participating school was expected to replicate to the fullest extent possible. Rather, ESI provided schools with funding, a broad set of content area and technical support resources, and a mutually supportive professional learning community. Programmatically, the initiative required that schools enhance or create activities within each of the three domains and CRE. Beyond this very broad framework of supports and programming domains, ESI allowed schools a great deal of discretion over the specific use of their resources and encouraged schools to experiment with activities and experiences that they believe would best meet the needs and circumstances of their students and staff. With this in mind, the evaluation's assessment of alignment was necessarily broad and attempted to capture the extent to which schools utilized their resources and developed activities in ways that were consistent with ESI's key programming domains and with the expectations of the DOE's ESI Central Team. Researchers worked closely with the Central Team to develop a five-dimensional rubric. Its elements are summarized in Table 2 below. Based on their scores on each element of the rubric, ESI schools were given a total alignment score of up to 15.

Assessing Student Participation

The third component of the implementation study assessed students' participation in the programming activities that were provided in the ESI schools. As noted above, some of these activities were either created or enhanced through ESI funding and supports, while others were already being offered at the time schools were selected for ESI. Regardless of the source of support, this aspect of the study utilized surveys to capture students' self-reported exposure to experiences that were both consistent with the ESI theory of action and likely to be associated with improvements in their developmental, engagement and school performance outcomes. The surveys were administered to students in ESI and

TABLE 2   Assessment of ESI Programming Alignment

ELEMENT	DATA SOURCE	SCORING
Representation of three programming domains— Captures the number of programs that were aligned with academic supports, youth development or college-focused school culture.	Activity questionnaire administered to principals and ESI liaisons	Reported at least one activity in only one domain. Reported at least one activity in two domains. Reported at least one activity in all three domains.
Evidence of culturally relevant education— Captures teachers' exposure to professional development sessions focused on culturally relevant education.	Interviews with teachers, principals and ESI liaisons	Neither teachers nor principal reported availability of CRE-related PD. Either teachers or principal reported availability of CRE-related PD. Both teachers and principal reported availability of CRE-related PD.
Population served—Identifies the number of programs explicitly serving Black and Latino male students.	Activity questionnaire administered to principals and ESI liaisons	No programs designed explicitly for Black and Latino males students . One program designed explicitly for Black and Latino males students. Two or more programs designed explicitly for Black and Latino males students.
Early college and career supports—Captures the availability college or career activities for 9th or 10th graders.	Activity questionnaire administered to principals and ESI liaisons	No college or career activities in grades 9 or 10. One college or career activities in grades 9 or 10. Two or more college or career activities in grades 9 or 10.
Attendance at liaison meetings—Indicates whether ESI school liaison and other staff attended the citywide ESI liaison meetings and events.	Attendance logs from ESI meetings and convenings	School was represented at two or fewer ESI liaison meetings. School was represented at three or four ESI liaison meetings. School was represented at five or more ESI liaison meetings.

Source: The Research Alliance for New York City Schools

comparison schools in April and May each year from the 2012–2013 through 2015–2016 school years (see below for more information about the comparison schools). These years correspond to Grades 9 through 12 for students who were in 9th grade in Fall 2012 (the first year of ESI implementation). These students are referred to as the 2012 Cohort. The years also correspond to Grades 9 through 11 for students who were in 9th grade in Fall 2013 (the second year of ESI implementation). These

TABLE 3   Participation Activities by ESI-Aligned Programming Domain

ACADEMIC SUPPORT ACTIVITIES	YOUTH DEVELOPMENT ACTIVITIES	COLLEGE AND CAREER PLANNING ACTIVITIES
Tutoring Programs	Student advisory programs	College Advising
Regents Exam Preparation Programs	Mentoring/Peer Mentoring Programs	College Trips
Advanced Placement/IB Classes	Youth Groups	Internships

Source: The Research Alliance for New York City Schools

students are referred to as the 2013 Cohort. With the exception of the 2013 version, the surveys asked students a series of questions about whether they participated in a variety of activities during the current school year.

Finally, in an effort to capture a general sense of students' exposure to culturally relevant materials and curricula, the surveys also included a question asking students whether their teachers "provide reading material that reflects my race, ethnicity and/or culture." There are two important issues that readers should keep in mind when interpreting the activity participation information from the surveys.

- The findings reflect information provided by students who completed a survey on the one or two days during the spring semester when it was administered in a given school in a given year. Thus, differences in the composition of the respondent samples may account for some of the differences in participation rates from grade to grade.
- The surveys were not able to capture every activity that might have been aligned with the ESI programming domains, nor even all of the activities that might have been supported with ESI resources. At the same time, the survey questions were generally framed in broad terms in an effort to capture a range of activities that fall under an overarching category like tutoring programs, college advising, student advisories, and so on.

Despite these limitations the surveys provide a reasonably accurate picture of the ESI-related activities that students in the ESI schools utilized from grade to grade.

Capturing Educator and Student Perspectives on ESI

Our assessment of ESI implementation was deepened by capturing students' and teachers' perspectives about key elements of ESI and their influence on the overall culture of the schools. This included student and teacher reflections on the challenges that young men of color face as they navigate the transition to and through high school and the ways in which ESI attempted to address those challenges. Over the course of the four-year implementation period, the research team compiled more than 500 hours of individual and focus group interviews with administrators, teachers, and students. We used an iterative, five-step process to code and analyze transcripts from every interview and focus group. This method was developed to lead researchers from initial reflections about how ESI operated in individual schools to the identification and fine-grained analysis of major themes across schools. This allowed us to closely analyze the responses of educators and identify broader patterns (in particular, those that might help explain impact findings).

IMPACT STUDY: DATA AND METHODS

The ESI impact study was designed to assess the degree to which implementation of ESI led to more productive experiences and better outcomes for the students enrolled in the ESI schools. At the heart of the impact study is a comparison between the experiences and outcomes of students in the ESI schools with those of similar students in similar schools that did not have access to ESI's resources and supports. Before moving on to an overview of the data sources and analytic methods that underlie the assessment of ESI impacts, therefore, this section first describes the process used to select schools that were as similar as possible to the ESI schools during the years leading up to the start of the initiative.

ESI and Non-ESI Comparison Schools

For each ESI school, we identified two comparison schools that were statistically most similar in terms of the demographic characteristics and middle school academic performance of 9th grade students who started high school during the four years prior to the 2012–2013 school year (the start of ESI). Comparison schools were also identified based on the trajectory of academic outcomes for the four prior cohorts of 9th grade students. The pool of potential comparison schools included those meeting one of the following requirements:

- Schools that were invited to and applied for ESI, but were not selected;
- Schools that were invited to ESI but did not apply, with 15 or more Black and Latino male students in 2009–2010, 2010–2011, and 2011–2012; or
- Schools that had more than 25 Black and Latino male students and more than 25 percent Black and Latino male students in the 2011–2012 school year.
- Schools that used the same admissions criteria as a given ESI school.

Table 4 provides a direct comparison between the participating ESI schools and the resulting non-ESI comparison schools. For the purposes of this report, the comparison focuses on Black and Latino young men in the two groups of schools. The measures presented in the table reflect averages for incoming Black and Latino 9th graders over the four years prior to the start of ESI implementation in the 2012–2013 school year. The table shows these students' demographic characteristic and Grade 8 outcomes. It also shows the cumulative outcomes that these students achieved over their four years of high school.

Overall, Table 4 exhibits a high degree of similarity between the ESI and non-ESI schools. Differences between the two groups of schools are generally small and very few are statistically significant. The similarity in the population of Black and Latino young men in the two groups of schools over the four year prior to ESI implementation provides confidence that subsequent differences that may emerge are likely to be due

TABLE 4   Pre-ESI Characteristics and Outcomes for Black and Latino Young Men in ESI and Non-ESI Comparison Schools

STUDENT CHARACTERISTICS AND OUTCOMES	ESI SCHOOLS	COMPARISON SCHOOLS	ESTIMATED DIFFERENCE
Background Characteristics			
Home Language			
English	68.3	63.1	5.2
Not English	31.7	36.9	−5.2
Age (at start of Grade 9)	14.9	15.0	0.0
Overage for Grade 9	34.9	37.0	-2.0
8th Grade Outcomes			
Enrolled in a NYC Public School	92.1	90.8	1.3
Attendance Rate	90.6	90.0	0.6
ELA Test Scores			
Z-Score	−0.374	−0.404	0.030
Missing	13.4	14.3	−0.9
Math Test Scores			
Z-Score	−0.345	−0.385	0.039
Missing	11.7	12.8	−1.1
Services			
Free/Reduced Price Lunch	66.0	64.5	1.5
English Language Services	9.0	10.0	−1.0
Special Education Services	18.7	18.6	0.2
Cumulative high school outcomes (grades 9–12)			
Attendance Rate	85.6	84.7	0.9
Credits Earned	45.1	44.7	0.4
Suspensions			
Any Suspensions (%)	24.4	24.9	−0.6
Any Level 1 Suspensions (%)	13.7	14.5	−0.8
Any Level 2 Suspensions (%)	17.6	16.9	0.7
High School Graduation			
Any Diploma	70.5	67.9	2.6
Regents Diploma	64.5	61.7	2.8
Local Diploma	6.1	6.2	−0.1
NYS APM	13.0	11.8	1.2
College Enrollment			
Any College	36.2	33.0	3.2
4-Year College	21.9	19.4	2.4
2-Year College	14.3	13.5	0.8
Number of Schools	40	80	

Source: Research Alliance calculations based on data obtained from the NYC Department of Education.

Note: "Missing" represents the percentage of students for whom data for a given variable or outcome are not available.

to the supports and services provided by ESI. Similarly, they also provide confidence that a lack of subsequent differences are unlikely to be due to pre-existing differences between the two groups of schools.

Assessing Differences between ESI and Non-ESI Schools in Activity Participation, Perceptions of School and Self, and Preparation for Post-Secondary Transitions

Our study examined students' experiences along three dimensions of ESI's theory of action that are associated with the initiative's services and supports and students' subsequent experiences. First, it examines the degree to which students in ESI schools were more likely than those in non-ESI schools to participate in a range of activities that were aligned with the ESI programming domains. Second, it assesses the extent to which students' perceptions of ESI schools and school culture differed from those of students in non-ESI schools in ways that are aligned with ESI goals. This also includes indicators of students' assessment of their own academic self-concept and critical thinking skills. Third, the analysis focuses on students' goals for post-secondary education and work and the steps they took toward those goals.

Student Survey Samples

The evaluation's assessment in these three areas utilizes data from the surveys that were administered to students in the ESI schools and to students in up to 40 of the non-ESI comparison schools. As noted above, these data are available for two cohorts of incoming 9th grade students (those entering in Fall 2012 and Fall 2013, respectively) for each year through the Spring of 2016. This provides four full years of survey data (expected Grades 9 through 12) for the 2012 cohort and three full years (expected Grades 9–11) for the 2013 cohort.

Survey data are available for all 40 of the participating ESI schools. The number of non-ESI schools that administered student surveys differed from year to year. We were able to gain agreement for participation from 15 comparison schools in 2013, 22 in 2014, 20 in 2015, and 27 in 2016. The analyses of survey data focus only on the ESI schools for which survey data were also available for the accompanying non-ESI comparison school. In all, by combining samples across cohorts, survey data are available for students in Grades 9–12 for the following samples of ESI comparison schools:

- *Grade 9:* 25 ESI schools and 26 non-ESI comparison schools
- *Grade 10:* 27 ESI schools and 27 non-ESI comparison schools
- *Grade 11:* 29 ESI schools and 30 non-ESI comparison schools
- *Grade 12:* 27 ESI schools and 27 non-ESI comparison schools

Survey response rates differed somewhat between ESI and comparison schools. Response rates also declined as students moved from Grade 9 through Grade 12, particularly in the ESI schools. In Grade 9, approximately 83 percent of the Black and Latino young men who were enrolled in the ESI schools responded to the survey, compared to 76 percent of those enrolled in the comparison schools. By Grade 12, 52 percent of the Black and Latino young men who were enrolled in the ESI schools responded to the survey, compared to 65 percent of those enrolled in the comparison schools. Because not all Black and Latino young men responded to the survey each year, the results may not be representative of the full population of those students. However, among those who did respond, the characteristics of respondents in the ESI schools are very similar to those of students in the comparison schools. This high degree of similarity bolsters confidence that differences in self-reported participation and students' perceptions are likely to be due to ESI rather than stemming from background characteristics and prior experiences.

The focus on these samples enabled a rigorous assessment of differences and similarities in survey-based measures for the subset of ESI schools and those of a directly comparable group of non-ESI schools. In doing so, the analyses attempted to shed light on ESI influence on important aspects of students' experiences during high school. Below we offer several important cautions about the degree to which differences that may emerge between ESI and non-ESI comparison schools based on the student survey data can in fact be attributed to the influence of ESI resources and supports.

Measures from the Student Surveys

In addition to questions about student participation in ESI-aligned activities, the surveys included a wide range of items that aimed to capture important aspects of students' assessments of themselves and their school environment. Table 5 provides a list of the constructs that were developed from the student responses and the list of the survey items that were combined to create the measures. The surveys asked students to indicate their level of agreement, or assess the degree of the truth, (on a scale from 1 to 4) for each of these items. The student ratings for each cluster of items were then averaged to create the measures used in the analysis. Additional measures were constructed that reflect the percentage of students who, on average, affirmed or strongly affirmed a majority of the items include in the construct. Each of these items and the accompanying constructs and measures are available for ESI and non-ESI schools for Grades 9 through 12.

The student surveys also included batteries of items that asked students about their educational goals, their plans following high school graduation, and the steps that have taken to pursue those plans. Most of these items were direct responses about specific goals, plans, and activities (e.g., plans to attend college, earn a BA, or get a job; completing a college application or financial aid forms). In addition, the survey included an eight-item list of questions about conversations that students had with adults (both in and outside of schools) regarding their future. These items were used to construct an overall measure of "engagement with adults about future planning" focusing especially on college and careers. This measure was scored on a scale from one to four, and an additional metric was created to capture the percentage who had an overall positive level of engagement with adults about future planning.

Assessing Differences between ESI and Comparison Schools

The analyses used statistical regression models in which the average of a given survey measure for the sample of ESI schools was compared with the average for the accompanying non-ESI comparison schools.

TABLE 5   Measures of Students' Perceptions of School and Self

CONSTRUCT	ITEMS
Academic Self-Concept	I am confident in my academic abilities.
	I do well in school.
	I learn new concepts quickly.
	I am successful in school.
	I am confident in my ability to succeed in school.
Critical Thinking	I can easily express my thoughts on a problem.
	I usually use multiple source of information before making a decision.
	I compare ideas when thinking about a topic.
	I keep my mind open to different ideas when planning to make a decision.
	I am able to tell the best way of handling a problem.
Sense of Fair Treatment	The punishment for breaking school rules is the same no matter who you are.
	If a rule is broken, students know what kind of punishment will follow.
	All students are treated fairly when they break school rules.
	The rules are strictly enforced.
	The rules are fair.
	Everyone knows the rules for student conduct.
Perceptions of Racial/ Gender/Cultural Climate	I have been disrespected or mistreated by an adult because of my race, ethnicity, or nationality.
	I have been disrespected or mistreated by an adult at this school because of my gender.
	There is a lot of tension between different races, ethnicities, and nationalities.
Sense of Belonging in School	I feel comfortable at this school.
	I am a part of this school.
	I am committed to this school.
	I am supported at this school.
	I am accepted at this school.

Source: ESI evaluation student survey, developed by the Research Alliance for New York City Schools.

The models included variables that controlled for ancillary differences among the groups of schools based on student demographic characteristics, 8th grade test scores in math and English Language Arts, 8th grade attendance, and eligibility for services including free or reduced priced lunch, English language learning supports, and special education services. Analyses were conducted separately for the Grade 9 through 12 samples. There are two important factors that readers should keep in mind when interpreting differences and similarities between ESI and comparison schools based on the student survey data.

- As noted above, survey data were available only for a subset of the comparison schools. In addition, within ESI and comparison schools, survey data are only available for a subset of students who were enrolled at the time of survey administration. This means that differences between ESI and comparison schools that may emerge from analyses of the survey data could reflect differences in the characteristics of the respondents rather than to the influence of ESI services and supports.
- The analyses do not account for pre-existing differences and similarities between the ESI and comparison schools on the measures captured by the student surveys. Thus, it is possible that differences, and similarities, that may be observed after ESI implementation may actually reflect differences or similarities on the measures even before the ESI schools began implementation.

These important limitations are mitigated somewhat by the study design and analysis strategies used to produce the findings. In addition to the school-level similarities that stem from the matching process, additional analyses show a high degree of similarity between the background characteristics and middle school outcomes of survey respondents from the ESI and comparison schools. The analyses of the survey data also rely on multiple regression models that account for differences between ESI and non-ESI schools that may be due to student demographic characteristics, family background, and prior levels achievement and school engagement. Survey results for the full sample of ESI schools as well as those for the subset of ESI and comparison schools show a high degree of similarity. These similarities and the analytic framework provide a moderate level of confidence that differences that emerge between the two groups of schools are due to the subsequent resources and supports provided by ESI rather than other pre-existing student and school conditions and characteristics.

In short, while alternative interpretations of differences in the survey-based measures of ESI and non-ESI student experiences and perceptions cannot be ruled out, the analyses do provide useful insights into ESI's likely contribution, or lack of contribution, to changes in those experiences and perceptions.

Assessing ESI Impacts on Key Antecedents to College, High School Graduation, and College Readiness and Enrollment

Our study of ESI's impact focused on a range of outcomes that are important indicators of student engagement and performance during high school as well as critical antecedents to preparing for and enrolling in college. They draw on data from school district administrative records which are available for all ESI schools and for 80 non-ESI comparison schools. The administrative records are available for the 2012–2013 school year, the first year of ESI implementation, through the 2015–2016 school year. These years correspond to Grades 9–12 for students who were in the 2012 Cohort and to Grades 9–11 for students in the 2013 Cohort. College enrollment data are also available for Fall 2016 for students in the 2012 Cohort.

In addition to data for the years of ESI implementation, the administrative records also include data for up to four years prior to the start of ESI for each of the ESI schools and each of the non-ESI comparison schools. These pre-ESI data enable the analyses to account for differences in student outcomes or trends in those outcomes that might otherwise appear as subsequent differences that emerged after ESI began implementation. These administrative records data capture student attendance, credit accumulation, Regents examination scores, suspensions, mobility, high school graduation and diploma status, and college enrollment status. Following is a more detailed description of the methodology used to analyze ESI impacts on these outcomes.

Impact Analysis Methodology

The impact analyses are based on strong methods designed to maximize confidence in an assessment of ESI's added value or causal influence on student outcomes. They utilize what is known as Comparative Interrupted Time Series (CITS) analysis. CITS analysis accounts both for school characteristics that remain consistent over time (e.g., feeder patterns, location, and school culture) and for system-wide effects that could be occurring as ESI is implemented (e.g., district-wide improvements to curriculum or increased district funding). This is important because an improvement in participating schools' academic performance after the introduction of ESI might be due to ESI, but it also might be due to system-wide reforms, budget increases, or other external events. CITS allows us to distinguish between these possible causes by comparing ESI schools with others that did not have the benefit of ESI resources and supports during this period, but which are part of the NYC school system, and thus would be affected by any systemic influences.

The CITS analyses focuses on changes over time in outcomes for students in the ESI schools and compares those changes with changes for the same outcomes for similar students in similar comparison schools. Specifically, the analytic models estimate trends in student outcomes during the years leading up to the start of ESI, as well as deviations from those trends for students enrolled in the schools during the period when ESI was being implemented. The models also estimate trends and deviations for comparison schools, which reflect the influence of other factors on similar high schools during the same period. The differences in deviations from historical trends between ESI schools and comparison schools represent the impact of ESI over and above other potential influences. Finally, the CITS methodology used in this report has additional features that account for other factors that may mask or exaggerate the impact of ESI on student outcomes. These include statistical adjustments that account for changes over time and differences across schools in student characteristics. The analytic models account for the modest

differences between ESI and comparison schools in the respective trajectories of student outcomes from the pre-ESI period.

While CITS is a strong method for estimating ESI's impacts on student outcomes, it does have limitations for inferences about ESI's causal
influence on those outcomes. Most notably are influences that may derive
from unmeasured pre-existing differences between the ESI and comparison schools. These may derive from the fact that the ESI schools were
targeted specifically as potential beneficiaries of the initiative's resources
and supports. Further, among the 65 or so high schools that were sufficiently motivated to apply for ESI, only 40 were selected to participate.
The identification of comparison schools and the CITS analyses attempt
to account for many of the factors that went into the selection of schools
for ESI *and* that may also have influenced subsequent student outcomes.
However, there may be some unaccounted factors that led schools to
apply and be selected *and* that also influenced subsequent student outcomes. We recognize that the analyses may not fully account for them,
if they exist.

NOTES

CHAPTER 1

1. Gloria Ladson-Billings, "From the Achievement Gap to the Education Debt: Understanding Achievement in U.S. Schools," *Educational Researcher* 35, no. 7 (2006): 3–12.
2. Jacqueline J. Irvine. "Foreword," in *Culture, Curriculum and Identity in Education*, ed. H. R. Milner (New York: Palgrave Macmillan, 2010), xi–xvi.
3. H. R. Milner IV, "Beyond a Test Score: Explaining Opportunity Gaps in Educational Practice," *Journal of Black Studies* 43, no. 6 (2012): 693–718.
4. Shaun R. Harper & Associates, *Succeeding in the City: A Report from the New York City Black and Latino Male High School Achievement Study* (Philadelphia: University of Pennsylvania, Center for the Study of Race and Equity in Education, 2014); Tyrone Howard, Terry La Mont, Oscar Navarro, Brian Woodwood, Kenius Watson, Bianco Haro, and Adrian Huerta, *The Counter Narrative: Reframing Success of High Achieving Black and Latino Males in Los Angeles County* (Los Angeles: UCLA Black Male Institute, 2017).
5. H. Richard Milner IV and Tyrone C. Howard, "Counter-Narrative as Method: Race, Policy and Research for Teacher Education," *Race Ethnicity and Education* 16, no. 4 (2013): 536–61, doi:10.1080/13613324.2013.817772; Theresa Perry, Claude Steele, and Asa G. Hilliard, *Young, Gifted, and Black: Promoting High Achievement Among African-American Students* (Boston: Beacon Press, 2003); J. L. Wood and Shaun R. Harper, *Advancing Black Male Student Success from Preschool Through PhD* (Sterling, VA: Stylus, 2015); Anne Gregory, Russel Skiba, and Pedro Noguera, "The Achievement Gap and the Discipline Gap: Two Sides of the Same Coin?" *Educational Researcher* 39, no. 1 (2010): 59–68; Edward Fergus, Pedro Noguera, and Margary Martin, *Schooling for Resilience: Improving the Life Trajectory of Black and Latinx Boys* (Cambridge, MA: Harvard Education Press, 2014).
6. Monique Morris, *Pushout: The Criminalization of Black Girls in Schools* (New York: New University Press, 2016).
7. Travis J. Bristol, "Teaching Boys: Toward a Theory of Gender Relevant Pedagogy," *Gender and Education* 27, no. 1 (2015): 53–68; James E. Davis and Will J. Jordan, "The Effects of School Context, Structure, and Experiences on African American Males in Middle and High School," *Journal of Negro Education* 63, no. 4 (1994): 570–87; Decoteau J. Irby, "Revealing Racial Purity Ideology: Fear of Black-White Intimacy as a Framework for Understanding School Discipline in Post-*Brown*

Schools," *Educational Administration Quarterly* 50, no. 5 (2014): 783–95; Edward W. Morris, "'Tuck in That Shirt!' Race, Class, Gender, and Discipline in an Urban School," *Sociological Perspectives* 48, no. 1 (2005): 25–48; Carla R. Monroe, "Misbehavior or Misinterpretation?" *Kappa Delta Pi Record* 42, no. 4 (2006): 161–65; Pedro A. Noguera, "Schools, Prisons, and Social Implications of Punishment: Rethinking Disciplinary Practices," *Theory into Practice* 42, no. 4 (2003): 341–50; Anthony A. Peguerol and Zahra Shekarkhar, "Latino/a Student Misbehavior and School Punishment," *Hispanic Journal of Behavioral Sciences* 33, no. 1 (2011): 54–70; Russell J. Skiba, Robert S. Michael, Abra C. Nardo, and Reece L. Peterson, "The Color of Discipline: Sources of Racial and Gender Disproportionality in School Punishment," *Urban Review* 34, no. 4 (2002): 317–42. Victor M. Rios, *Punished: Policing the Lives of Black and Latino Boys.* (New York: New York University Press, 2011).

8. Walter S. Gilliam, Angela N. Maupin, Chin R. Reyes, Maria Accavitti, and Frederick Shic, "Do Early Educators' Implicit Biases Regarding Sex and Race Relate to Behavior Expectations and Recommendations of Preschool Expulsions and Suspensions?" (brief, Yale Child Study Center, New Haven, CT, 2016), https://medicine.yale.edu/childstudy/zigler/publications/Preschool%20Implicit%20Bias%20Policy%20Brief_final_9_26_276766_5379_vl.pdf.

9. Oscar Barbarin, Iheoma U. Iruka, Chistine Harradine, Donna-Marie C. Winn, Marvin K. McKinney, and Lorraine C. Taylor, "Development of Social-Emotional Competence in Boys of Color: A Cross-Sectional Cohort Analysis from Pre-K to Second Grade," *American Journal of Orthopsychiatry* 83, nos. 2–3 (2013): 145–55, doi:10.1111/ajop.12023.

10. Douglas Downey and Shana Pribesh, "When Race Matters: Teachers' Evaluations of Students' Classroom Behavior," *Sociology of Education* 77, no. 4 (2004): 267–82, doi:10.1177/003804070407700401; La Vonne I. Neal, Audrey D. McCray, Gwendolyn Webb-Johnson, and Scott T. Bridgest, "The Effects of African American Movement Styles on Teachers' Perceptions and Reactions," *Journal of Special Education* 37, no. 1 (2003), 49–57, http://web.pdx.edu/~jhumn/Neal%20et.%20al.pdf.

11. Tyrone C. Howard, *Black Male(d): Peril and Promise in the Education of African American Males* (New York: Teachers College Press, 2014); Alfredo J. Artiles, Janette K. Klingner, and William F. Tate, "Representation of Minority Students in Special Education: Complicating Traditional Explanations," *Educational Researcher* 35, no. 6 (2006): 3–5, doi:10.3102/0013189x035006003; Wanda J. Blanchett, "Disproportionate Representation of African American Students in Special Education: Acknowledging the Role of White Privilege and Racism," *Educational Researcher* 35, no. 6 (2006): 24–28, doi:10.3102/0013189x035006024; Carla O'Connor and Sonia D. Fernandez, "Race, Class, and Disproportionality: Reevaluating the Relationship Between Poverty and Special Education Placement," *Educational Researcher* 35, no. 6 (2006): 6–11, doi:10.3102/0013189x035006006; Edward Fergus, "Common Causes of Disproportionality" (Special Education Newsletter, California Department of Education, 2010), http://www.calstat.org/publications/article_detail.php?a_id=128&nl_id=19; Donna Y. Ford, "Multicultural Issues: Underrepresentation of Culturally Different Students in Gifted Education: Reflections About Current Problems and Recommendations for the Future," *Gifted Child*

Today 33, no. 3 (2010): 31–35; Gilman W. Whiting, "From At Risk to At Promise: Developing Scholar Identities Among Black Males," *Journal of Secondary Gifted Education* 17, no. 4 (2006): 222–29, doi:10.4219/jsge-2006-407; Eboni M. Zamani-Gallaher and Vernon C. Polite, *The State of the African American Male* (East Lansing: Michigan State University Press, 2010).

12. Alfredo J. Artiles and Stanley C. Trent, "Overrepresentation of Minority Students in Special Education," *Journal of Special Education* 27, no. 4 (1994): 410–37, doi:10.1177/002246699402700404; Lloyd M. Dunn, "Special Education for the Mildly Retarded—Is Much of it Justifiable?" *Exceptional Children* 35, no. 1 (1968): 5–22, doi:10.1177/001440296803500101.

13. Emily Style, "Curriculum as Window and Mirror" (briefing paper, Listening for All Voices, Summit, NJ, 1988), https://nationalseedproject.org/images/documents/Curriculum_As_Window_and_Mirror.pdf.

14. *Digest of Education Statistics, 2016* (Washington, DC: National Center for Education Statistics, 2016).

15. Ulrich Boser, *Teacher Diversity Revisited: A New State-by-State Analysis* (Washington, DC: Center for American Progress, 2014).

16. Seth Gershenson, Stephen Holt, and Nicholas Papageorge, "Who Believes in Me? The Effect of Student-Teacher Demographic Match on Teacher Expectations" (Research Paper No. 2633993, School of Public Affairs, American University, Washington, DC, 2015), doi:10.2139/ssrn.2633993; Seth Gershenson, Cassandra M. D. Hart, Constance A. Lindsay, and Nicholas W. Papageorge, "The Long-Run Impacts of Same-Race Teachers" (Discussion Paper Series No. 10630, IZA Institute of Labor Economics, Bonn, March 2017), doi:10.3386/w25254; Thomas S. Dee, "Teachers, Race and Student Achievement in a Randomized Experiment," *Review of Economics and Statistics* 86, no. 1 (2004): 195–210; Anna J. Egalite, Brian Kisida, and Marcus A. Winters, "Representation in the Classroom: The Effect of Own-Race Teachers on Student Achievement," *Economics of Education Review* 45 (2015): 44–52, doi:10.1016/j.econedurev.2015.01.007.

17. Gershenson et al., "Who Believes in Me?" 3.

18. *Demographics and Work Experience: A Statistical Portrait of New York City's Public School Teachers* (New York: New York City Independent Budget Office, 2014), http://www.ibo.nyc.ny.us/iboreports/2014teacherdemographics.pdf.

19. "How Many Male Teachers of Color Work in NYC?" *NYU Steinhardt at a Glance*, April 3, 2017, https://research.steinhardt.nyu.edu/site/research_alliance/2017/04/03/how-many-male-teachers-of-color-work-in-nyc/.

20. Frank Edwards, Hedwig Lee, and Michael H. Esposito, "Risk of Being Killed by Police Use of Force in the United States by Age, Race-Ethnicity, and Sex," *Proceedings of the National Academy of Sciences* 116, no. 34 (2019): 16793–98, doi:10.31235/osf.io/kw9cu.

21. Ronald B. Mincy, *Black Males Left Behind* (Washington, DC: Urban Institute, 2006); Pedro A. Noguera, *The Trouble with Black Boys . . . and Other Reflections on Race, Equity, and the Future of Public Education* (Hoboken, NJ: John Wiley & Sons, 2009); Pedro A. Noguera, Aída Hurtado, and Edward Fergus, *Invisible No More: Understanding the Disenfranchisement of Latinx Men and Boys* (London: Routledge, 2013); Whiting, "From At Risk to At Promise."

22. Sharif El-Mekki interview by Rose Pierre-Louis, "Changing the Narrative for Black Boys and Men" (podcast, McSilver Institute for Poverty Policy and Research, January 11, 2020, https://mcsilver.nyu.edu/black-boys-and-men-changing-the-narrative-2/.

23. "Don't Just Focus on Abolishing the School-to-Prison Pipeline: We Should Also Build the School-to-Activism Pipeline," *Philly's 7th Ward* (blog), November 20, 2017, https://phillys7thward.org/2017/11/dont-just-focus-abolishing-school-prison-pipeline-also-build-school-activism-pipeline/.

24. Selcuk R. Sirin, "Socioeconomic Status and Academic Achievement: A Meta-Analytic Review of Research," *Review of Educational Research* 75, no. 3 (2005): 417–53, doi:10.3102/00346543075003417.

25. "Child Poverty in America 2012: National Analysis," Children's Defense Fund, 2013, https://www.childrensdefense.org/wp-content/uploads/2018/08/child-poverty-in-america-2012.pdf.

26. US Census Bureau, "Quick Facts: New York City, New York," https://www.census.gov/quickfacts/newyorkcitynewyork.

27. Richard Fry and Jeffrey S. Passel, *Latinx Children: A Majority Are U.S.-Born Offspring of Immigrants* (Washington, DC: Pew Hispanic Center, 2009).

28. Alma F. Ada, "The Pajaro Valley Experience: Working with Spanish-Speaking Parents to Develop Children's Reading and Writing Skills in the Home Through the Use of Children's Literature," in *Minority Education: From Shame to Struggle*, ed. T. Skutnabb-Kangas and J. Cummins (Philadelphia: Multilingual Matters, 1998), 223–38; Krista M. Perreira and India J. Ornelas, "The Physical and Psychological Well-Being of Immigrant Children," *The Future of Children* 21, no.1 (2011): 195–218; Alejandro Portes and Rubén G. Rumbaut *Legacies: The Story of the Immigrant Second Generation* (Berkeley: University of California Press, 2001); Carola Suarez-Orozco and Marcelo Suarez-Orozco, *Children of Immigration* (Cambridge, MA: Harvard University Press, 2001).

29. Jerry E. Garrett and Shannon Holcomb, "Meeting the Needs of Immigrant Students with Limited English Ability," *Education Resources Information Center* 35, no. 1 (2005): 49–62; Judy Smith-Davis, "The New Immigrant Students Need More Than ESL" *Education Digest: Essential Readings Condensed for Quick Review* 69, no. 8 (2004): 21–26, https://eric.ed.gov/?id=EJ740555; Michelle L. Spomer and Emory L. Cowen, "A Comparison of the School Mental Health Referral Profiles of Young ESL and English-Speaking Children," *Journal of Community Psychology* 29, no. 1 (2001): 69–82, doi:10.1002/1520-6629(200101)29:1<69::aid-jcop5>3.0.co;2-v.

30. Reva Jaffe-Walter, *Coercive Concern: Nationalism, Liberalism, and the Schooling of Muslim Youth* (Redwood City, CA: Stanford University Press, 2016); Laurie Olsen, *Made in America* (New York: The New Press, 1997); Angela Valenzuela, *Subtractive Schooling* (Albany: State University of New York Press, 1997).

31. Adriana Villavicencio, Dyuti Bhattacharya, and Brandon Guidry, "Moving the Needle: Exploring Key Levers to Boost College Readiness for Black and Latino Males in NYC" (report, Research Alliance for New York City Schools, New York, 2013).

32. Laurie M. Brotman, Esther Calzada, Keng-Yen Huang, Sharon Kingston, Spring Dawson-McClure, Dimitra Kamboukos, Amanda Rosenfelt, Amihai Schwab,

and Eva Petkova, "Promoting Effective Parenting Practices and Preventing Child Behavior Problems in School Among Ethnically Diverse Families from Underserved, Urban Communities," *Child Development* 82, no. 1 (2011), 258–76, doi:10.1111/j.1467-8624.2010.01554.x.

33. Ivory Toldson, *Breaking Barriers 2: Plotting the Path Away from Juvenile Detention and Toward Academic Success for School-Age African American Males* (Washington, DC: Congressional Black Caucus Foundation, 2011).

34. Ivory Toldson and Chance D. Lewis, *Challenge the Status Quo: Academic Success Among School-Age African American Males* (Washington, DC: Congressional Black Caucus Foundation, 2012), https://www.cbcfinc.org/oUploadedFiles/CTSQ.pdf.

35. "Test Results," New York City Department of Education, 2019, https://infohub.nyced.org/reports/academics/test-results.

36. James J. Kemple, *The Condition of New York City High Schools: Examining Recent Trends and Looking Toward the Future* (New York: Research Alliance for NYC Schools, 2013).

37. *Black Lives Matter: The Schott 50 State Report on Public Education and Black Males* (Quincy, MA:Schott Foundation for Public Education, 2015), http://schottfoundation.org/resources/black-lives-matter-schott-50-state-report-public-education-and-black-males.

38. Thomas Bailey and Sung-Woo Cho, "Developmental Education in Community Colleges Prepared for the White House Summit on Community Colleges" (issue brief, Community College Research Center, Teachers College at Columbia University, New York, 2010), https://ccrc.tc.columbia.edu/media/k2/attachments/developmental-education-community-colleges.pdf.

39. John Michael Lee Jr. and Tafaya Ransom, *The Educational Experience of Young Men of Color: A Review of Research, Pathways and Progress* (New York: College Board Advocacy and Policy Center, 2011); John Michael Lee Jr. and Tafaya Ransom, *College Readiness and Completion for Young Men of Color: 2012 State of Black America: Occupy the Vote to Educate, Employ, and Empower* (New York: National Urban League, 2012).

40. William G. Bowen, Matthew M. Chingos, and Michael S. McPherson. *Crossing the Finish Line: Completing College at America's Public Universities* (Princeton, NJ: Princeton University Press, 2009).

41. "About MBK Communities," MBK Alliance, https://www.obama.org/mbka2/about-mbk-communities/.

42. Joscha Legewie and Jeffrey Fagan, "Aggressive Policing and the Educational Performance of Minority Youth," *American Sociological Review* 84, no. 2 (2019): 220–47, doi:10.1177/0003122419826020.

43. Ibid.; Amanda Geller and Jeffrey Fagan, "Police Contact and the Legal Socialization of Urban Teens," *RSF: The Russell Sage Foundation Journal of the Social Sciences* 5, no. 1 (2019), 26, doi:10.7758/rsf.2019.5.1.02.

44. "Why We Can't Wait: Women of Color Urge Inclusion In 'My Brother's Keeper'" (letter), African American Policy Forum, 2014, https://aapf.org/2014; Kimberle W. Crenshaw, "The Girls Obama Forgot," *New York Times*, July 29, 2014, https://www.nytimes.com/2014/07/30/opinion/Kimberl-Williams-Crenshaw-My-

Brothers-Keeper-Ignores-Young-Black-Women.html; Dani McClain, "'Black Women, Like Black Men, Scar': Conversation on My Brother's Keeper Heats Up," *The Nation*, June 18, 2014, https://www.thenation.com/article/archive/black-women-black-men-scar-conversation-my-brothers-keeper-heats/; "Inclusion of Girls In My Brother's Keeper," *NewsOne*, June 19, 2014; J. B Wogan, "My Brother's Keeper Is Great, but What About the Girls?" *Governing*, May 15, 2015, https://www.governing.com/topics/urban/gov-brothers-keeper-black-girls-obama.html.

45. Michael J. Dumas, "My Brother as 'Problem,'" *Educational Policy* 30, no. 1 (2015): 95, doi:10.1177/0895904815616487.

46. Adriana Villavicencio, Sarah Klevan, and James J. Kemple, "The Expanded Success Initiative: Challenges and Progress in the Pursuit of College and Career Readiness for Black and Latino Young Men" (report, Research Alliance for New York City Schools, New York, 2018).

47. Ibid.

48. Ronald F. Ferguson, *Aiming Higher Together: Strategizing Better Educational Outcomes for Boys and Young Men of Color* (New York: Urban Institute, 2016), https://www.urban.org/sites/default/files/publication/80481/2000784-Aiming-Higher-Together-Strategizing-Better-Educational-Outcomes-for-Boys-and-Young-Men-of-Color.pdf; Fergus et al., *Schooling for Resilience*; Derrick M. Gordon, Derek Iwamoto, Nadia Ward, Randolph Potts, and Elizabeth Boyd, "Mentoring Urban Black Middle-School Male Students: Implications for Academic Achievement," *Journal of Negro Education* 78, no. 3 (2009): 277–89.

49. Villavicencio et al., "The Expanded Success Initiative."

50. Our study was funded by The Fund for Public Schools, which raises funds from foundations, businesses, and individuals to support New York City's schools. More details about the study can be found in the appendix.

51. Pseudonyms are used throughout.

52. Salvador Vidal-Ortiz and Juliana Martínez, "Latinx Thoughts: Latinidad with an X," *Latino Studies* 16 (2018): 384–95.

53. Christopher L. Busey and Carolyn Silva, "Troubling the Essentialist Discourse of Brown in Education: The Anti-Black Sociopolitical and Sociohistorical Etymology of Latinxs as a Brown Monolith," *Educational Researcher* 2, no. 10 (2020): 1–11; Gustavo Lopez and Ana Gozales-Barrere, "Afro-Latino: A Deeply Rooted Identity Among U.S. Hispanics," Pew Research Center, March 1, 2016, https://www.pewresearch.org/fact-tank/2016/03/01/afro-latino-a-deeply-rooted-identity-among-u-s-hispanics/.

54. Michael J. Dumas and J. D. Nelson, "(Re)Imagining Black Boyhood: Toward a Critical Framework for Educational Research," *Harvard Educational Review* 86, no. 1 (2016): 27–47.

55. Rosalind S. Chou and Joe R. Feagin, *Myth of the Model Minority: Asian Americans Facing Racism*, 2nd ed. (London: Routledge, 2015).

56. Lillian Dunn, Elise Corwin, and John Duval, "Creating a Movement, Not a Moment: New York City's Efforts to Implement an Initiative Focused on Young Men of Color" (report, New York City Department of Education, New York, 2016), https://esinyc.com/creating-a-movement-2/.

CHAPTER 2

1. Interview data from ESI program leaders and participants were derived from the Research Alliance evaluation, which spanned 2012–16. Names of school staff and students are withheld by mutual agreement.

2. James Kemple, "Strategies to Reduce Inequality," in *Education Reform in New York City: Ambitious Change in the Nation's Most Complex School System*, ed. Jennifer A. O'Day, Catherine S. Bitter, and Louis M. Gomez (Cambridge, MA: Harvard Education Press, 2011).

3. Harold Bloom and Rebecca Unterman, *Sustained Positive Effects on Graduation Rates Produced by New York City's Small Public High Schools of Choice* (New York: MDRC, 2012).

4. John A. Powell, Stephen Menendian, and Wendy Ake, *Targeted Universalism: Policy and Practice* (Berkeley, CA: Haas Institute for a Fair and Inclusive Society, 2019), www.haasinstitute.berkeley.edu/targeteduniversalism.

5. Lillian Dunn, Elise Corwin, and John Duval. "Creating a Movement, Not a Moment: New York City's Efforts to Implement an Initiative Focused on Young Men of Color" (report, New York City Department of Education, 2016), https://esinyc.com/wp-content/uploads/2016/06/ESI-District-Narrative-for-posting.pdf.

6. NYC DOE, "Expanded Success Initiative: Design Challenge Overview" (application packet), 2012.

7. Clifford Adelman, *Answers in the Tool Box: Academic Intensity, Attendance Patterns, and Bachelor's Degree Attainment* (Washington, DC: US Department of Education, 1999), http://www2.ed.gov/pubs/Toolbox/toolbox.html; see also Ellen Foley, Jacob Mishook, Joanne Thompson, Michael Kubiak, Jonathan Supovitz, and Mary Kaye Rhude-Faust, *Leading Indicators for Education* (Providence, RI: Annenberg Institute for School Reform at Brown University, 2008), http://annenberginstitute.org/sites/default/files/product/206/files/LeadingIndicators.pdf; Marvin Lynn, "Examining Teachers' Beliefs About African American Male Students in a Low-Performing High School in an African American School District," *Teachers College Record* 112, no. 1 (2010): 289–330; David E. Kirkland, "Books Like Clothes: Engaging Young Black Men with Reading," *Journal of Adolescent & Adult Literacy* 55, no. 3 (2011): 199–208; Jeannie Oakes, *Beyond Tracking: Multiple Pathways to College, Career, and Civic Participation* (Cambridge, MA: Harvard Education Press, 2008); William C. Symonds, Robert Schwartz, and Ronald F. Ferguson, *Pathways to Prosperity: Meeting the Challenge of Preparing Young Americans for the 21st Century* (Cambridge, MA: Pathways to Prosperity Project, Harvard University Graduate School of Education, 2011), http://www.gse.harvard.edu/news_events/features/2011/Pathways_to_Prosperity_Feb2011.pdf.

8. William G. Tierney, Thomas Bailey, Jill Constantine, Neal Finkelstein, and Nicole Farmer Hurd, *Helping Students Navigate the Path to College: What High Schools Can Do* (Washington, DC: Institute of Education Services, US Department of Education, 2009), http://educationnorthwest.org/webfm_send/1061; Mathew Militello, Jason Schweid, and John Carey, "Sí se Puede en Colaboración! Increasing College Placement Rates of Low-income Students," *Teachers College Record* 113, no. 7 (2011): 1435–76; Ivory A. Toldson, *Breaking Barriers: Plotting the Path to Academic Success for School-Age African-American Males* (Washington, DC:

Congressional Black Caucus Foundation, 2008), http://www.cbcfinc.org/images/pdf/breaking_barriers.pdf; Tony Fabelo, Michael D. Thompson, Martha Plotkin, Dottie Carmichael, Miner P. Marchbanks III, and Eric A. Booth, "Breaking Schools' Rules: A Statewide Study of How School Discipline Relates to Students' Success and Juvenile Justice Involvement" (report, Council of State Governments Justice Center, New York, 2011), http://knowledgecenter.csg.org/drupal/system/files/Breaking_School_Rules.pdf; Tiffany Jones, Estela M. Bensimon, and Alicia C. Dowd, *Using Data and Inquiry to Build Equity-Focused College-Going Cultures* (Washington, DC: National College Access Network, 2011), http://www.collegeaccess.org/2011_Boston_Toolkit.aspx; John Bean, "Nine Themes of College Student Retention," in *College Student Retention: Formula for Student Success*, ed. Alan Seidman (Santa Barbara, CA: Greenwood, 2009): 215–43; Mandy Savitz-Romer, Joie Jager-Hyman, and Ann Coles, "Removing Roadblocks to Rigor: Linking Academic and Social Supports to Ensure College Readiness and Success" (report, Institute for Higher Education Policy, Washington, DC, 2009), http://www.ihep.org/research/publications/removing-roadblocks-rigor-linking-academic-and-social-supports-ensure-colleg-0; Edward Smith, "The Role of Social Supports and Self-Efficacy in College Success" (brief, Institute for Higher Education Policy, Washington, DC, 2010), http://www.ihep.org/research/publications/role-social-supports-and-self-efficacy-college-success; David Miller, "Man Up: Recruiting and Retaining African American Male Mentors" (report, Urban Leadership Institute, 2008), https://bma.issuelab.org/resources/14715/14715.pdf.

9. Pedro A. Noguera, *The Trouble with Black Boys . . . and Other Reflections on Race, Equity, and the Future of Public Education* (Hoboken, NJ: John Wiley & Sons, 2009); Carol M. Lieber, "Increasing College Access Through School-Based Models of Postsecondary Preparation, Planning and Support" (report, Educators for Social Responsibility, Cambridge, MA, 2009), http://esrnational.org/esr/wp-content/uploads/2009/05/increasing-college-access-hi-res.pdf; Patricia McDonough, "Building a College Culture: Needs, Goals, Principles, and a Case Study" (UCLA Graduate School of Education), http://www.sandi.net/cms/lib/CA01001235/Centricity/Domain/25/BuildingACollegeCulture.pdf; J. B Scramm, "High Schools as Launch Pads: How College-Going Culture Improves Graduation Rates for Low-Income High Schools" (white paper, College Summit, Washington, DC, 2008), http://www.collegesummit.org/images/uploads/WhitePaperfull.pdf; *Eight Components of College and Career Readiness Counseling*, College Board Advocacy and Policy Center, 2011, http://nosca.collegeboard.org/tools-resources; "Next Generation Career and Technical Education" (report, NYC Mayoral Task Force, New York, 2008), http://schools.nyc.gov/NR/rdonlyres/91B215BF-21F8-4E11-9676-8AFCFBB170E0/0/NYC_CTE_728_lowres.pdf; Anne Bowles and Betsy Brand, "Learning Around the Clock: Benefits of Expanded Learning Opportunities for Older Youth" (report, American Youth Policy Forum, Washington, DC, 2009).

10. Figure 2.1 and the description of the theory of action are reproduced with permission from Adriana Villavicencio, Sarah Klevan, and James J. Kemple, "The Expanded Success Initiative Challenges and Progress in the Pursuit of College and Career Readiness for Black and Latino Young Men" (report, Research Alliance for New York City Schools, New York, 2013).

11. These school performance summaries have been replaced by "School Quality Snapshots."
12. Sarah Klevan, Adriana Villavicencio, and Suzanne Wulach, "Preparing Black and Latinx Young Men for College and Careers" (report, Research Alliance for New York City Schools, New York, 2013).
13. Shawn Dove interview by Rose Pierre-Louis, "Black Boys and Men: Changing the Narrative" (podcast, McSilver Institute for Poverty Policy and Research, New York University, January 11, 2020), https://soundcloud.com/nyumcsilver/s2-episode-2-we-are-the-iconic
14. Na'ilah S. Nasir and Jarvis G. Givens, "We Dare Say Love: Black Male Student Experiences and the Possibilities Therein," in *"We Dare Say Love": Supporting Achievement in the Educational Life of Black Boys*, ed. Christopher P. Chatmon (New York: Teachers College Press, 2019), 2.
15. Michael J. Dumas, "'Losing an Arm': Schooling as a Site of Black Suffering," *Race Ethnicity and Education* 17, no. 1 (2013): 1–29, doi:10.1080/13613324.2013.850412; Christopher P. Chatmon, Shawn Ginwright, and Gregory Hodge, "The Roots and Routes of Oakland's African American Male Achievement Initiative (AAMA)," in Chatmon, ed., *"We Dare Say Love,"* 22.
16. The Million Hoodie March in New York City took place three weeks later on March 21, 2012.
17. Scott M. Stringer, *Teacher Residencies: Supporting the Next Generation of Teachers and Students* (New York: Bureau of Policy and Research, NYC Comptroller, 2019), https://comptroller.nyc.gov/wp-content/uploads/documents/Teacher-Residencies.pdf.

CHAPTER 3

1. Michael Lipsky, *Street-Level Bureaucracy: The Dilemmas of the Individual in Public Service.* (New York: Russell Sage Foundation, 1980).
2. Interview data from ESI program leaders and participants were derived from the Research Alliance evaluation, which spanned 2012–16. Names of school staff and students are withheld by mutual agreement.
3. The Fund for Public Schools issued a request for proposals to thousands of external vendors. Several individuals within the district central office reviewed the applications using a rubric. They also built in an appeals process.

CHAPTER 4

1. Brittany Aronson and Judson Laughter, "The Theory and Practice of Culturally Relevant Education," *Review of Educational Research* 86, no. 1 (2016): 163–206, doi:10.3102/0034654315582066; Hilary G. Conklin, "Modeling Compassion in Critical, Justice-Oriented Teacher Education," *Harvard Educational Review* 78, no. 4 (2008): 652–74, doi:10.17763/haer.78.4.j80j17683q870564; Geneva Gay, *Culturally Responsive Teaching: Theory, Research, and Practice* (New York: Teachers College Press, 2000); Gary R. Howard, *We Can't Teach What We Don't Know: White Teachers, Multiracial Schools*, 2nd ed. (New York: Teachers College Press, 2006); Tyrone C. Howard, "Who Really Cares? The Disenfranchisement of African American Males in PreK–12 Schools: A Critical Race Theory Perspective,"

Teachers College Record 110, no. 5 (2008): 954–85; Gloria Ladson-Billings, "But That's Just Good Teaching! The Case for Culturally Relevant Pedagogy," *Theory into Practice* 34, no. 3 (1995): 159–65, doi:10.1080/00405849509543675; Sonia Nieto and Patty Bode, *Affirming Diversity: The Sociopolitical Context of Multicultural Education* (New York: Pearson Education, 2008); Django Paris, "Culturally Sustaining Pedagogy," *Educational Researcher* 41, no. 3 (2012): 93–97, doi:10.3102/0013189x12441244; Alison G. Dover, "Teaching for Social Justice: From Conceptual Frameworks to Classroom Practices," *Multicultural Perspectives* 15, no. 1 (2013): 3–11, doi:10.1080/15210960.2013.754285.

2. Gloria Ladson-Billings, "Toward a Theory of Culturally Relevant Pedagogy," *American Educational Research Journal* 32, no. 3 (1995): 469.

3. Gay, *Culturally Responsive Teaching*, 31.

4. Alison G. Dover, "Teaching for Social Justice: From Conceptual Frameworks to Classroom Practices," *Multicultural Perspectives* 15, no. 1 (2013): 161, doi:10.1080/15 210960.2013.754285.

5. In 2012, Django Paris asserted an alternative term by defining culturally sustaining pedagogy as one that "seeks to perpetuate and foster—to sustain—linguistic, literate, and cultural pluralism as part of the democratic project of schooling" ("Culturally Sustaining Pedagogy," 93). Since this initiative was designed in 2011 and began in 2012, however, trainers, schools, and educators largely used the terms *culturally relevant* and/or *culturally responsive*.

6. Lina Cherfas, Rebecca Casciano, and Michael Anthony Wiggins, "It's Bigger Than Hip-Hop: Estimating the Impact of a Culturally Responsive Classroom Intervention on Student Outcomes," *Urban Education* (2018): 1–34; Yoonjung Choi, "Teaching Social Studies for Newcomer English Language Learners: Toward Culturally Relevant Pedagogy," *Multicultural Perspectives* 15, no. 1 (2013): 12–18, doi:10.1080/15210960.2013.754640; Marta Civil and Leslie H. Khan, "Mathematics Instruction Developed from a Garden Theme," *National Council of Teachers of Mathematics* 7 (March 2001): 400; Thomas Dee and Emily Penner, "The Causal Effects of Cultural Relevance: Evidence from an Ethnic Studies Curriculum" (Working Paper No. 16-01, Center for Education Policy Analysis, Stanford University, Palo Alto, CA, 2016); Jeff Duncan-Andrade, "Gangstas, Wankstas, and Ridas: Defining, Developing, and Supporting Effective Teachers in Urban Schools," *International Journal of Qualitative Studies in Education* 20, no. 6 (2007): 617–38, doi:10.1080/09518390701630767; Barbara Nykiel-Herbert, "Iraqi Refugee Students: From a Collection of Aliens to a Community of Learners: The Role of Cultural Factors in the Acquisition of Literacy by Iraqi Refugee Students with Interrupted Formal Education," *Multicultural Education* 17, no. 3 (2010): 2–14; Rassamichanh Souryasack and Jin Sook Lee, "Drawing on Students' Experiences, Cultures and Languages to Develop English Language Writing: Perspectives from Three Lao Heritage Middle School Students," *Heritage Language Journal* 5, no. 1 (2007): 79–97.

7. Interview data from ESI program leaders and participants were derived from the Research Alliance evaluation, which spanned 2012–16. Names of school staff and students are withheld by mutual agreement.

8. "Demographics and Work Experience: A Statistical Portrait of New York City's Public School Teachers," New York City Independent Budget Office, 2014, http://

www.ibo.nyc.ny.us/iboreports/2014teacherdemographics.pdf.

9. Eduardo Bonilla-Silva, *Racism Without Racists*, 5th ed. (New York: Rowman & Littlefield, 2017).

10. Aronson and Laughter, "The Theory and Practice of Culturally Relevant Education"; Gay, *Culturally Responsive Teaching*; Nieto and Bode, *Affirming Diversity*.

11. Chezare A. Warren, "Towards a Pedagogy for the Application of Empathy in Culturally Diverse Classrooms," *Urban Review*, 46, no. 3 (2013): 395–419.

12. Jamilia J. Blake, Bettie R. Butler, Chance W. Lewis, and Alicia Darensbourg, "Unmasking the Inequitable Discipline Experiences of Urban Black Girls: Implications for Urban Educational Stakeholders," *Urban Review* 43, no. 1 (2010): 90–106, doi:10.1007/s11256-009-0148-8; Anne Gregory, Russell J. Skiba, and Pedro A. Noguera, "The Achievement Gap and the Discipline Gap," *Educational Researcher* 39, no. 1 (2010): 59–68, doi:10.3102/0013189x09357621; Monique Morris, *Pushout: The Criminalization of Black Girls in Schools* (New York: New Press, 2018); Jennifer A. Sughrue, "Zero Tolerance for Children: Two Wrongs Do Not Make a Right," *Educational Administration Quarterly* 39, no. 2 (2003): 238–58, doi:10.1177/0013161x03251154; John M. Wallace Jr., Sara Goodkind, Cynthia M. Wallace, and Jerald G. Bachman, "Racial, Ethnic, and Gender Differences in School Discipline among U.S. High School Students: 1991–2005," *Negro Education Review* 59, nos. 1–2 (2008): 47–62; Alicia C. Insley, "Suspending and Expelling Children from Educational Opportunity: Time to Reevaluate Zero Tolerance Policies," *American University Law Review* 50 (January 2001): 1040–73.

13. Johanna Miller, Udi Ofer, Alexander Artz, Tara Bahl, Tara Foster, Deinya Phenix, Nick Sheehan, and Holly A. Thomas, "Education Interrupted: The Growing Use of Suspensions in New York City's Public Schools" (report, New York Civil Liberties Union, New York, 2011), http://www.nyclu.org/files/publications/Suspension_Report_FINAL_noSpreads.pdf.

14. Chezare A. Warren, "Empathy, Teacher Dispositions, and Preparation for Culturally Responsive Pedagogy," *Journal of Teacher Education* 69, no. 2 (2018): 169–83.

15. Chezare A. Warren, "Conflicts and Contradictions: Conceptions of Empathy and the Work of Good-Intentioned Early Career White Female Teachers," *Urban Education* 50, no. 5 (2014): 572–600.

16. The featured case studies are from Tony Laing and Adriana Villavicencio, "Culturally Relevant Education: A Guide for Educators: The Research Alliance for NYC Schools" (guide, NYU Steinhardt, New York, 2016).

17. Aronson and Laughter, "The Theory and Practice of Culturally Relevant Education," 5.

18. Jahque Bryan-Gooden, Megan Hester, and Leah Q. Peoples, "Culturally Responsive Curriculum Scorecard" (report, Metropolitan Center for Research on Equity and the Transformation of Schools, New York University, 2019), https://research.steinhardt.nyu.edu/scmsAdmin/media/users/atn293/ejroc/CRE-Rubric-2018-190211.pdf; "Racial Equity Analysis Tool," Seattle Public Schools, 2020, https://www.seattleschools.org/UserFiles/Servers/Server_543/File/District/Departments/DREA/racial_equity_analysis_tool.pdf; Edward Fergus and Roey Ahram, "Addressing Racial/Ethnic Disproportionality in Special Education" (report, Metropolitan Center for Urban Education, NYU Steinhardt, 2011), https://www.racialequitytools

.org/resourcefiles/dataanalysisworkbook.pdf; Todd Lacher, "Action for Access: Do Your Students Have Access?" Center for Assessment and Policy Development, https://www.racialequitytools.org/resourcefiles/lacher.pdf; Just Partners, Inc., "Advancing the Mission: Tools for Equity, Diversity, and Inclusion" (report, Annie E. Casey Foundation, 2009), https://www.racialequitytools.org/resourcefiles/caseyann.pdf.

19. "Equitable Classroom Practices Observation Checklist," Great Lakes Equity Center, 2010, https://greatlakesequity.org/resource/equitable-classroom-practice-observation-checklist.

20. Brendan Bartanen and Jason Grissom, "School Principal Race and the Hiring and Retention of Racially Diverse Teachers" (Working Paper No. 19-59, Annenberg Institute for School Reform, Brown University, 2019), https://www.edworkingpapers.com/ai19-59; Hua-Yu S. Cherng and Peter F. Halpin, "The Importance of Minority Teachers," *Educational Researcher* 45, no. 7 (2016): 407–20, doi:10.3102/0013189x16671718; Dan Goldhaber, Roddy Theobald, and Christopher Tien, "The Theoretical and Empirical Arguments for Diversifying the Teacher Workforce: A Review of the Evidence" (report, Center for Education Data and Research, Seattle, 2015), https://www.cedr.us/papers/working/CEDR%20WP%202015-9.pdf; Scott E. Page, "Making the Difference: Applying a Logic of Diversity," *Academy of Management Perspectives* 21, no. 4 (2007): 6–20, doi:10.5465/amp.2007.27895335; Katherine W. Phillips, "How Diversity Works," *Scientific American*, October 2014, 43–47; Genevieve Siegel-Hawley, "How Non-Minority Students Also Benefit from Racially Diverse Schools" (report, National Coalition on School Diversity, Washington, DC, 2012), https://www.school-diversity.org/pdf/DiversityResearchBriefNo8.pdf; Ana M. Villegas and Jacqueline J. Irvine, "Diversifying the Teaching Force: An Examination of Major Arguments," *Urban Review* 42, no. 3 (2010):175–92, doi:10.1007/s11256-010-0150-1; Amy S. Wells, Lauren Fox, and Diana Cordova-Cobo, "How Racially Diverse Schools and Classrooms Can Benefit All Students" (report, The Century Foundation, February 9, 2016), https://tcf.org/content/report/how-racially-diverse-schools-and-classrooms-can-benefit-all-students/.

21. Seth Gershenson, Cassandra M. D. Hart, Constance A. Lindsay, and Nicholas W. Papageorge, "The Long-Run Impacts of Same-Race Teachers" (Discussion Paper Series No. 10630, IZA Institute of Labor Economics, Bonn, March 2017), doi:10.3386/w25254.

CHAPTER 5

1. Urie Bronfenbrenner, *The Ecology of Human Development: Experiments by Nature and Design* (Cambridge, MA: Harvard University Press, 1979); Jenny Onyx and Paul Bullen, "Measuring Social Capital in Five Communities," *Journal of Applied Behavioral Science* 36, no. 1 (2000): 23–42, doi:10.1177/0021886300361002; Robert D. Putnam, *Bowling Alone: The Collapse and Revival of American Community* (New York: Simon & Schuster, 2001).

2. See Jean A. Baker, Tara Terry, Robert Bridger, and Anne Winsor, "Schools as Caring Communities: A Relational Approach to School Reform," *School Psychology Review* 26, no. 4 (1997): 586–602, doi:10.1080/02796015.1997.12085888; Terry De Jong, "A Framework of Principles and Best Practice for Managing Student

Behaviour in the Australian Education Context," *School Psychology International* 26, no. 3 (2003): 353, doi:10.1177/0143034305055979; Sue Roffey, *Changing Behaviour in Schools: Promoting Positive Relationships and Wellbeing* (Thousand Oaks, CA: Sage, 2010); Sue Roffey, "Developing Positive Relationships in Schools," in ibid. Quote from Urie Bronfenbrenner, *Making Human Beings Human: Bioecological Perspectives on Human Development* (Thousand Oaks, CA: Sage, 2005), 262.

3. Jeffrey Cornelius-White, "Learner-Centered Teacher-Student Relationships Are Effective: A Meta-Analysis," *Review of Educational Research* 77, no. 1 (2007): 113–43, doi:10.3102/003465430298563; Dana L. Haynie and Wayne D. Osgood, "Reconsidering Peers and Delinquency: How Do Peers Matter?" *Social Forces* 84, no. 2 (2005): 1109–130, doi:10.1353/sof.2006.0018; Kirabo Jackson, Shanette C. Porter, John Q. Easton, Alyssa Blanchard, and Sebastián Kiguel, "School Effects on Socio-Emotional Development, School-Based Arrests, and Educational Attainment" (Working Paper No. 226-0220, CALDER, Washington, DC, 2020), https://caldercenter.org/publications/school-effects-socio-emotional-development-school-based-arrests-and-educational; Catherine Riegle-Crumb, "More Girls Go to College: Exploring the Social and Academic Factors Behind the Female Postsecondary Advantage Among Hispanic and White Students," *Research in Higher Education* 51, no. 6 (2010): 573–93, doi:10.1007/s11162-010-9169-0; Ryan S. Wells, Tricia Seifert, Ryan D. Padgett, Sueuk Park, and Paul D. Umbach, "Why Do More Women Than Men Want to Earn a Four-Year Degree? Exploring the Effects of Gender, Social Origin, and Social Capital on Educational Expectations," *Journal of Higher Education* 82, no. 1 (2011): 1–32, doi:10.1353/jhe.2011.0004; Maureen T. Hallinan, "Teacher Influences on Students' Attachment to School," *Sociology of Education* 81, no. 3 (2008): 271–83, doi:10.1177/003804070808100303.

4. David L. DuBois, Nelson Portillo, Jean E. Rhodes, Naida Silverthorn, and Jeffrey C. Valentine, "How Effective Are Mentoring Programs for Youth? A Systematic Assessment of the Evidence," *Psychological Science in the Public Interest* 12, no. 2 (2011), 57–91, doi:10.1177/1529100611414806; Lillian T. Eby, Tammy D. Allen, Sarah C. Evans, Thomas Ng, and David DuBois, "Does Mentoring Matter? A Multidisciplinary Meta-Analysis Comparing Mentored and Non-Mentored Individuals," *Journal of Vocational Behavior* 72, no. 2 (2008): 254–67, doi:10.1016/j.jvb.2007.04.005; Susan Jekielek, Kristin A. Moore, Elizabeth C. Hair, and Harriet J. Scarupa, "Mentoring: A Promising Strategy for Youth Development" (report, Child Trends Research Brief, Washington, DC, 2002).

5. Thomas A. DiPrete and Claudia Buchmann, *The Rise of Women: The Growing Gender Gap in Education and What It Means for American Schools* (New York: Russell Sage Foundation, 2013); Peggy C. Giordano, "Relationships in Adolescence," *Annual Review of Sociology* 29 (2003): 257–81; Jan N. Hughes, Timothy A. Cavell, and Victor Willson, "Further Support for the Developmental Significance of the Quality of the Teacher-Student Relationship," *Journal of School Psychology* 39, no. 4 (2001): 289–301, doi:10.1016/s0022-4405(01)00074-7; Crumb, "More Girls Go to College"; Wells et al., "Why Do More Women Than Men?"

6. Edward Fergus, Pedro Noguera, and Margary Martin, *Schooling for Resilience: Improving the Life Trajectory of Black and Latinx Boys* (Cambridge, MA: Harvard Education Press, 2014).

7. Oscar Barbarin, "Mentally Healthy and Safe Schools," in *A Call for Change: Providing Solutions for Black Male Achievement*, ed. M. Casserly, S. Lewis, C. Simon, R. Uzzell, and M. Palacios (Washington, DC: Council of the Great City Schools, 2012), 282–309.

8. Ronald B. Mincy, *Black Males Left Behind* (Washington, DC: Urban Institute, 2006); Pedro A. Noguera, *The Trouble with Black Boys . . . and Other Reflections on Race, Equity, and the Future of Public Education* (Hoboken, NJ: John Wiley & Sons, 2009); Edward Fergus, "Common Causes of Disproportionality," *Special Education Newsletter*, California Department of Education, 2010; Fergus et al., *Schooling for Resilience*; Ivory Toldson, *Breaking Barriers: Plotting the Path to Academic Success for School-Age African-American Males* (Washington, DC: Congressional Black Caucus Foundation, 2008).

9. Interview data from ESI program leaders and participants were derived from the Research Alliance evaluation, which spanned 2012–16. Names of school staff and students are withheld by mutual agreement.

10. Michael V. Singh, "Resisting the Neoliberal Role Model: Latino Male Mentors' Perspectives on the Intersectional Politics of Role Modeling," *American Educational Research Journal* 20, no. 10 (2020): 1–32.

11. Valerie L. Johnson, Patricia Simon, and Eun-Young Mun, "A Peer-Led High School Transition Program Increases Graduation Rates Among Latino Males," *Journal of Educational Research* 107, no. 3 (2014): 186–96.

12. Iesha Jackson, Yolanda Sealey-Ruiz, and Wanda Watson, "Reciprocal Love: Mentoring Black and Latino Males Through an Ethos of Care," *Urban Education* 49, no. 4 (2014): 394–417.

13. "The Boys Aren't Broken, the Systems Are: Changing the Narrative About Young Men of Color," *Voices in Urban Education* no. 48 (2018): 39.

14. Decoteau J. Irby, "Revealing Racial Purity Ideology: Fear of Black-White Intimacy as a Framework for Understanding School Discipline in Post-*Brown* Schools," *Educational Administration Quarterly* 50, no. 5 (2014): 783–95, doi:10.1177/0013161x14549958; Decoteau J. Irby, "Mo' Data, Mo' Problems: Making Sense of Racial Discipline Disparities in a Large Diversifying Suburban High School," *Educational Administration Quarterly* 54, no. 5 (2018): 693–722, doi:10.1177/0013161x18769051; Alicia C. Insley, "Suspending and Expelling Children from Educational Opportunity: Time to Reevaluate Zero Tolerance Policies," *American University Law Review* 50 (2001): 1040–73; Pedro A. Noguera, "Schools, Prisons, and Social Implications of Punishment: Rethinking Disciplinary Practices," *Theory into Practice* 42, no. 4 (2003): 341–50.

15. Anne Gregory, Russel Skiba, and Pedro Noguera, "The Achievement Gap and the Discipline Gap: Two Sides of the Same Coin?" *Educational Researcher* 39, no. 1 (2010): 59–68.

16. Emily Arcia, "Achievement and Enrollment Status of Suspended Students: Outcomes in a Large, Multicultural School District," *Education and Urban Society* 38, no. 3 (2006): 359–69, doi:10.1177/0013124506286947; Tamela M. Eitle and David J. Eitle, "Inequality, Segregation, and the Overrepresentation of African Americans in School Suspensions," *Sociological Perspectives* 47, no. 3 (2004): 269–87, doi:10.1525/sop.2004.47.3.269; Tony Fabelo, Michael D. Thompson, Martha

Plotkin, Dottie Carmichael, Miner P. Marchbanks III, and Eric A. Booth, *Breaking Schools' Rules: A Statewide Study of How School Discipline Relates to Students' Success and Juvenile Justice Involvement* (New York: Council of State Governments Justice Center, 2011), https://knowledgecenter.csg.org/kc/system/files/Breaking_School_Rules.pdf; Gregory et al., "The Achievement Gap and the Discipline Gap"; Anne Gregory and Rhona S. Weinstein, "The Discipline Gap and African Americans: Defiance or Cooperation in the High School Classroom?" *Journal of School Psychology* 46, no. 4 (2008): 455–75, doi:10.1016/j.jsp.2007.09.001.

17. Russel W. Rumberger and Daniel J. Losen, "The Hidden Costs of California's Harsh School Discipline and the Localized Economic Benefits from Suspending Fewer High School Students" (report, Center for Civil Rights Remedies and California Dropout Research Project, Los Angeles, 2017), http://www.schooldisciplinedata.org/ccrr/docs/CostofSuspensionReportFinal.pdf.

18. "Resilient Kids, Safer Schools," NYC DOE, 2013, https://www.schools.nyc.gov/school-life/safe-schools/resilient-kids-safer- schools#:~:text=Restorative%20Justice%20Practices%20de%2Demphasize,of%20a%20school's%20daily%20practice.

19. Hilary Lustick, "Culturally Responsive Restorative Discipline," *Educational Studies* 56, no. 6 (2020): 555–83, doi:10.1080/00131946.2020.1837830.

20. Case studies are from Tony Laing and Adriana Villavicencio, "Creating Supportive Bonds of Brotherhood: A Guide for Educators" (guide, Research Alliance for New York City Schools, New York, 2016), https://research.steinhardt.nyu.edu/scmsAdmin/media/users/sg158/PDFs/esi_practice_guides/Brotherhood_Practice Guide.pdf; Linda Tigani, Tony Laing, and Adriana Villavicencio, "Learning Out Loud: Elevating Student Voices in Education" (report, Research Alliance for New York City Schools, New York, 2016), https://research.steinhardt.nyu.edu/scmsAdmin/media/users/ks191/Learning_Out_Loud/Learning_Out_Loud_Guide.pdf.

CHAPTER 6

1. Britany Aronson and Judson Laughter, "The Theory of and Practice of Culturally Relevant Education: A Synthesis of Research Across Content Areas," *Review of Educational Research* 86, no. 1 (2016): 163–206; Thomas Dee and Emily Penner, "The Causal Effects of Cultural Relevance: Evidence from an Ethnic Studies Curriculum" (Working Paper No. 16-01, National Bureau of Economic Research, Cambridge, MA, 2016), https://www.nber.org/system/files/working_papers/w21865/w21865.pdf; Edward Smith, "The Role of Social Supports and Self-Efficacy in College Success," Institute for High Education Policy, 2010, http://www.ihep.org/research/publications/role-social-supports-and-self-efficacy-college-success.

2. Interview data from ESI program leaders and participants were derived from the Research Alliance evaluation, which spanned 2012–16. Names of school staff and students are withheld by mutual agreement.

3. Adriana Villavicencio, Dyuhti Bhattacharya, and Brandon Guidry, "Moving the Needle: Exploring Key Levers to Boost College Readiness Among Black and Latinx Males in New York City" (report, Research Alliance for New York City Schools, New York, 2013), https://research.steinhardt.nyu.edu/research_alliance/publications/moving_the_needle.

4. Thomas Bailey and Sung-Woo Cho, "Issue Brief: Developmental Education in Community Colleges Prepared for the White House Summit on Community College" (report, Community College Resource Center, New York, 2010), http://ccrc.tc.columbia.edu/media/k2/attachments/developmental-education-community-colleges.pdf.

5. Vanessa Coca, "New York City Goes to College: A First Look" (report, Research Alliance for New York City Schools, New York, 2014), https://research.steinhardt.nyu.edu/research_alliance/publications/nyc_goes_to_college_first_look.

6. Expanded Success, "Expanded Success Initiative," *Vimeo*, 2014, https://vimeo.com/87308558.

7. Karisma Morton and Catherine Riegle-Crumb, "Is School Racial/Ethnic Composition Associated with Content Coverage in Algebra?" *Educational Researcher* 49, no. 6 (2020): 441–47, https://doi.org/10.3102/0013189X20931123; "New Data from U.S. Department of Education Highlights Educational Inequities Around Teacher Experience, Discipline and High School Rigor," US Department of Education, 2012, https://www.ed.gov/news/press-releases/new-data-us-department-education-highlights-educational-inequities-around-teache.

8. Ivory Toldson, *Breaking Barriers: Plotting the Path to Academic Success for School-Age African-American Males* (Washington, DC: Congressional Black Caucus Foundation, 2008).

9. iMentor is a school-based mentoring program that places public high school students in New York City in one-to-one relationships with college-educated mentors. Pairs are matched for three to four years and exchange weekly emails and meet monthly in person.

10. James J. Kemple, Micha D. Segeritz, and Nickisha Stephenson, "Building On-Track Indicators for High School Graduation and College Readiness: Evidence from New York City," *Journal of Education for Students Placed at Risk* 18, no. 1 (2013): 7–28.

11. James J. Kemple, *Career Academies: Impacts on Work and Educational Attainment* (New York: MDRC, 2004), https://www.mdrc.org/publication/career-academies-impacts-work-and-educational-attainment; James J. Kemple, *Career Academies: Long-Term Impacts on Work, Education, and Transitions to Adulthood* (New York: MDRC, 2008), https://www.mdrc.org/publication/career-academies-long-term-impacts-work-education-and-transitions-adulthood.

12. Case studies are from Tony Laing and Adriana Villavicencio, "Early Exposure to and Preparation for College: A Guide for Educators" (report, Research Alliance for New York City Schools, New York, 2016), https://research.steinhardt.nyu.edu/scmsAdmin/media/users/sg158/PDFs/esi_practice_guides/EarlyCollege_Practice Guide.pdf; Tony Laing and Adriana Villavicencio, "Improving Academic Readiness for College: A Guide for Educators" (report, Research Alliance for New York City Schools, New York, 2016), https://research.steinhardt.nyu.edu/scmsAdmin/media/users/sg158/PDFs/esi_practice_guides/Academics_PracticeGuide.pdf.

13. Elaine Allensworth and Nate Schwartz, "School Practices to Address Student Learning Loss" (report, Annenberg Institute at Brown University, Providence, RI, 2020), https://annenberg.brown.edu/sites/default/files/EdResearch_for_Recovery_Brief_1.pdf.

14. Kemple et al., "Building On-Track Indicators."

CHAPTER 7

1. Interview data from ESI program leaders and participants were derived from the Research Alliance evaluation, which spanned 2012–16. Names of school staff and students are withheld by mutual agreement.

2. Shaun R. Harper and associates, "Succeeding in the City: A Report from the New York City Black and Latino Male High School Achievement Study" (report, Center for the Study of Race and Equity in Education, Philadelphia, 2014), https://works .bepress.com/sharper/53/.

3. *School Interventions That Work: Targeted Support for Low-Performing Students* (Washington, DC: Alliance for Excellent Education, 2017); Hunter R. Boylan, "Targeted Intervention for Developmental Education Students (T.I.D.E.S.)," *Journal of Developmental Education* 32, no. 3 (2009): 14–18, 20, 22–23.

4. Lillian Dunn, Elise Corwin, and John Duval, "Creating a Movement, Not a Moment: New York City's Efforts to Implement an Initiative Focused on Young Men of Color" (report, NYC DOE, 2016).

5. Geoffrey D. Borman, Gina M. Hewes, Laura T. Overman, and Shelly Brown, "Comprehensive School Reform and Achievement: A Meta-Analysis," *Review of Educational Research* 74, no. 2 (2004): 125–230.; Mark Dynarski, "Interpreting the Evidence from Recent Federal Evaluations of Dropout-Prevention Programs," in *Dropouts in America: Confronting the Graduation Rate Crisis*, ed. Gary Orfield (Cambridge, MA: Harvard Education Press, 2004); Denise Gottfredson, Amanda Cross, Denise Wilson, Melissa Rorie, and Nadine Connell, "Effects of Participation in After-School Programs for Middle School Students: A Randomized Trial," *Journal of Research on Educational Effectiveness* 3 (June 2010): 282–313, doi:10.1080/19345741003686659; Susan Zief, Sherri Lauver, and Rebecca Maynard, "Impacts of After-School Programs on Student Outcomes: A Systematic Review for the Campbell Collaboration," *Campbell Collaboration* 2, no. 1 (2006), doi:10.4073/csr.2006.3.

6. "Evidence Summary for the Perry Preschool Project," 2017, https://evidence basedprograms.org/document/perry-preschool-project-evidence-summary/; James J. Kemple, *Career Academies: Long-Term Impacts on Work, Education, and Transitions to Adulthood* (New York: MDRC, 2008), https://www.mdrc.org/ publication/career-academies-long-term-impacts-work-education-and-transitions-adulthood.

7. Delonte Harrod, "COVID-19, Racism Are Dual Crises for Black Americans," *Medscape*, June 10, 2020, https://www.medscape.com/viewarticle/932128; Xenia S. Bion, "Racism Fuels Double Crisis: Police Violence and COVID-19 Disparities," California Health Care Foundation, June 8, 2020, https://www.chcf.org/blog/ racism-fuels-double-crisis-police-violence-covid-19-disparities/; "Coronavirus and Police Brutality Roil Black Communities," *New York Times*, June 8, 2020, https:// www.nytimes.com/2020/06/07/us/politics/blacks-coronavirus-police-brutality .html; "Addressing Law Enforcement Violence as a Public Health Issue," American Public Health Association, https://www.apha.org/policies-and-advocacy/public-health-policy-statements/policy-database/2019/01/29/law-enforcement-violence.

8. "Addressing Law Enforcement Violence as a Public Health Issue."

9. "Health Equity Considerations and Racial and Ethnic Minority Groups," Center for Disease Control, https://www.cdc.gov/coronavirus/2019-ncov/community/health-equity/race-ethnicity.html.

10. David B. Tyack and Larry Cuban, *Tinkering Toward Utopia: A Century of Public School Reform* (Cambridge, MA: Harvard University Press, 1997).

11. Bettina L. Love, *We Want to Do More Than Survive: Abolitionist Teaching and the Pursuit of Educational Freedom* (Boston: Beacon Press, 2019).

12. Amna A. Akbar, "The Left Is Remaking the World," *New York Times*, July 11, 2020, https://www.nytimes.com/2020/07/11/opinion/sunday/defund-police-cancel-rent.html.

13. Frederick Douglass, "West India Emancipation" speech, 1857, https://rbscp.lib.rochester.edu/4398.

ACKNOWLEDGMENTS

Mi madre. No hay suficientes palabras para expresar mi gratitud por todas las maneras en las que me has apoyado en esta trayectoria y muchas otras. Habiéndome criado tú sola, conseguiste inculcar en mí la autoestima para ir en busca de mis sueños, a la vez que me proveíste de un ejemplo inigualable de ética laboral y compromiso por causas justas. Tu decisión de dejar a tu hermosa tierra natal y tu amorosa familia para inmigrar a este país, siendo una joven madre y sabiendo poco inglés, me alentaron a hacerle frente a mis temores y dudas. Tu inteligencia e ingenio para sacar adelante tu propio negocio sirviendo a latinos y otros inmigrantes por 25 años, me inspiraron a usar lo que tengo para reciprocar. Tu valentía al permitirme viajar 3,000 millas sola, cuando apenas había entrado a los primeros meses de mis 18 años de vida lo hicieron todo posible. Espero que mi vida y mi trabajo te llenen de orgullo.

My sisters. I will always count myself as blessed, because to know your fierce love and warmth is to have a protective sphere around me daily. Kathy Chavez, Lory Lozano, and Emily Saenz—once cheerleaders in real life, you have been my biggest cheerleaders since the day I came home from the hospital. Thank you for always making me feel like I was capable of anything and for celebrating my wins and my losses like they were your own. A special thanks to our big sis, Kathy, for rescuing my family during a pandemic so that I could write this book—and for doing it with so much joy my heart bursts just thinking about it.

My mentors. Gary Anderson, thank you for grounding my doctoral work in the types of critical questions that give meaning to education research and for guiding me through the program and long after. I'm grateful for our coffees and our friendship. Pedro Noguera, thank you for always making the time to provide direction, support, and advice for more than a decade, despite the many demands on your time. Monica Bryne-Jiminez, mi hermana in arms, thank you for your leadership, for reminding me that we are more than just our tenure packets and that there are many ways to make a difference. Edward Fergus, thank you for encouraging me to write this book, for always keeping it real, and for exemplifying the type of engaged scholar I aim to be. Thanks to each of you for inspiring me by your example and commitment to equity and justice. For that especially, I am grateful.

James Kemple and the Research Alliance. Jim—my mentor, my teacher, my friend—I know how fortunate I was to land at the Research Alliance. Thank you for taking a chance on me when I must have seemed totally green and unskilled. I will forever be indebted to the years I spent in our conference rooms learning from you what it means to do good research and what it looks like to be a good colleague. Of course, thank you for your ongoing guidance on this project. Your expertise, creativity, insight, and attention to detail has informed the study and my work in ways I'm sure I cannot enumerate.

I also want to acknowledge other past and present members of the Research Alliance who have supported this project since 2012 (and apologize to any who I fail to name). Sarah Klevan, thank you for being my steadfast partner on this project, for your impeccable skills in the field, for leading the research during my maternity leaves, and for attending to all of the minor details and major aspects of the work. Suzanne Wulach, thank you for sweating all the small stuff while never losing sight of what matters the most. Sahnah Lim, thank you for creating a system for surveying thousands of students every year. And Camille Lafayette, thank you for taking up her mantle with so much grace and aplomb. Tony

Laing, warm thanks for leading the case study work of this project and for your work with young people that is a model for us all. Thank you to the many staff members who I have had the privilege to work alongside on this project or who were gracious enough to provide our team with critical feedback along the way: Nathan Alexander, Christine Baker-Smith, Dyuti Bhattacharya, Vanessa Coca, Cheri Fancsali, Brandon Guidry, David Kang, Saskia Levy-Thompson, Lisa Merrill, Lori Nathanson, Rory Santaloci, Benjamin Schwab, and Micha Segeritz. Thank you to those who supported the work as graduate students—Micah Bart-Rogers, Andrea Alexandra Lopez-Barraza, Hilary Lustick, Amanda Kate McNulty, and Maxine Roca—as well as the great number of survey administrators in the field whose work may have only lasted a season but whose professionalism made a lasting impact. Michael Cohen and Jessica Vasseghi, even though you were never members of the Research Alliance, I consider you members of my team. Thank you for all of your hard work on this manuscript. A special thanks to Linda Tigani, whose contributions to the study elevated the quality and thoughtfulness of this project and who was generous enough to read multiple chapters of this book. Last but not least, thank you to Chelsea Farley, who, along with Shifra Goldenberg and Kayla Stewart, provided what must have amounted to thousands of hours of reading manuscripts, sitting in review meetings, providing feedback, and editing text. Your collective efforts have not only sharpened every publication but have permanently shaped my thinking and writing. And Kayla, you continued to support my work all the way to the end, even in a hurricane. Thank you ALL for making the work infinitely better. I couldn't imagine a better team.

Members of the ESI Team—Paul Forbes, Lillian Dunn, John Duval, Hector Calderon, Jevon Williams, Camille Kinlock, Elise Crown, and Richard Haynes—thank you for collaborating with us in this work and for making the research possible. Paul and Lillian, especially, thank you for your partnership. I will forever be indebted to your openness, your insight, and your commitment to the greatest aims of the initiative. *The Open Society Foundations and the Fund for Public Schools*, thank you for generously funding the evaluation. *The principals, teachers, students, and other staff members of the schools involved in this study,* thank you for letting our research team into your buildings year after year and for being generous with your time. Thank you most for your candor and for sharing your stories.

Special friends. Patricia Melecio, Adrienne Brown, Tanjila Islam, Nikki Stanley, Heather Grantham, Alexandra Morbitzer, Eileen Rivera, Elaine Delahoz, Jill Delahoz, Angus Mungal, and, of course, the one and only César Vargas—each of you keeps me sane, keeps me going, and keeps me growing. Thank you for being my chosen family. Jayne Fargnoli at Harvard Education Press, this book wouldn't have been possible without your support and friendship. Somehow, you managed to meet my internal resistance and external barriers with unwavering focus and encouragement. Thank you for being part of this journey. I couldn't have done it without you.

My daughters, Auset and Folasade Shabazz. You may have technically made this book more challenging to write, but you also provide me with so much joy and purpose that every one of my endeavors is graced with your magic. Thank you for the gift of being your mom. It is my greatest ambition to do it well.

Diallo Shabazz—my moon, my husband, friend, and companion. Thank you for being my biggest source of inspiration. Through your lifelong efforts and daily practice to better the world and all of those around you, you inspire me to be the best version of myself. This book is indebted to our thirteen years of conversations about education, your critical eye on almost everything I've written, and your unique insight into transformational change. Thank you for the sacrifices you made to support my writing this book. I know it wasn't easy, and I will always be grateful. Thank you for everything you do for our children, our families, and our communities.

ABOUT THE AUTHOR

Adriana Villavicencio is an assistant professor in the School of Education at the University of California, Irvine. Her research is focused on K–12 educational policy and practice that deepens or disrupts inequities for students of colors and their families. For nearly a decade, she served as a senior research associate and deputy director of the Research Alliance for New York City Schools at New York University, a research-practice partnership with the New York City Department of Education, and led many of its large-scale research projects on topics including computer science for underrepresented students, effective schooling for immigrant English learners, and racial justice programs in schools. She also served on the advisory board for the Young Women's Initiative; as a member New York State's Board of Regents Research Workgroup on Integration, Diversity and Equity; and as president of the Board of Directors for the Latino Alumni Association of Columbia University. Villavicencio is the author of numerous research reports, journal articles, and book chapters on equitable policy and practice in schools and regularly presents her research at national conferences and through a variety of both English- and Spanish-language television and online media. Prior to becoming a researcher, she taught high school English in East Oakland, California, and in Brooklyn, New York. She earned her PhD in education leadership and policy from the New York University Steinhardt School of Culture, Education, and Human Development. She also holds a MA in English education from Teachers College, Columbia University, and a BA in English from Columbia University.

INDEX